IMAGES
of America

MAPLETON

I0793179

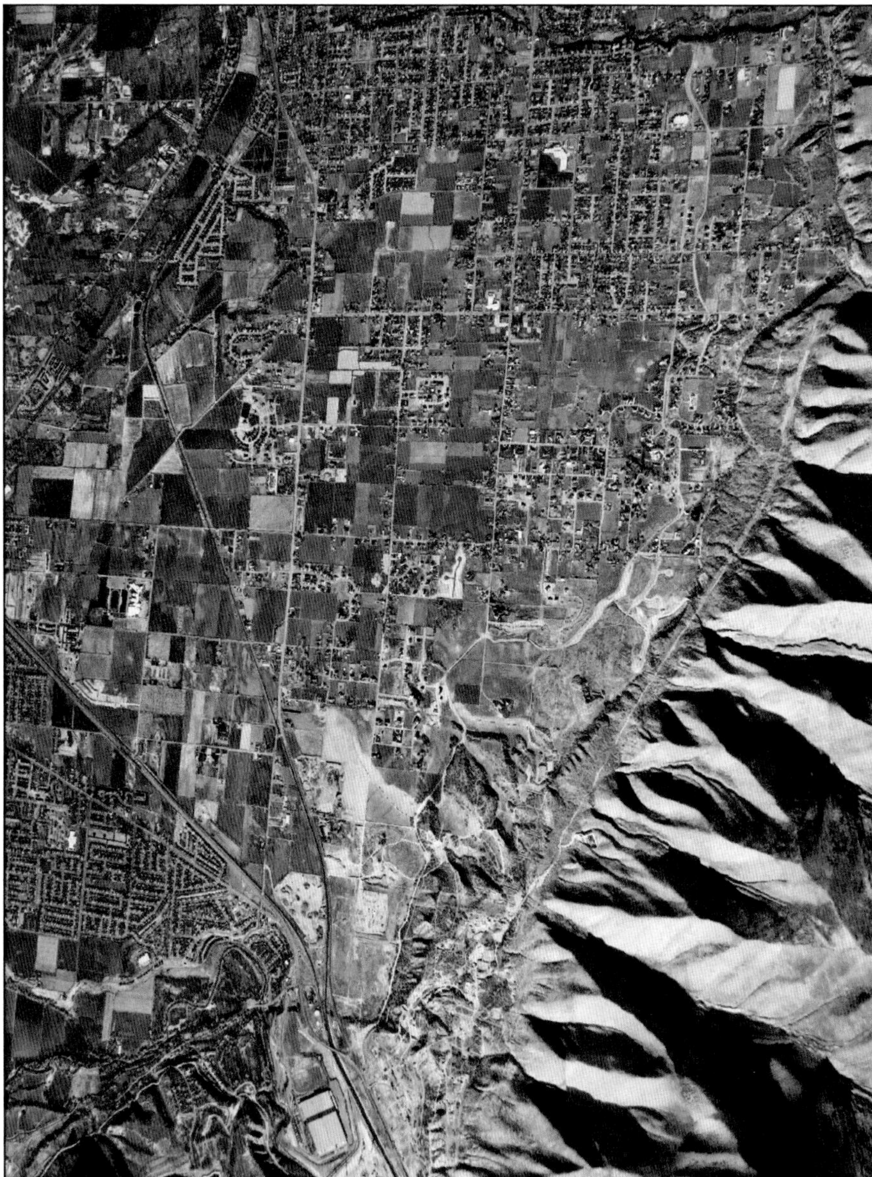

Bordered by Hobble Creek in the north and dominated by the 10,000-foot Sierra Bonita to the east, Mapleton, Utah, is a rural yet modern city and is a favored spot for families to raise both children and alfalfa. (Courtesy of Mapleton City.)

ON THE COVER: Aaron Wesley Matson's home, currently the Antonino residence, is found at 745 East 1200 North. The home was built in 1894; this photograph was taken in 1898 by George Edward Anderson and was preserved by Rell G. Francis. In front of the fence are, from left to right, Vera Matson, John, Cyrus, and Will (on horse). Behind the fence is Mabel, with Sarah Ann seated and Ella on the porch. In front of the home is Violet Moore, an adopted Maori girl from New Zealand who would later become Floyd Miner's grandmother. Next to Violet is Sara Birch Waters. (Courtesy of Floyd Miner.)

IMAGES
of America

MAPLETON

April Clawson and Kjirstin Youngberg

ARCADIA
PUBLISHING

Copyright © 2015 by April Clawson and Kjirstin Youngberg
ISBN 978-1-4671-3269-5

Published by Arcadia Publishing
Charleston, South Carolina

Printed in the United States of America

Library of Congress Control Number: 2014910319

For all general information, please contact Arcadia Publishing:
Telephone 843-853-2070
Fax 843-853-0044
E-mail sales@arcadiapublishing.com

Visit us on the Internet at www.arcadiapublishing.com

For the children of Mapleton, who will determine its future.

Contents

Acknowledgments

This book was a community-wide project. The Springville-Mapleton Pioneer Museum was a great resource. Staff members, particularly M. Lee Taylor, Helen Beardall, and Floyd Miner, were very helpful. To the Mapleton city employees who came and unlocked the Mapleton Museum and the basement section at the city building, we thank you. To those who came and visited and called and sent emails, we thank you for the advice, helpful hints, and the use of your photographs. We especially thank Dean Allan, MaryLyne Warren Witney, Collin Allan, Floyd Miner, Barbara Halverson Kissel, Gay Bennett McHargue, Richard Bills, Kay Bills, Mac Bills, Orpha Dee Bird Johnson, John S. Beardall, Angela Bleggi, Myra Richmond Miller, Colette Perry, M. Lee Taylor, J. Brent Haymond, Rolf and Tangie Walpole, Tyler Brinkerhoff, Mary Hjorth Fojtek, Ronald and Shirley Graves, Larry Clark, Franklin Ole Nielsen, Robert Carter, Carmen Oliver, Marie Wentz Turner, Susan Johnson, Wendy Sue Johnson, Kathleen Gividen Nelson Grace, and Jane Whiting Olsen.

Thanks go to Jay Smith, president of the Mapleton Sons of Utah Pioneers, for his guidance and direction. Particular thanks go to Ralph Kay Harmer and Wendell B. Johnson for the Mapleton history book. Also, thanks are owed to the Daughters of Utah Pioneers, Mapleton Camps, for continuing to preserve these historical records. We also appreciate Eric Brinkerhoff for his fun book about the early tales of Mapleton; a huge thank-you to Eric's maternal grandfather, Aaron Bruce Mendenhall Jr., who tirelessly preserved the heritage we have to honor today.

I want to expressly give thanks to my professor at Utah Valley University, Scott Abbott, who gave me the opportunity to write this book as my senior thesis project.

Thanks go to our families for putting up with us as we ignored them to finish this book.

I also thank Alyssa Jones at Arcadia Publishing for finding me. Thanks to Kjirstin for coming along for this adventurous ride. Unless otherwise noted, all images were taken by and appear courtesy of Kjirstin Youngberg.

Introduction

Mapleton is nestled due east of Utah Lake in a snug cove along the Wasatch Mountains. Pioneers arrived in Springville on September 18, 1850, after religious persecutions drove the Mormons to seek a place where they could practice their religion in freedom and safety. At first, the area was farmland used by the Springville residents.

Union Bench was the first name given, as the people had to be united to keep going under harsh conditions. Many described the first residents as being like a cooperative family with just a few occasional disagreements. Without the support of others, no one family could have survived on its own. At planting and harvest time, everyone helped their neighbors and shared labor to build homes and barns. Winters were brutally cold. Even the Native Americans left at the first sign of snow.

Early settlers had some altercations with the indigenous peoples and did not always understand their ways. Dean Tew told of his ancestors' attempts to help an elderly woman left to die in the elements. Barbara Jensen recalled a large bonfire where her father, Buss, watched as Native Americans burned the clothing he had gathered and donated to them. A.B. Mendenhall Jr. claimed Jimmy Wahnrodes sold his pinto pony several times to different people, only to have it always return to him. There were also cases of cooperation and trade as people learned to get along. These stories are told in Erik C. Brinkerhoff's book *Mapleton: A Collection of Folks' Tales*, published in 2006.

This book opens by showcasing what makes Mapleton unique today. There are still a handful of residents who are descendants of the original settlers. The 24th of July Pioneer Day Parade celebrates the 1847 arrival of pioneers in the Salt Lake Valley. People come from far and wide to enjoy this family event in Mapleton.

Chapter two describes the struggles of growing the community. A few businesses sprung up, including the Del Monte canning facility, which, though located in Spanish Fork, helped to give residents here a working income. Farming the land meant that water was a constant concern, but during the winter months, rain turns to snow, creating an environment ripe for family fun.

Our beginnings as a community are pictured in the last chapter. Pioneers endured many hardships—some we cannot even imagine today. Hunting, raising livestock, and farming were the staples of life. Everyone pulled together, and it has been said that "Everyone found out when somebody did something wrong." Community life meant that everyone knew you, your siblings and parents, and where you lived. Few held their tongues if a child needed correction.

These beautifully preserved memories are largely due to photographer George Edward Anderson, who lived in Springville. Anderson documented the families and activities in the area. Rell G. Francis helped to preserve these images.

Mapleton is said to be a magical place to raise a family. Even with the lack of a strong tax base, high water prices, and the many squabbles over growth, development, and land use, people stay. When times get tough, the people here continue to pull together. We hope you will enjoy this picturesque journey through Mapleton's past.

One

Mapleton Today and Yesterday

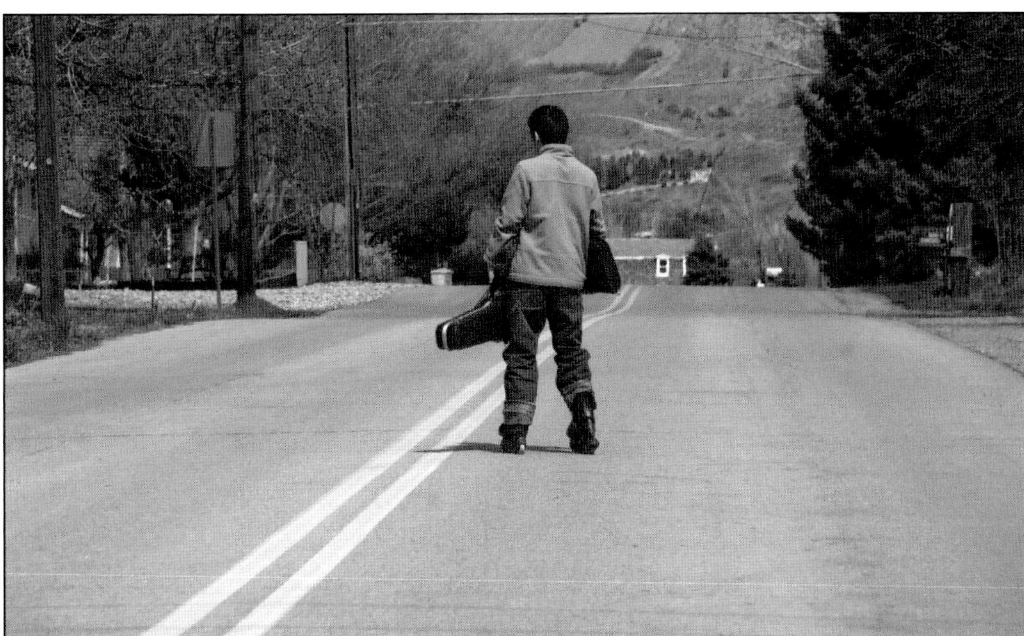

The oldest of Lia and Mark Huntington's seven children, 14-year-old Luke Huntington liked to rollerblade to Mapleton Junior High School. The family is relatively new to the city, having moved here in 2010. Luke loves many genres of music and studies classical violin. Fablehaven, Harry Potter, Percy Jackson, and the Michael Vey series are his recommended reads; two of his favorite authors are from Utah. Luke is currently a student at Maple Mountain High School.

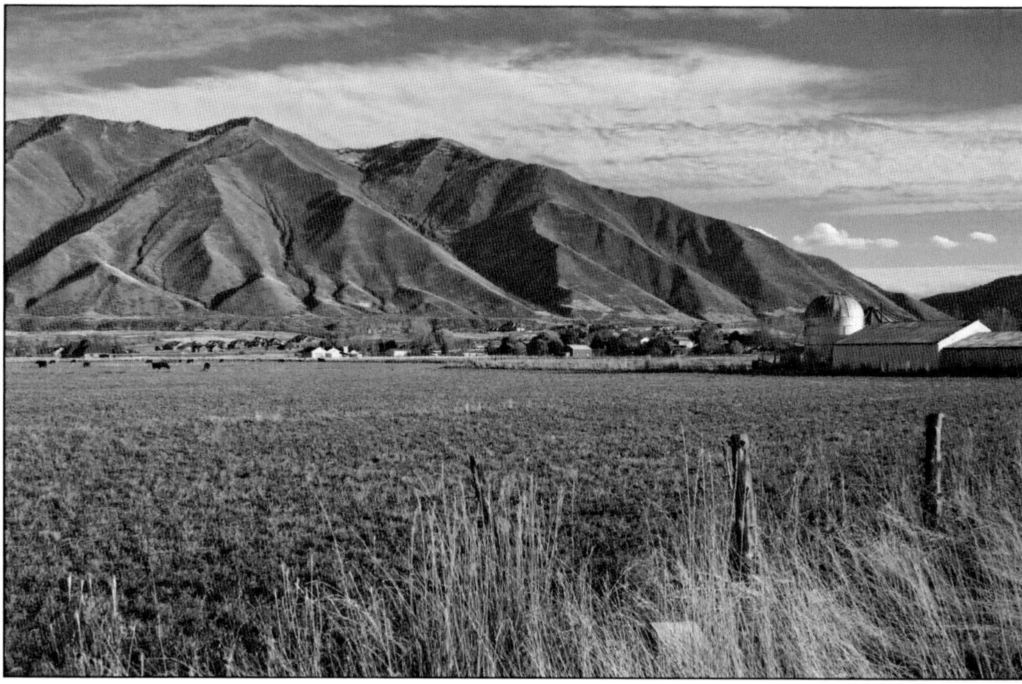

Southern Mapleton features many fields and farms. This 2010 photograph shows farms on the east side of Highway 89 and the lovely Sierra Bonita, which is also known as Maple Mountain. Spanish Fork Peak is another name for it, because the peak can be seen from the other side of the city, heading into Spanish Fork.

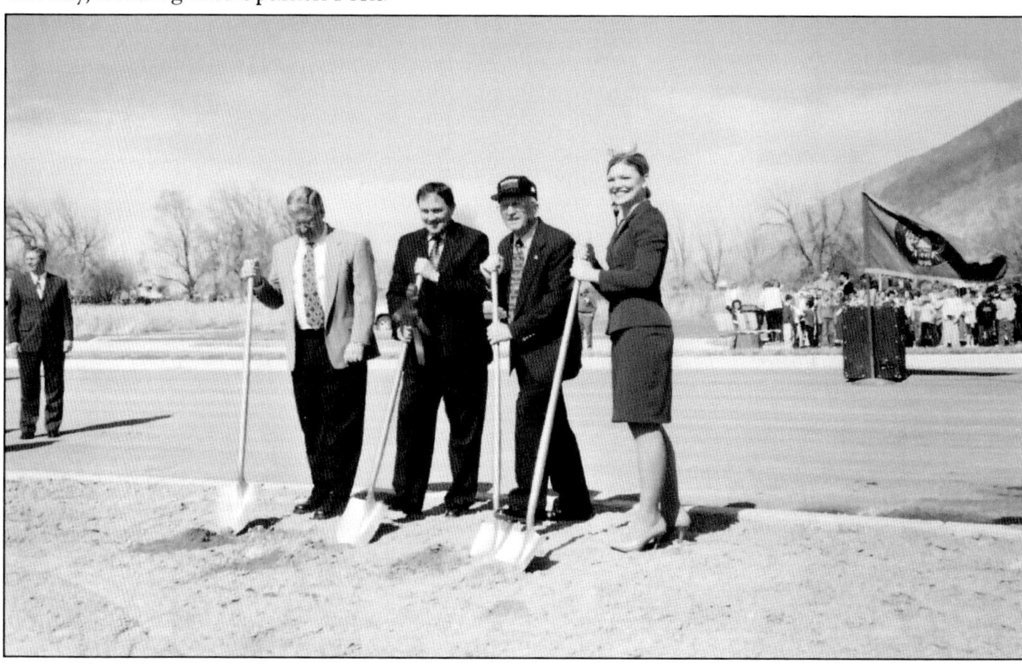

Pictured at the March 7, 2005, ground breaking ceremony for the city's new community center are, from left to right, city council member Ben Card, Lt. Gov. Gary Herbert, Mayor Dean Allan, and Miss Springville-Mapleton First Attendant Emily Jones. (Courtesy of Dean Allan.)

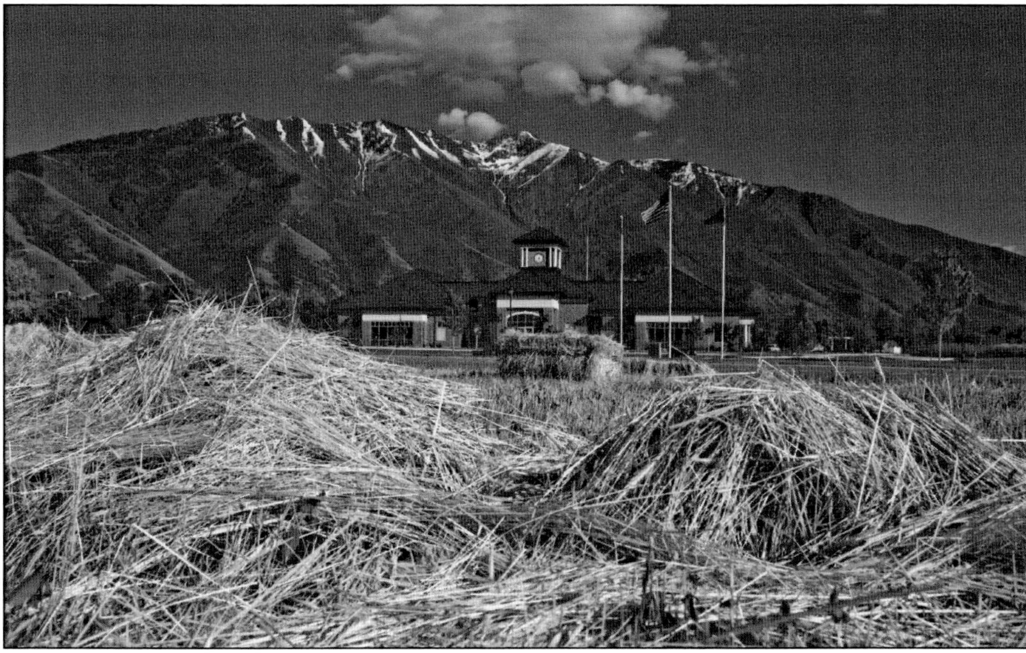

Mapleton City Building, seen here around 2011, is a modern, multiuse structure that includes a community center with a kitchen; spaces for a variety of classes, like ballet, yoga, and painting; a literacy center; and a senior citizens area. Across the street is a working hay field. Around the corner at 305 North Main Street is the new Mapleton Public Safety Building. (www.mapleton.org.)

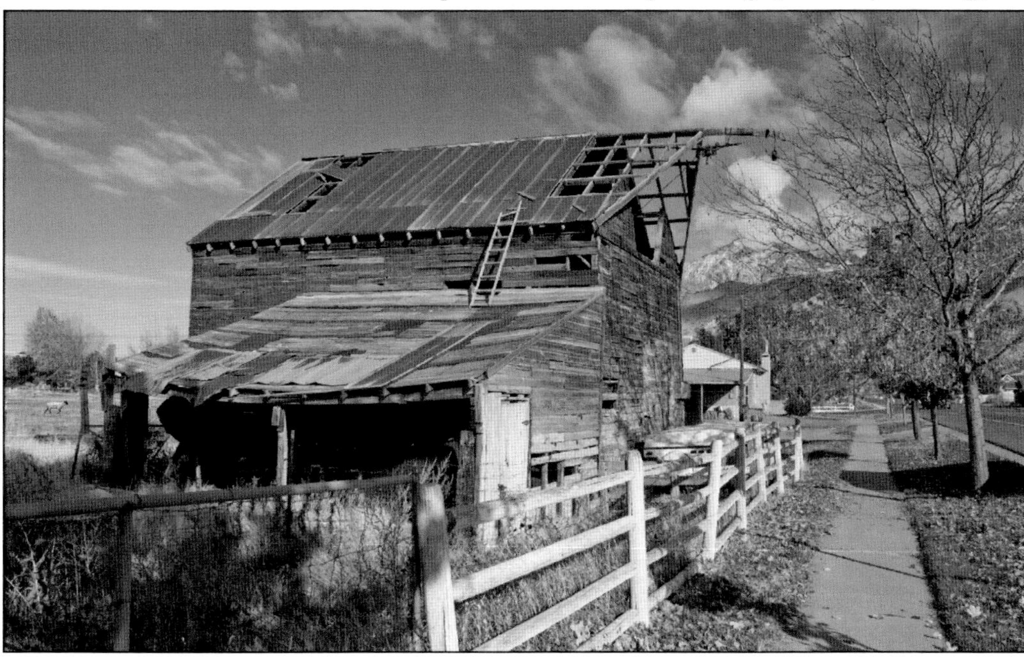

One of the Bona family barns was located on Main Street and 1600 North and was a favorite of photographers from all over the valley. It stood over 80 years until Hobble Creek's infamous canyon winds, along with heavy spring snow, helped collapse it in 2011. The Bona family was one of the founding Italian families who helped to settle Mapleton. (mapletonnews.com.)

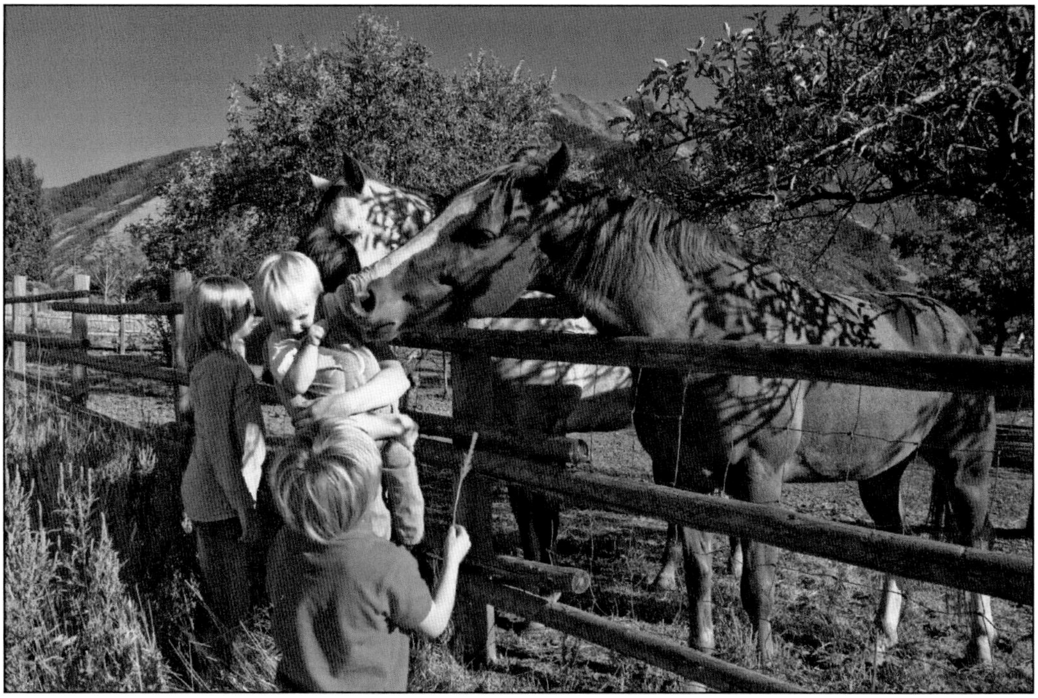

Pictured in the fall of 2010 are the children of Judith and Joe Everett. They are, from left to right, Ruth, Rachel, John (who is not at all sure he wants to be kissed by a horse), and Brigham. These children are descendants of the original Averett family who helped to establish the city. Since the name was pronounced Everett, the great-great-grandparents Charles and Hilda Marchbanks Averett decided in the 1920s to change the spelling to reflect the way it was pronounced.

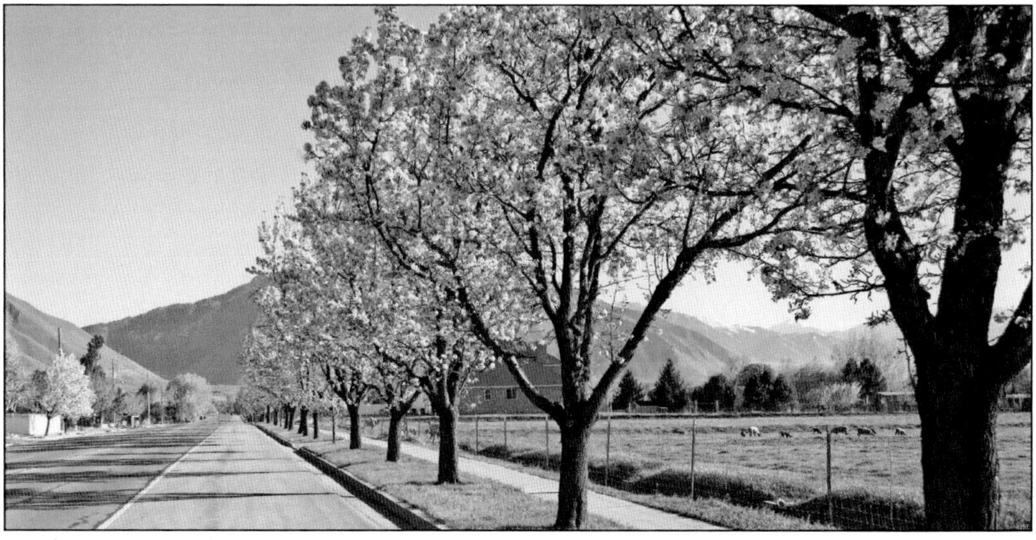

Mapleton is a proud part of the Tree City USA campaign, and the northwest side of Main Street is known as a Pioneer Heritage Tree Street. Maple trees with memorial plaques at the base honor the founding families of Mapleton. (www.arborday.org.)

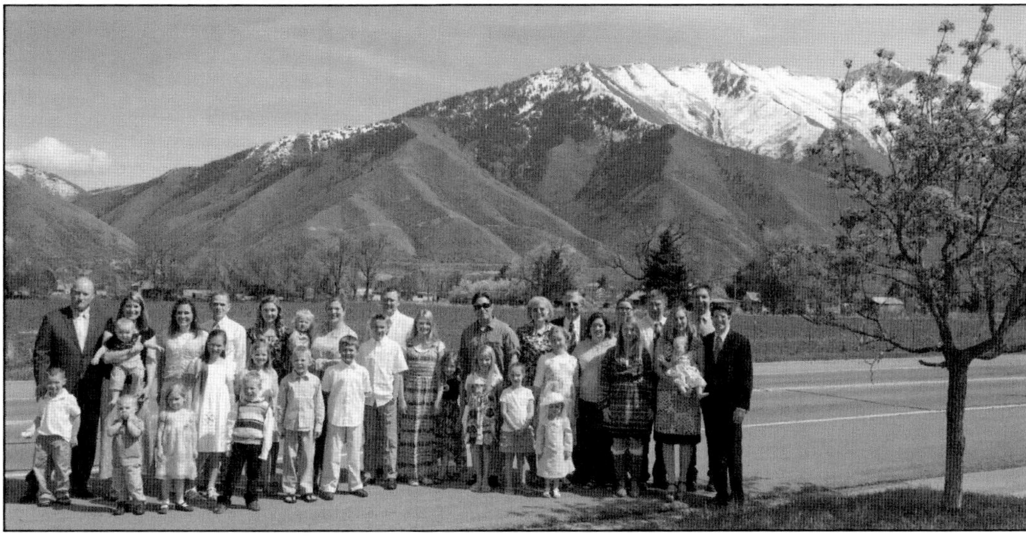

Pictured here in April 2014 are descendants of Stephen Chadwick Perry and his third wife, Mary Boggs. The Perry family is standing next to their Pioneer Heritage Tree planted in Stephen and Mary's honor, located on North Main Street.

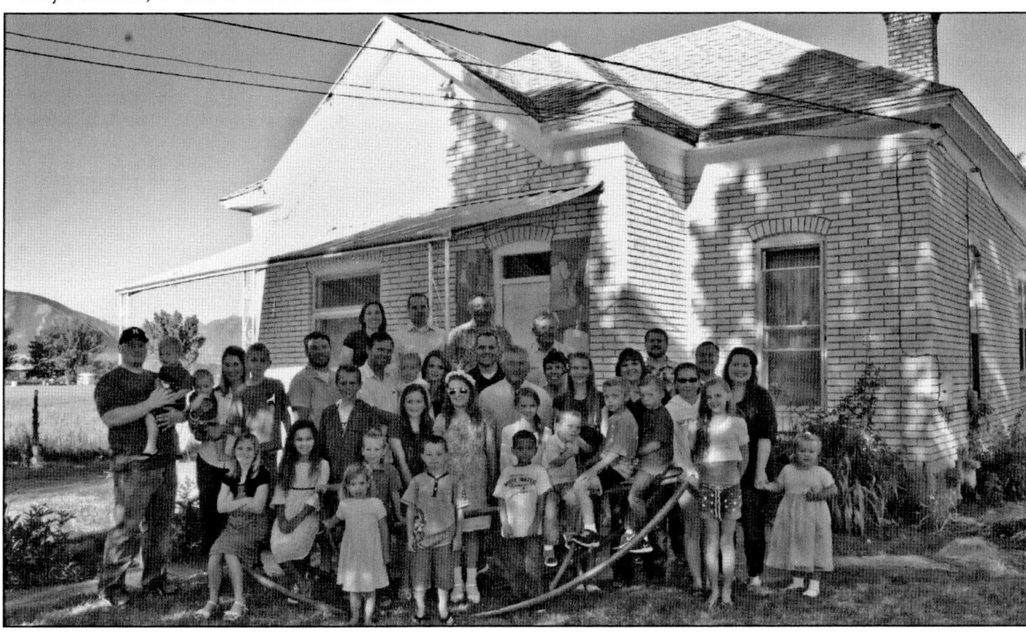

Another group of Perry family descendants gathered in June 2014 in front of the historic Marion Perry home; today, the home is no longer in the family. The house was built about 1907 on eight acres given to Marion Perry by his father, Stephen Chadwick Perry, from the original 160 acres Stephen homesteaded on the Mapleton Bench, originally called Union Bench. The home is located at 422 South Main Street. Marion brought his bride, Clara Elizabeth Larsen, there in 1910. Seven children were born to them in this home. Marion was a skilled horseman and trainer, and also dealt in hay and grain. In 1917, he contracted ptomaine poisoning and was partially crippled. He used his horses to get around and was loved and respected by all who knew him. Clara went to work after Marion's paralysis and became a licensed practical nurse at the Utah State Hospital, working there from 1941 to 1956.

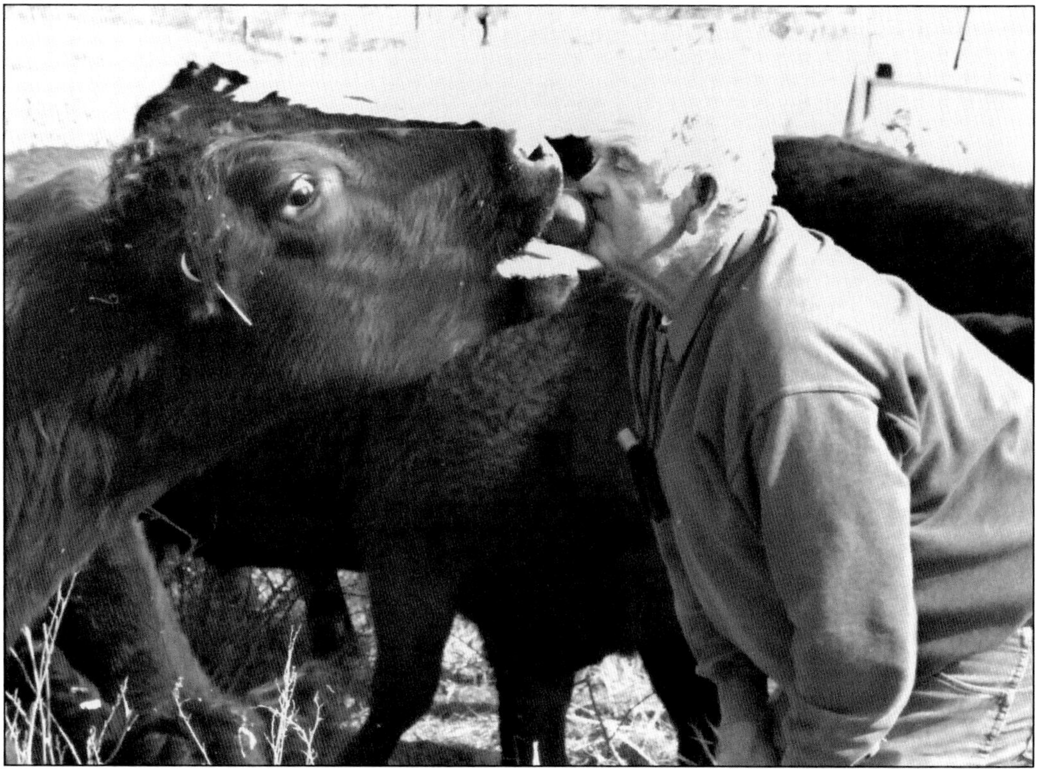

Richard "Dick" Bills is the oldest male native in Mapleton, born September 22, 1929, and is pictured here feeding his cow an apple in 2009. (Courtesy of Richard Bills.)

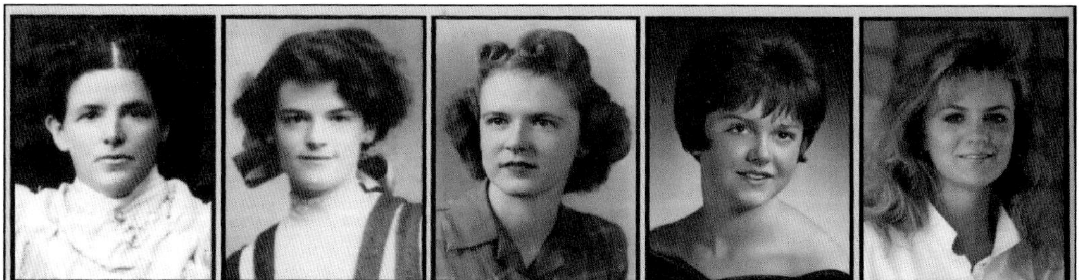

Five generations are seen here, with Orpha Dee Bird Johnson in the center. Orpha is the oldest native resident in Mapleton, born June 3, 1925, when Calvin Coolidge was president. From left to right are Rachel Hannah Thomas Banks, Lenore Banks Bird, Orpha Dee Bird Johnson, Brenda Johnson Hamilton, and Laura K. Hamilton Koepke. Perhaps the most famous of the Johnson family was Orpha's son Wendell, who, though paralyzed, became Mapleton's mayor and a gifted artist. (Courtesy of Orpha Dee Bird Johnson, www.wendellbjohnson.com.)

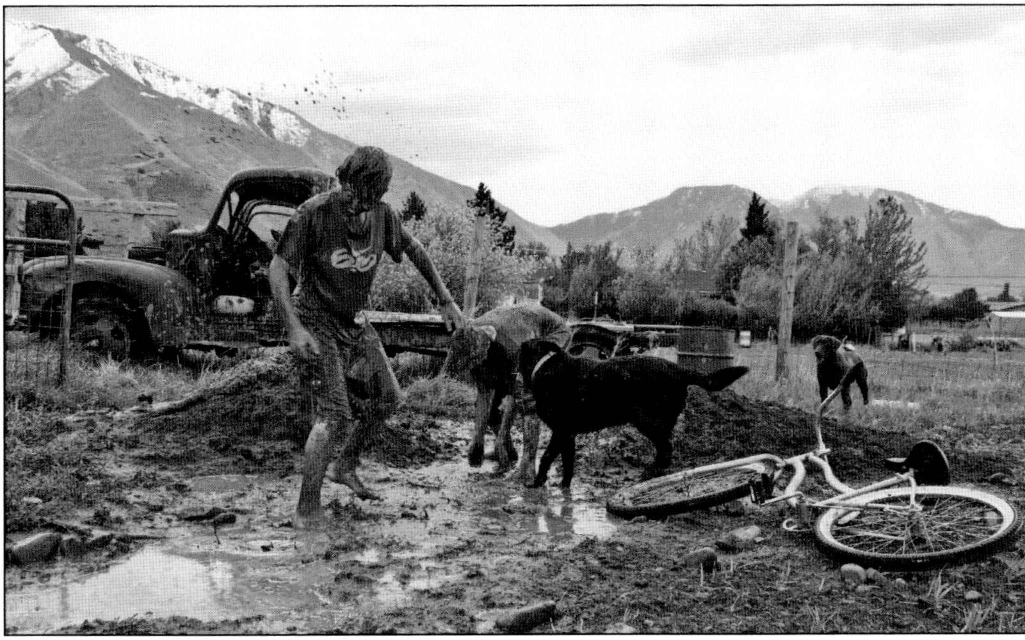

Mapleton boys Jacob Bleggi (left) and Connor Olson are seen in spring 2011 having a day of fun in the mud at the former residence of Jacob Bleggi. The original Bleggi descendants raised sheep and stock animals and helped Mapleton to flourish into the city it is today.

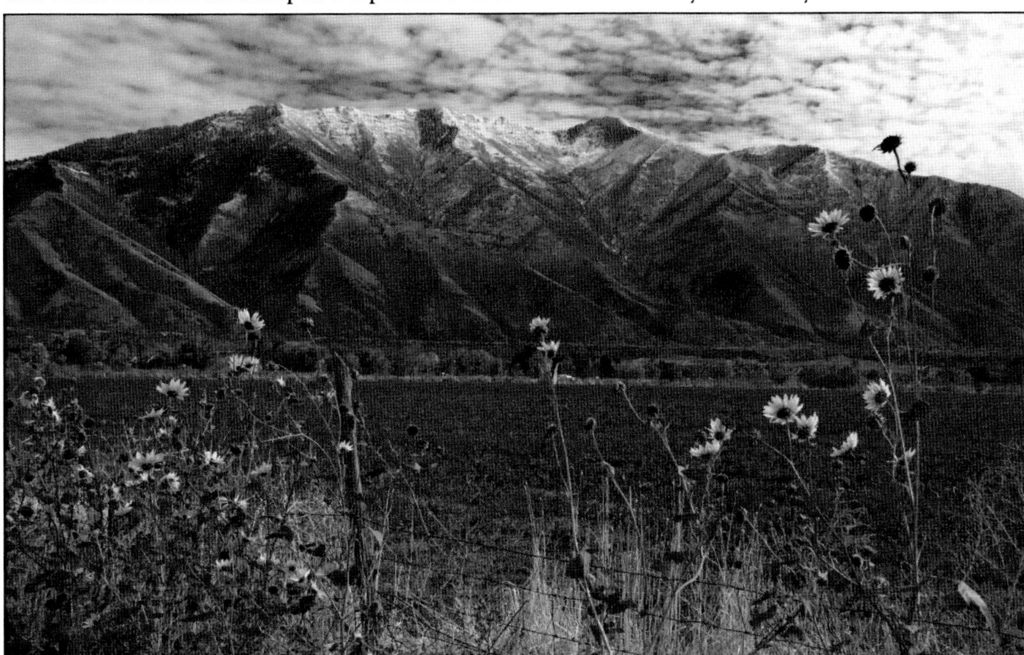

This 2012 photograph shows one of the few sheep pastures left in Mapleton as homes and church buildings are erected. Mapleton currently has eight chapels, two of them stake centers, with 22 separate wards or congregations. The only churches in Mapleton so far are for the Church of Jesus Christ of Latter-day Saints. A hiker recently claimed to have counted 34 steeples on a clear day from the mountain, while not seeing a single bar. (www.lds.org.)

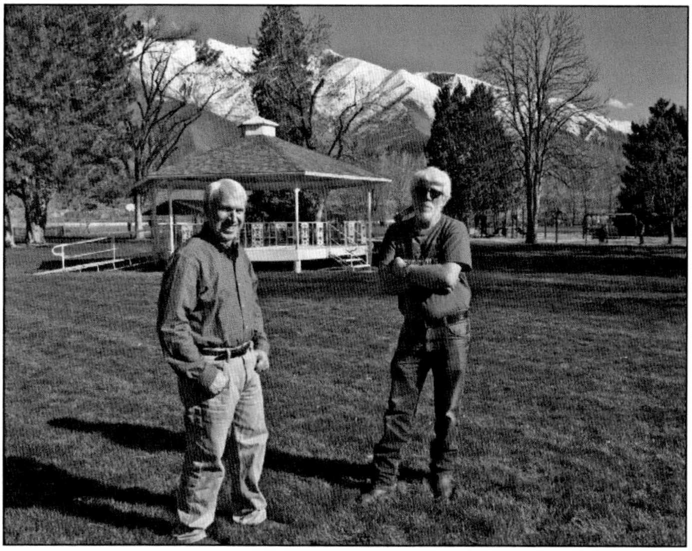

Mapleton business owners Richard Hjorth (left), owner of Hjorth Brothers Inc., and Steve Kappas, owner of Monogram Station, are pictured at the Mapleton City Park in April 2014. In the background is a gazebo built by Frank Johnson and a host of volunteers in 1983.

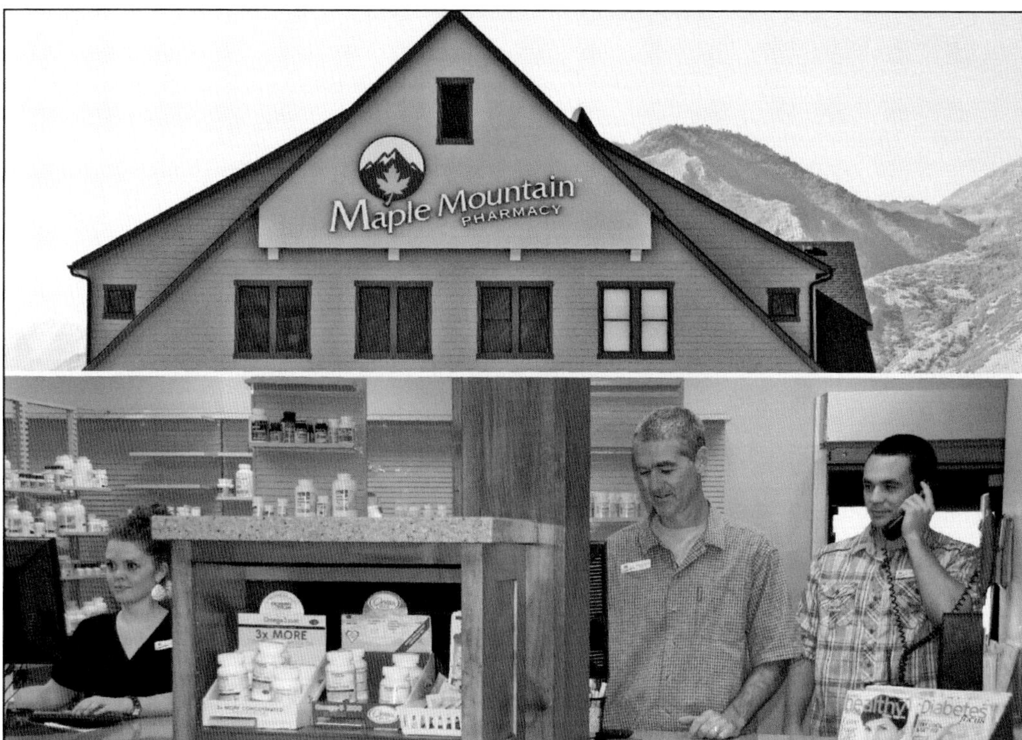

Maple Mountain Pharmacy opened in 2013. It is located at 724 South and 1600 West (Highway 89). The store features a gift shop with toys, games, jewelry, scented soaps, and an assortment of fun party items, including unique greeting cards and helium balloons. There is also an ice cream and smoothie fountain with hot food for a fun date. Pictured are, from left to right, Leslee Nance, pharmacist Mike Johnson, and Zach Johnson. (www.maplemountainpharmacy.com.)

These children are enjoying a wedding reception at the home of Chris and Claudia Cannon in 2010. From left to right are Shale Walker, Elliott Cannon, and Ruby Cannon.

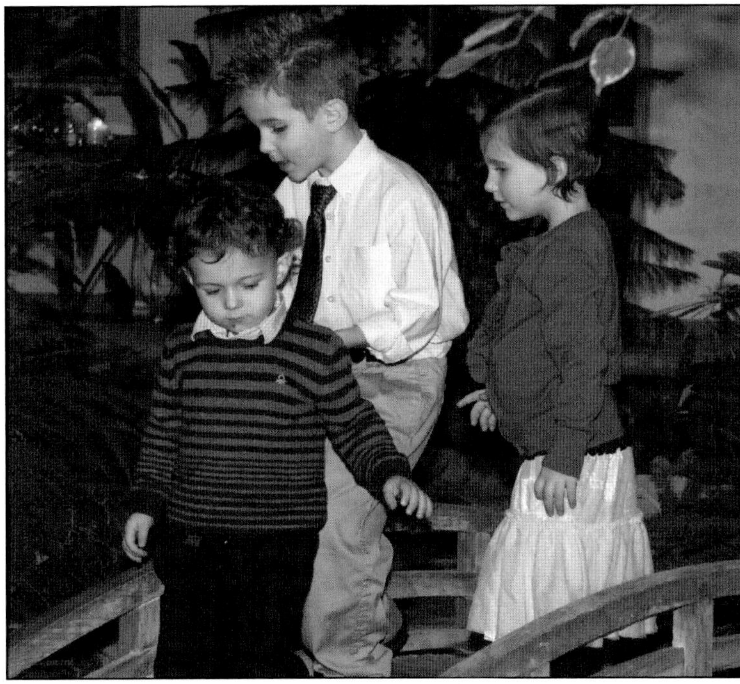

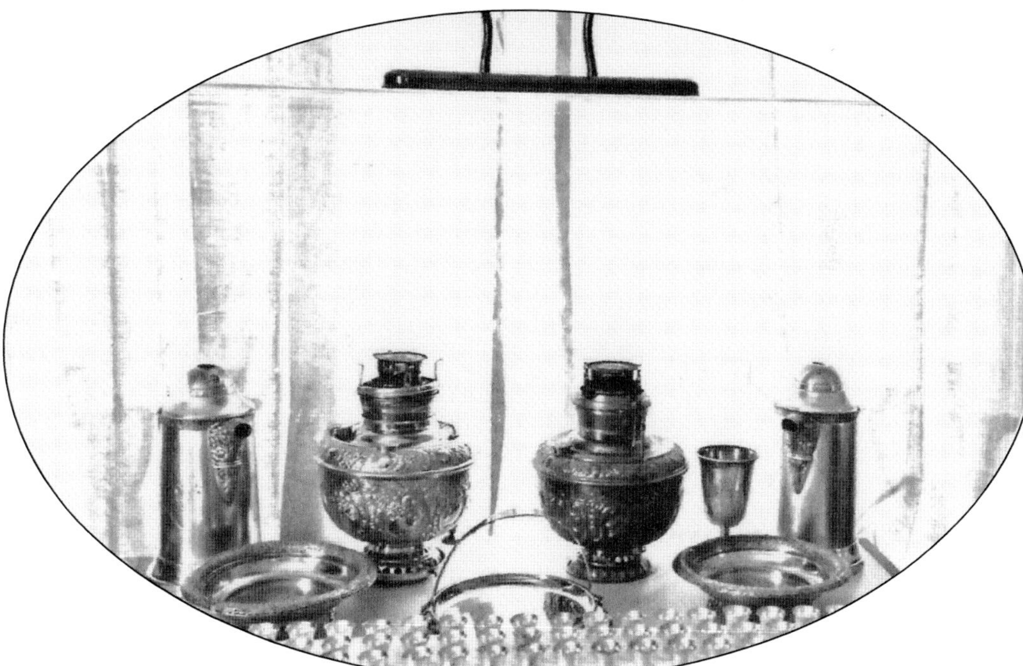

Seen today at the Mapleton City Historical Museum, this sacrament set for the Church of Jesus Christ of Latter-day Saints was from the first church building in Mapleton in 1893. The sacrament is a weekly ritual for members. In the first row are 70 silver sacrament cups. The second row features three bread trays. In the third row are a silver pitcher, silver coal oil lamp, bronze oil lamp, communal goblet, and a second water pitcher. Above everything is a sacrament tray for the small cups. (April Clawson photograph.)

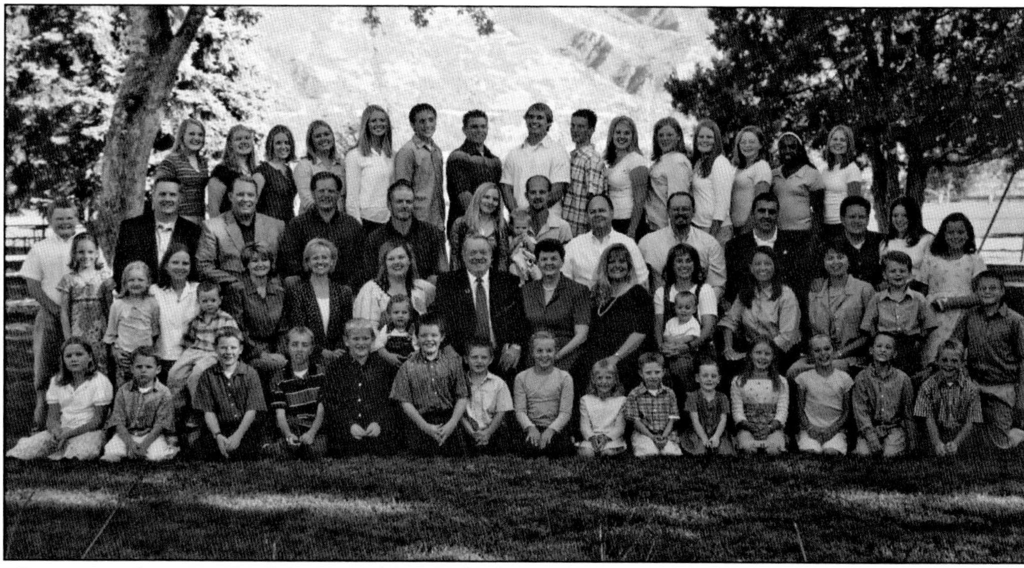

This group photograph of the Ronald and Shirley Graves family was taken to honor and celebrate the couple's 50th wedding anniversary in 2003. Ronald and Shirley have volunteered their time and talents in various capacities. (Courtesy of Ronald and Shirley Graves.)

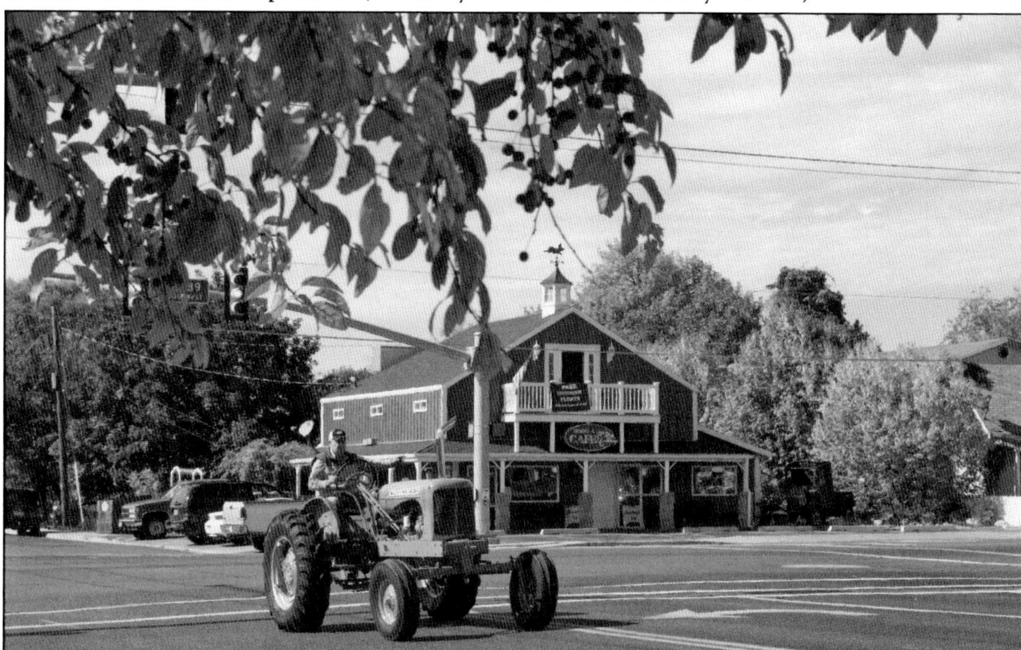

The intersection of Highway 89 and West Maple Street has plenty of activity in the autumn, as this scene from 2011 demonstrates. The red Model A Café is in the background. Maple Mountain Insurance Company has replaced it. Mapleton has two stoplights, three gas stations, a few large businesses, and quite a number of small businesses. Additionally, the Chevron gas station, with the added convenience store and Subway restaurant, is now open on the northeast corner, and due north on Highway 89 are the Family Pet Hospital and the Mapleton Floral and Gift Shop, a popular place for the local high school students.

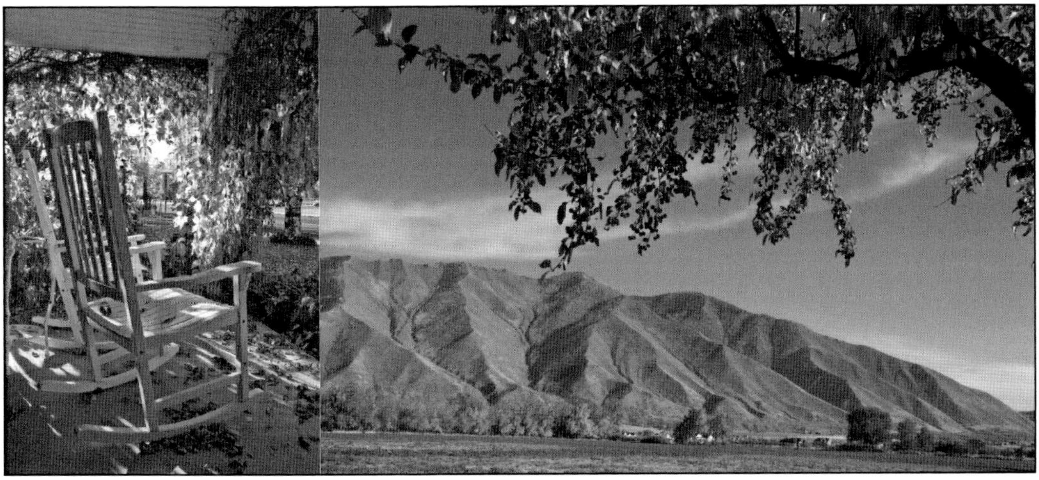

Rockers invite visitors to come sit and enjoy the beautiful scenery of Maple Mountain from the Main Street corner.

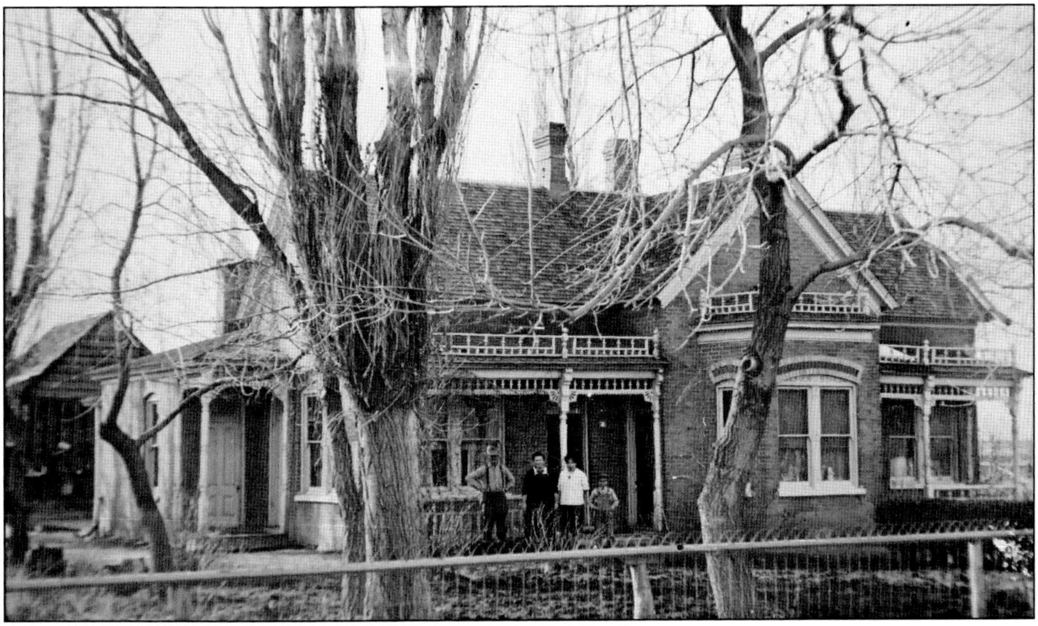

This c. 1892 photograph shows John Henry and Emma Sarah Kelsey Lee with their children, Ronald and Thelma Lee, in front of their home at 597 North 300 West in Mapleton. They built the home during the summer while they lived in a tent across the street. John served as the town water master, and Emma was a member of the Daughters of Utah Pioneers. (Courtesy of Larry Clark.)

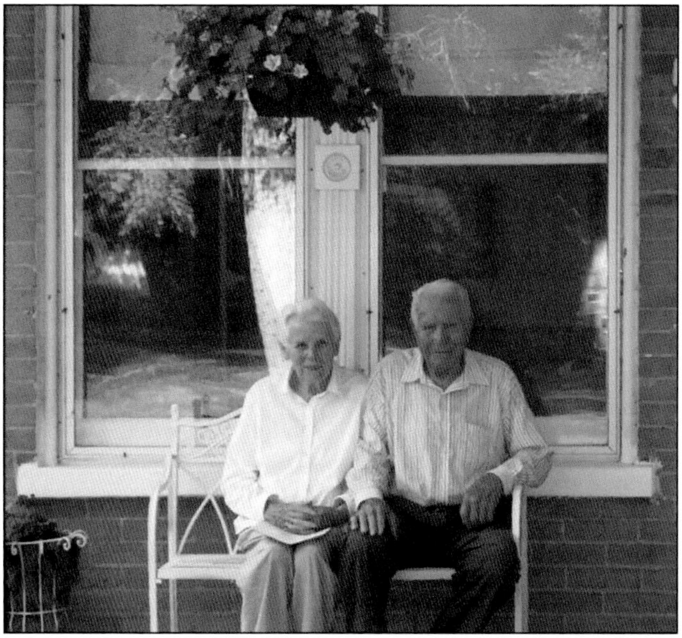

Seen here is the same 1892 Mapleton home but in July 2011 with Lois Clark, a descendant of the Lees, and her husband, Merlin "Wayne" Clark, who are not the current owners of the home. Wayne and Lois are the parents of seven children and retired to Mapleton. (Courtesy of Larry Clark.)

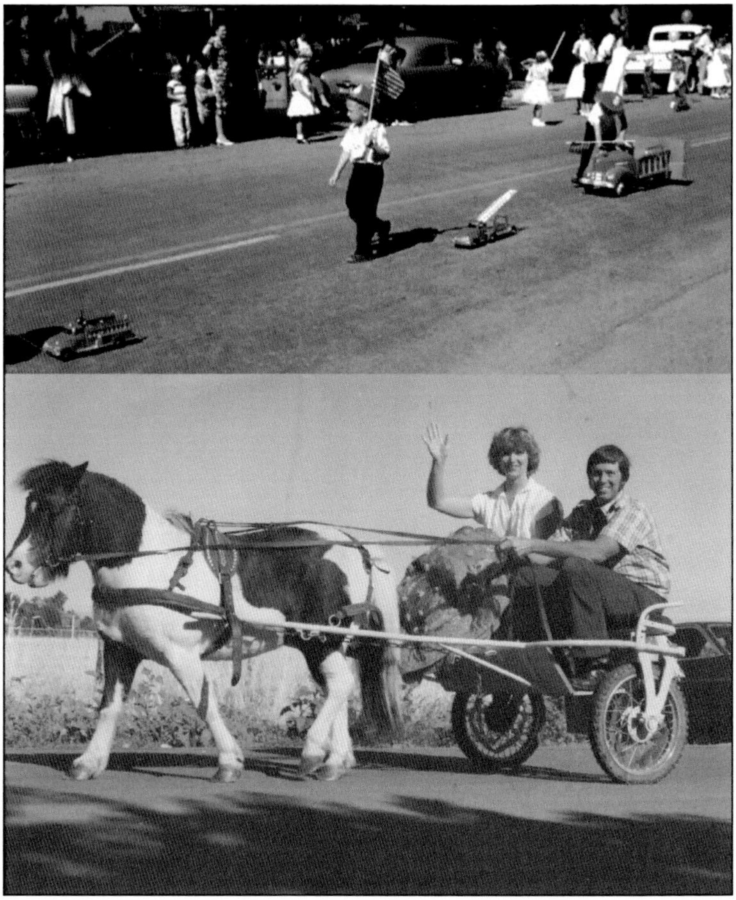

At top, in Mapleton's 24th of July Parade in 1956, Richard Hjorth is pulling his new fire truck from his fifth birthday. At bottom, Seabisquit the Shetland pony is pulling a cart in the July 24 parade in the late 1960s. Seabisquit was a favorite entry in the parade for 20 years. Dianne Wittusen and her husband, Ron, guide the cart and pony on the parade route. (Top, courtesy of Mary Hjorth Fojtek; bottom, courtesy of Richard Bills.)

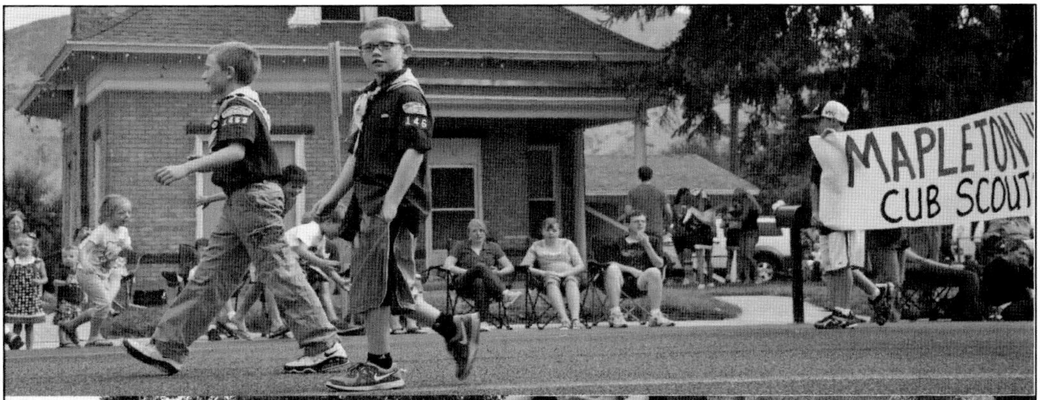

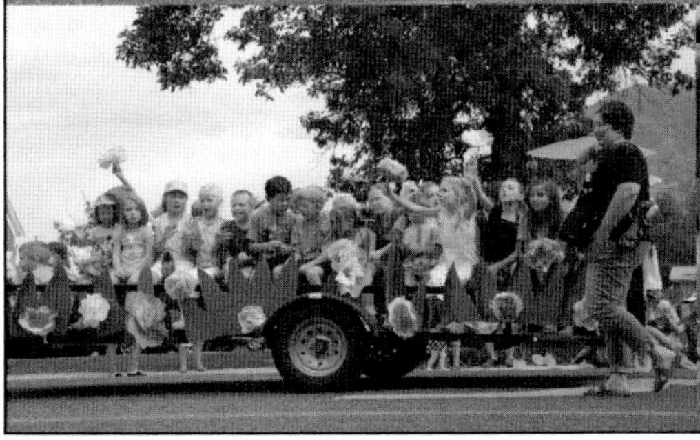

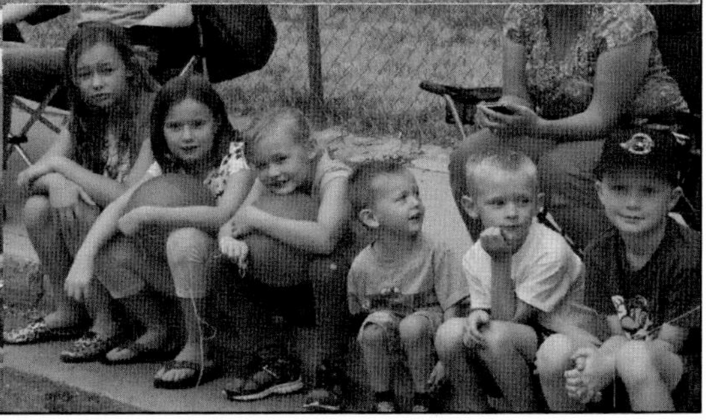

Pictured here are scenes from Mapleton's 24th of July Parade. Mapleton has a rich heritage, and the annual parade, held on a state holiday, honors the pioneers' arrival into Salt Lake Valley and the beginnings of the state. This pioneer celebration is the biggest yearly event in the city. Festivities begin at sunrise and run into the late evening with a popular concert and fireworks show.

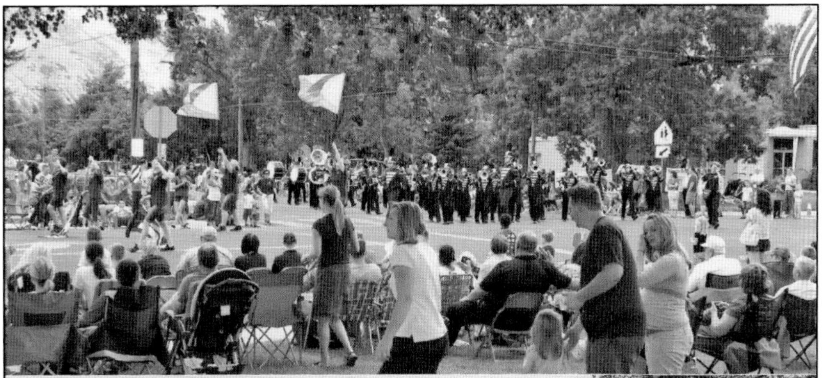

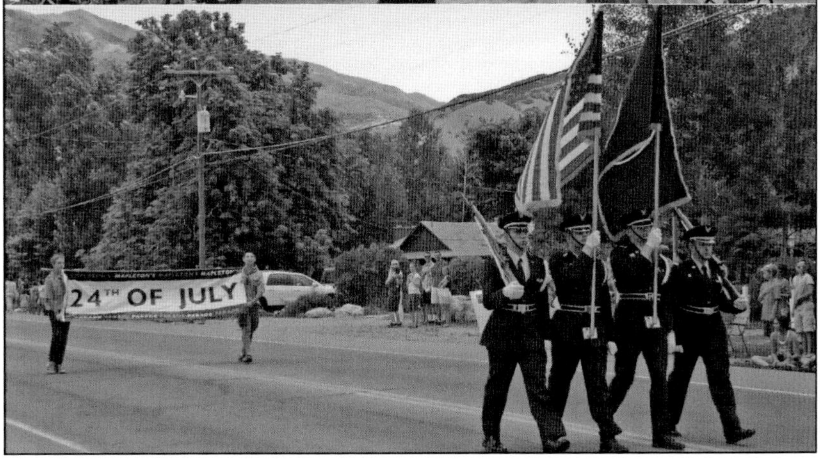

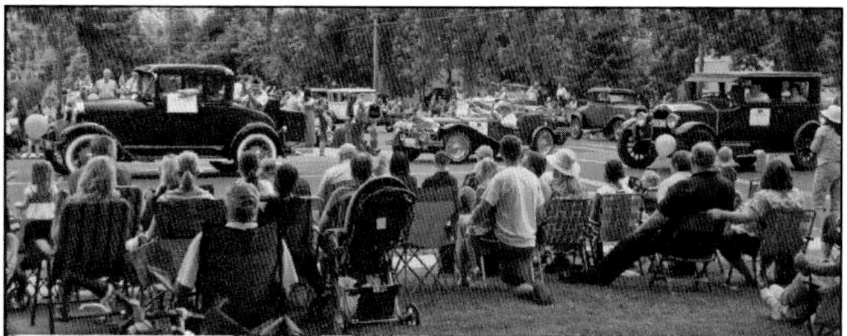

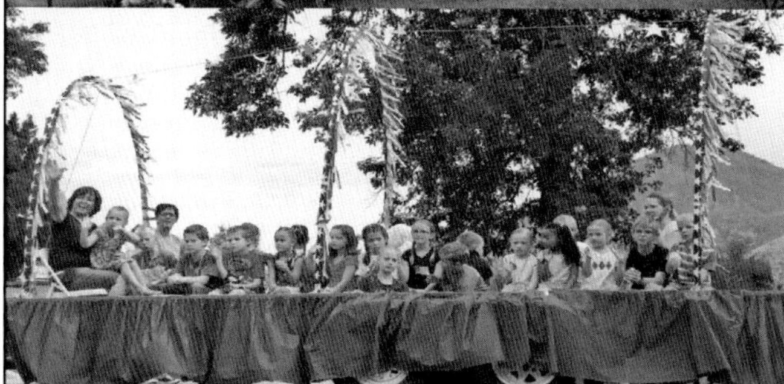

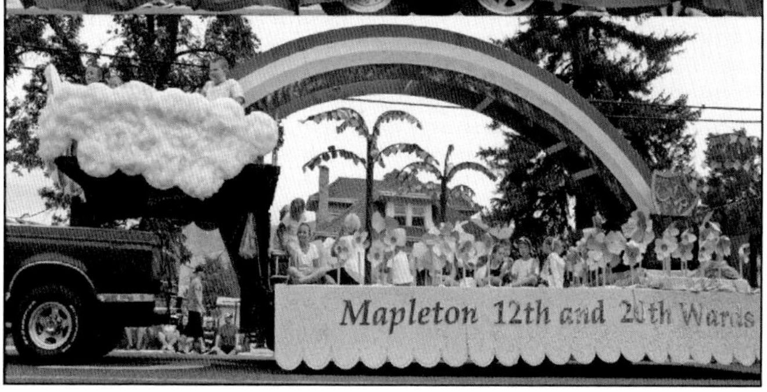

Pictured here are crowds enjoying Mapleton's 24th of July Parade, including participants from the 12th and 20th Wards, Mapleton North Stake, of the Church of Jesus Christ of Latter-day Saints.

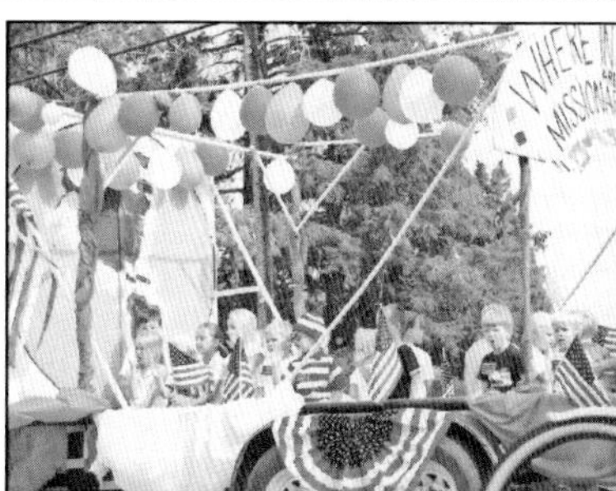

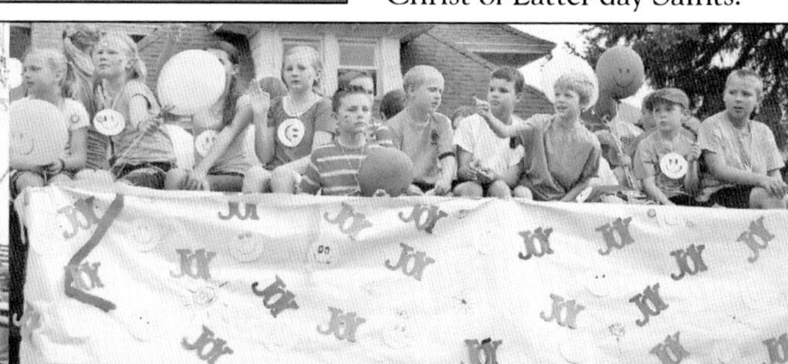

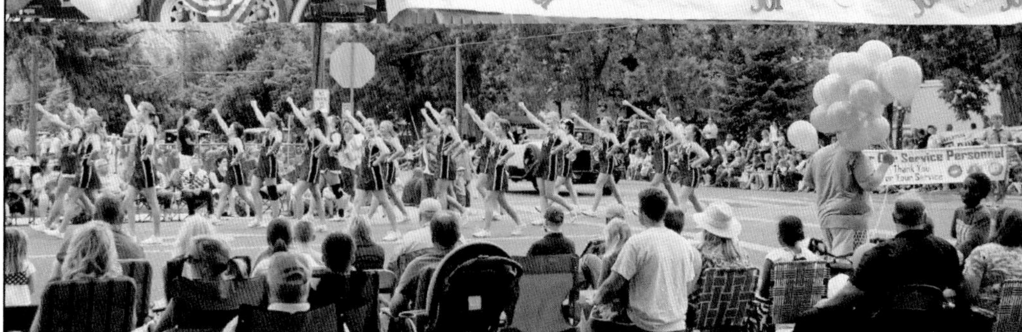

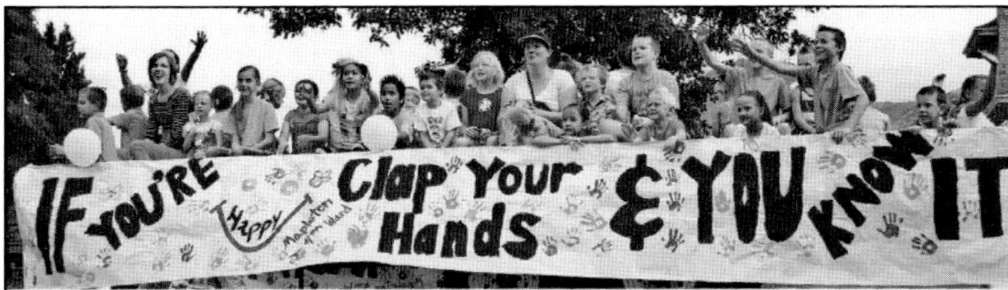

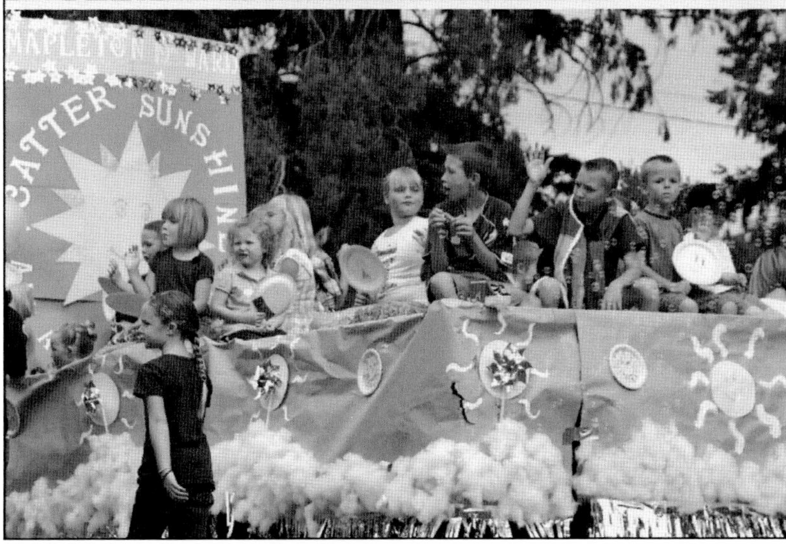

Parade participants celebrate at Mapleton's 24th of July Parade, including members from the 4th and 19th Wards, Mapleton Stake, of the Church of Jesus Christ of Latter-day Saints.

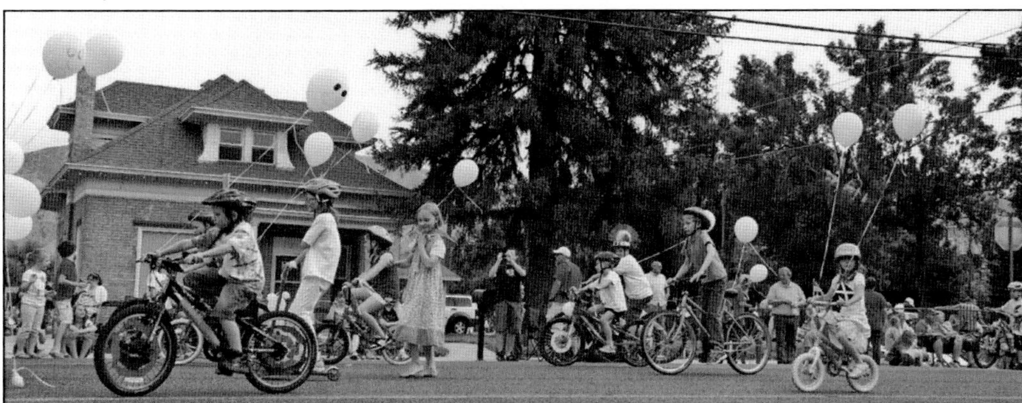

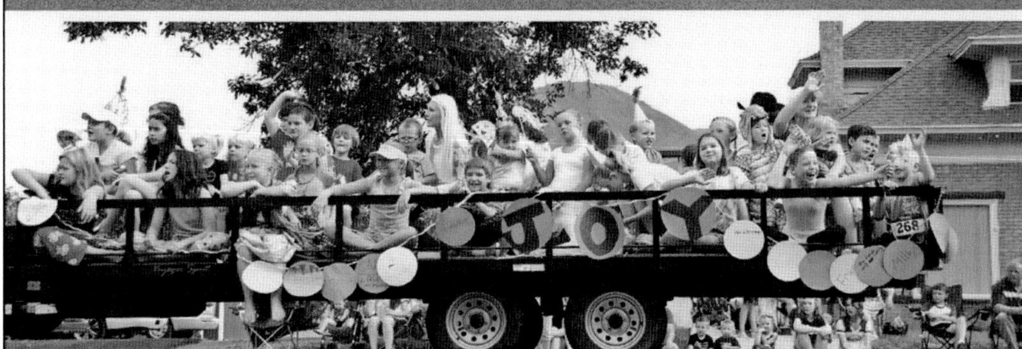

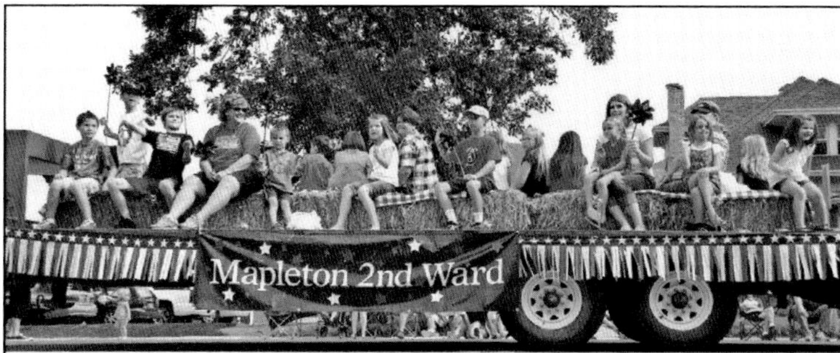

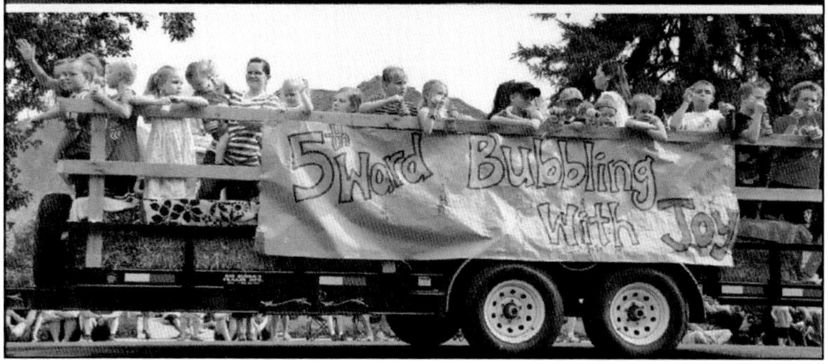

Pictured at Mapleton's 24th of July Parade are members from the 2nd and 5th Wards, Mapleton North Stake, of the Church of Jesus Christ of Latter-day Saints.

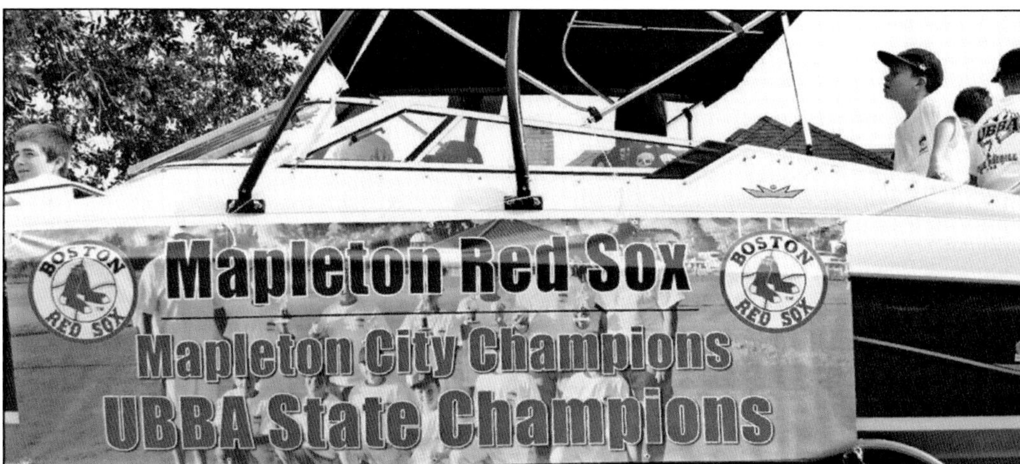

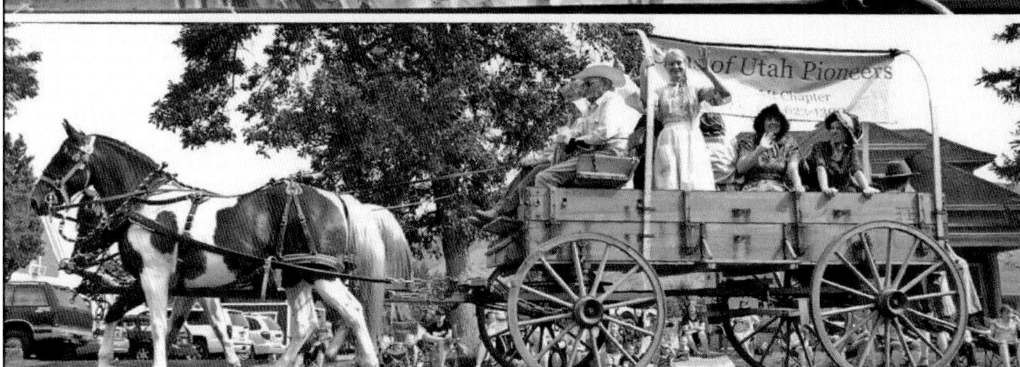

Mapleton's 24th of July Parade featured floats honoring the Mapleton Red Sox state champion baseball team and the Sons of Utah Pioneers.

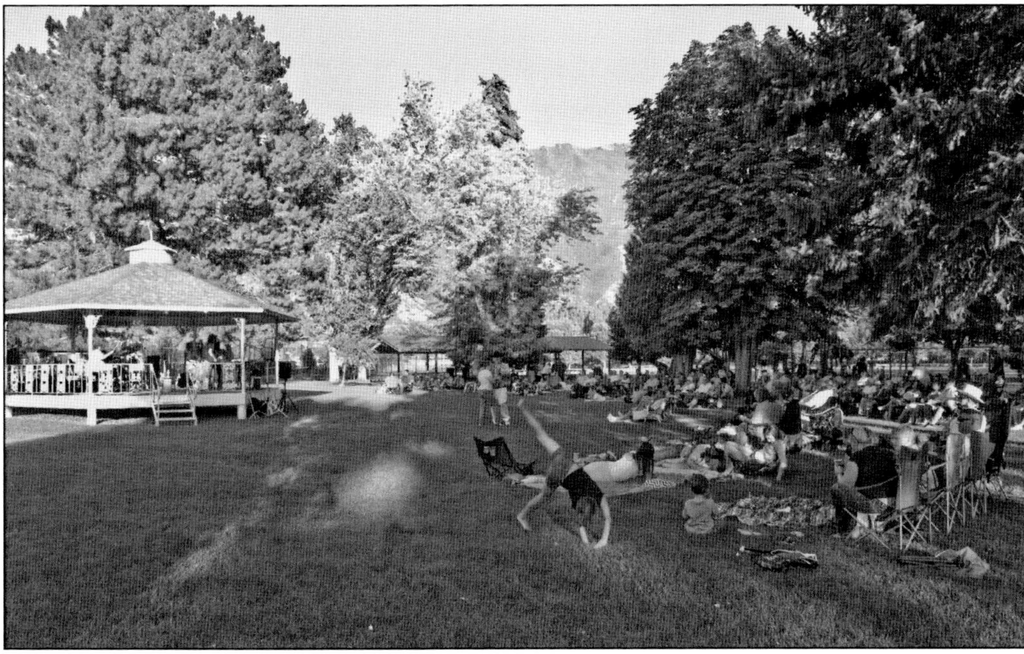

Mapleton's Summer Concerts in the Park have started attracting crowds. This July 7, 2014, concert featured the family-friendly band Midlife Crisis.

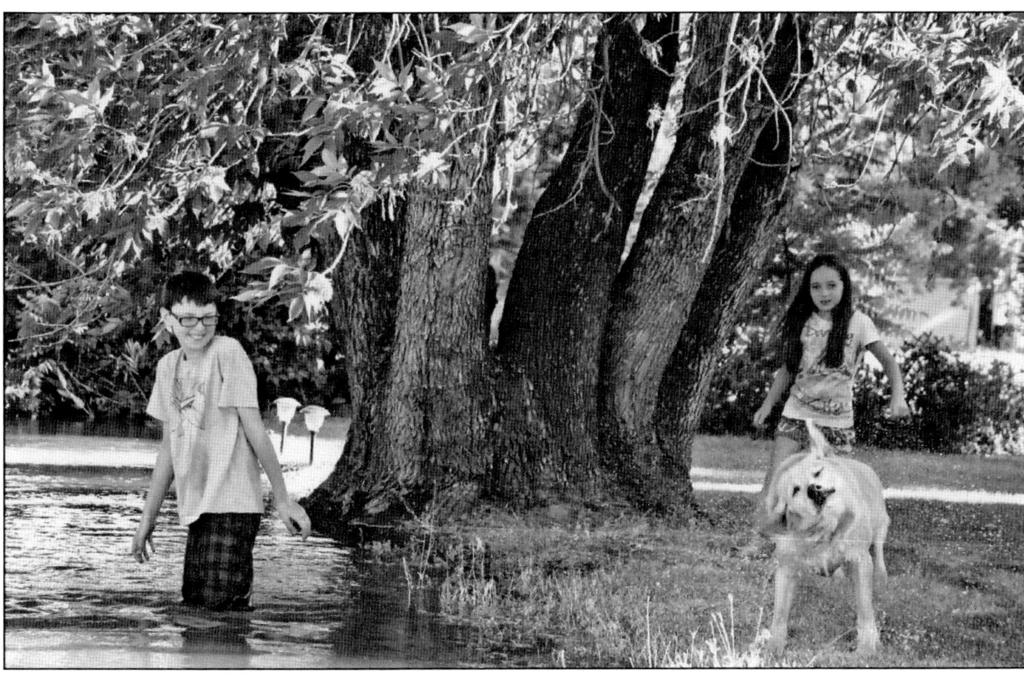

Amanda and Shawn Bagley's children, 11-year-old Garrett (left) and seven-year-old Olivia, enjoy the cool water on a hot summer day on July 8, 2014. Indie, their golden retriever, does not care who gets wet. Shawn was born and raised in Mapleton and decided to raise his children here, too.

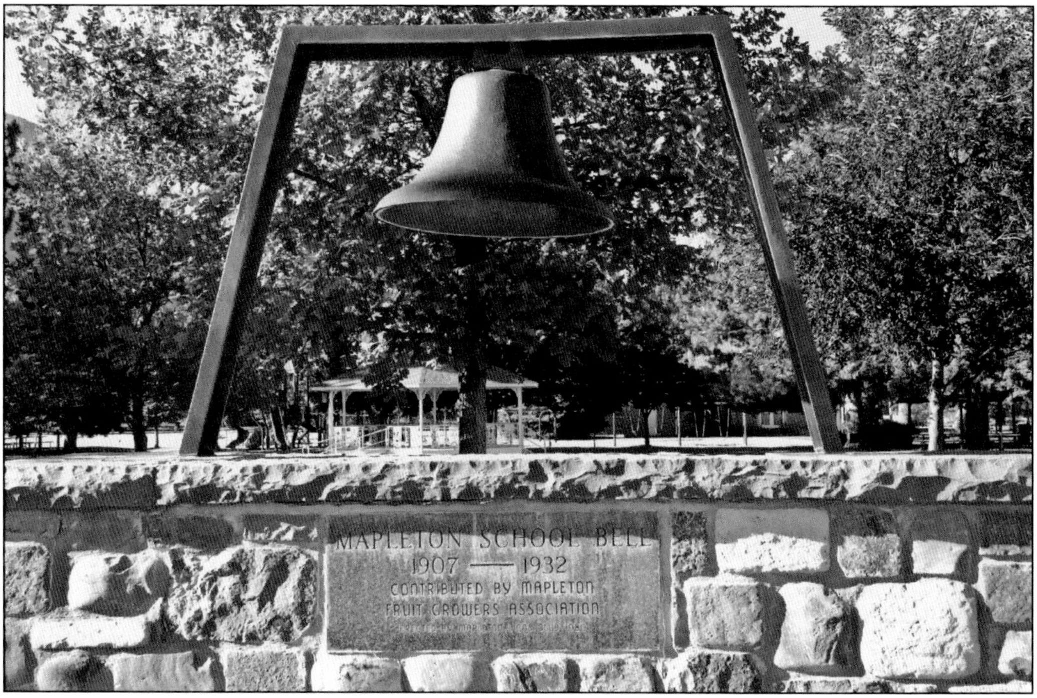

The original Mapleton School bell is now displayed in a memorial at the Mapleton City Park, at the corner of Main and Maple Streets, seen here in June 2014. The bell was used at the school and also to call firemen until a siren could be installed at the fire station. Located in the park is the Amusement Hall, and across from the park on Main Street is the historic "Old White Church." Mapleton Elementary School, Hobble Creek Elementary School, and Mapleton Junior High School are the only schools in the city. Private and charter school options are available in neighboring cities, and Mapleton also has quite a few families that prefer homeschooling.

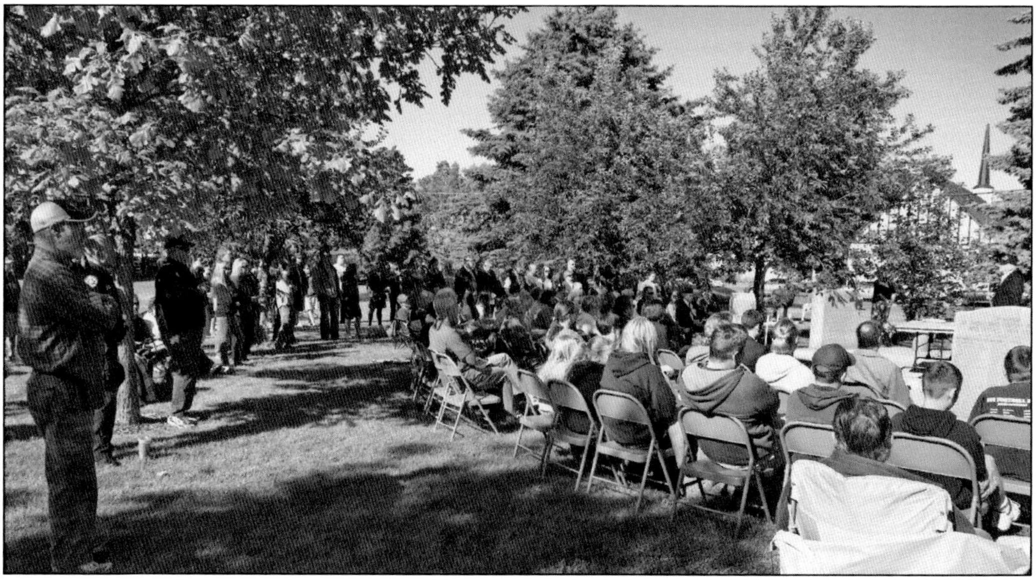

Citizens gather at the city park for Memorial Day Remembrance in 2012.

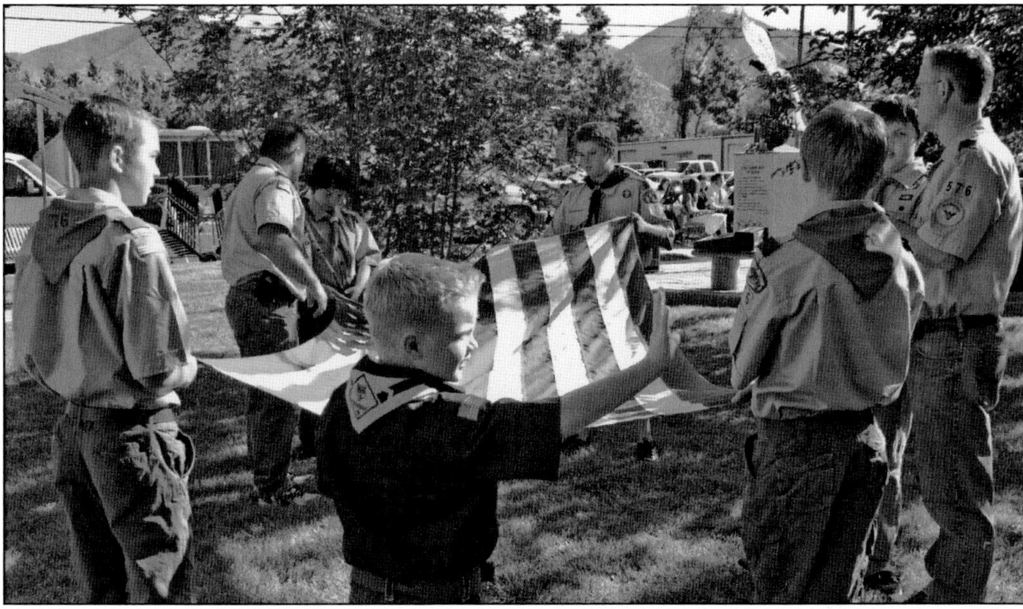

The Annual Memorial Day Remembrance is hosted at the Mapleton City Park. Pictured in 2012 are Mapleton's 11th Ward Boy Scouts and a Cub Scout, represented by Mapleton North Stake of the Church of Jesus Christ of Latter-day Saints.

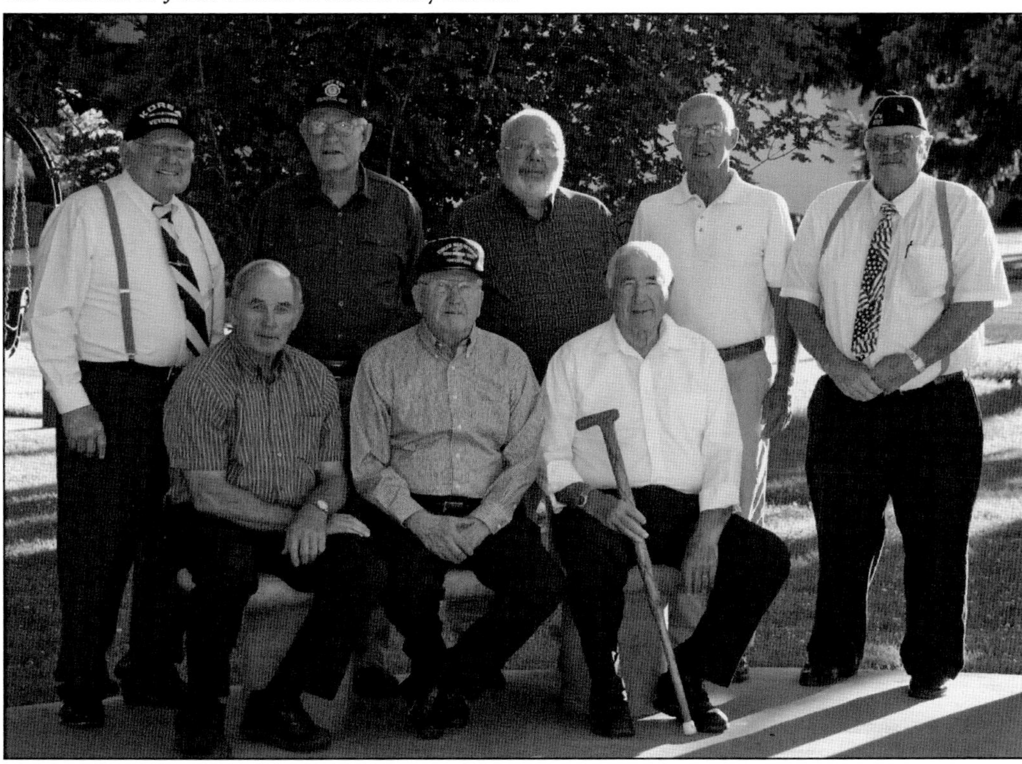

Mapleton veterans have their picture taken in July 2014 at the Mapleton City Park War Memorial site on Maple Street. Pictured are, from left to right, (first row) Mac Bills, Dean Allan, and Blaine Hales; (second row) Ervin Denna, Fred Hurst, Ron Perry, Morris Warren, and Wynn Everett.

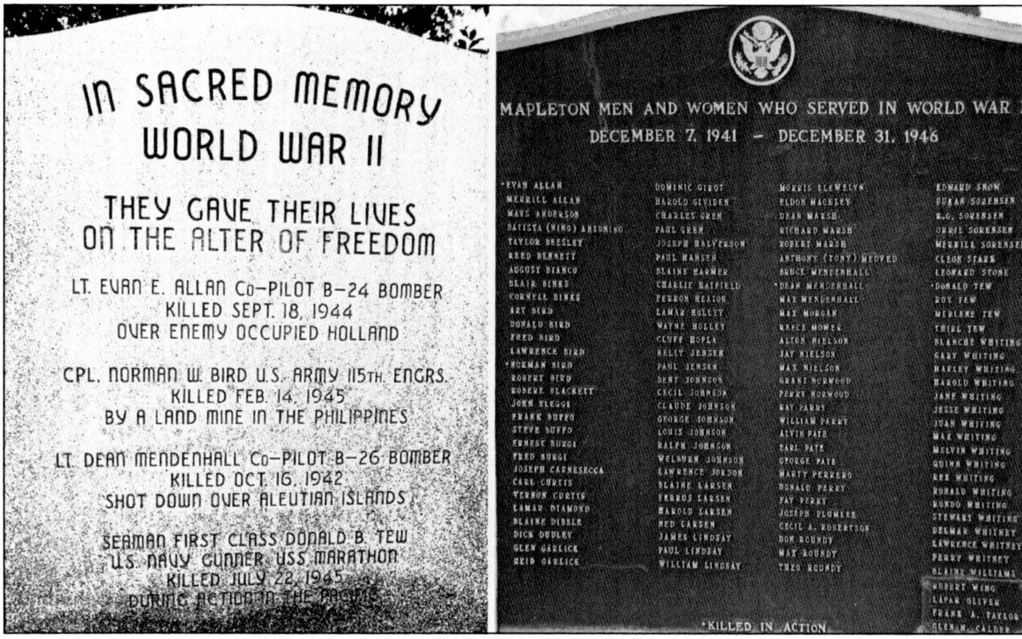

Mapleton's war memorials seen here pay homage to those who served in World War II, the Korean War, and the Vietnam War. Additional names not listed are Rondo Whiting and Ruth Jensen.

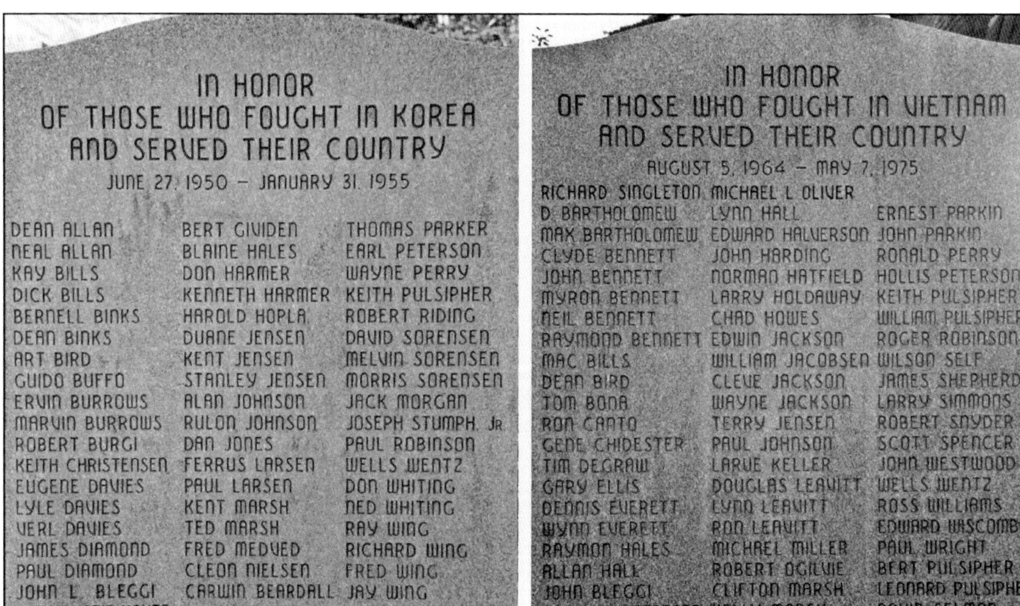

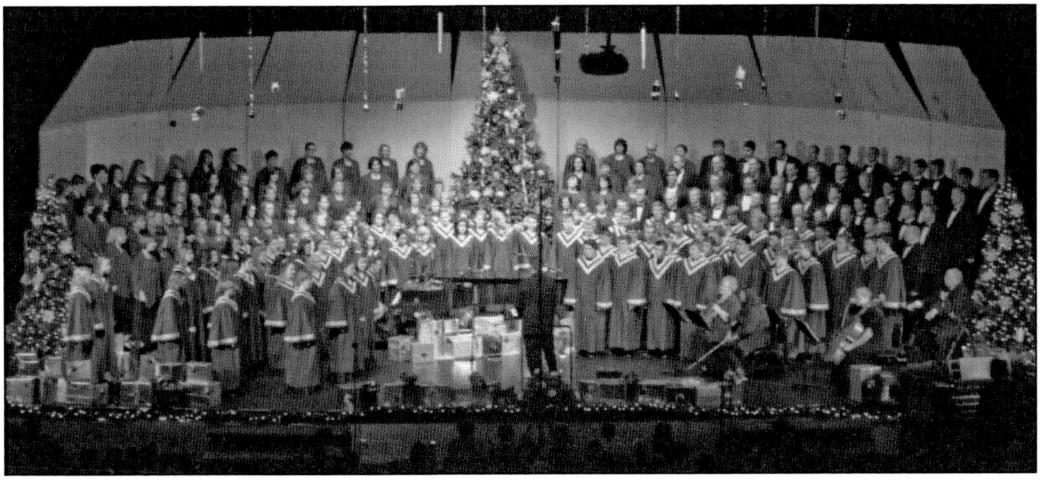

Here is the 2012 Mapleton Chorale Christmas Concert with the Maple Mountain High School choir. Formed in 1994 by Hal and Dianna Black, Suzie Judd, Steve Roden and Sherrie Dunford, the Mapleton Chorale is an audition-based community choral group. It has been called "Utah's Best Kept Secret," and has been a launching pad for many singers and one conductor, Ryan Murphy, who graduated to the Mormon Tabernacle Choir. The Mapleton Chorale also tours and was chosen to perform at the Lincoln Center in New York City for the 10-year September 11 memorial concert in 2011. The conductor featured here is Cory Mendenhall, who now conducts the Utah Millennial Choir & Orchestra and continues as the music director at Maple Mountain High School in Spanish Fork. Chris Downard will direct the Mapleton Chorale for the 2015 season.

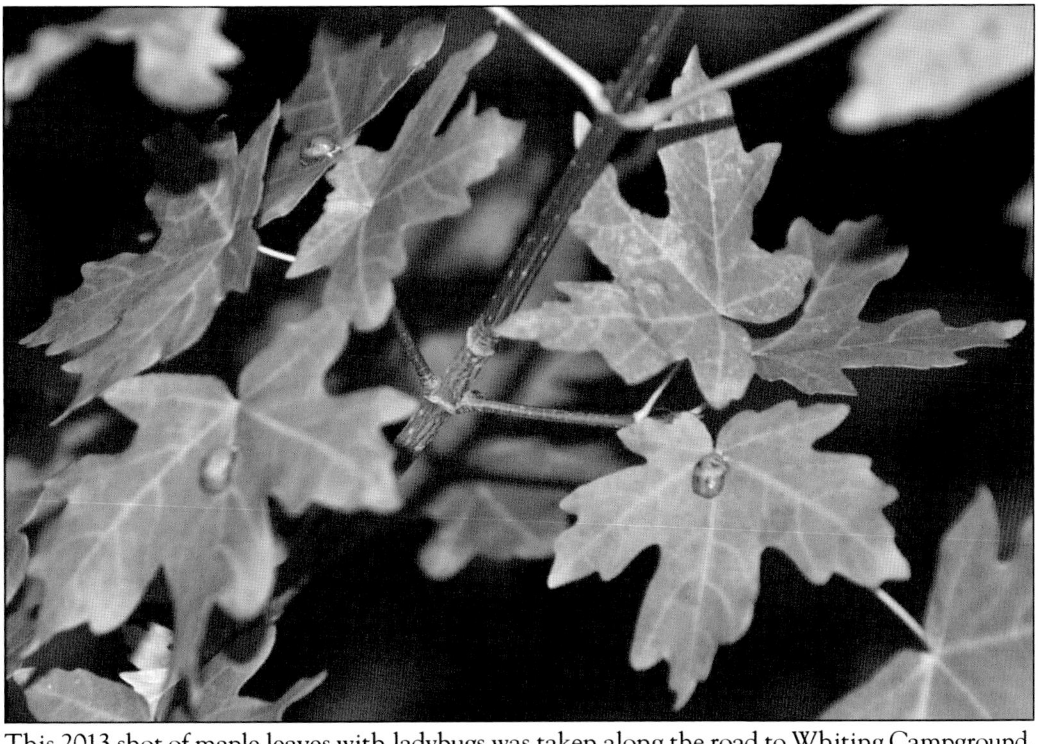

This 2013 shot of maple leaves with ladybugs was taken along the road to Whiting Campground.

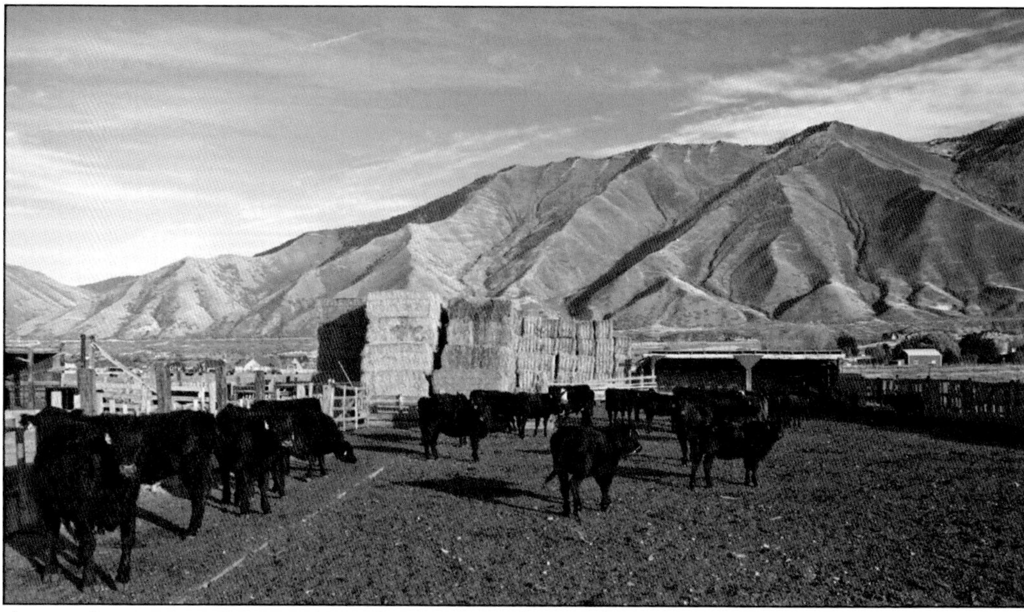

A vanishing pastoral view of Mapleton is seen here. The area, which has remained somewhat rural, is rapidly suburbanizing in the wake of development, but modern-day livestock drives still go down the streets in order to get animals to their grazing pastures.

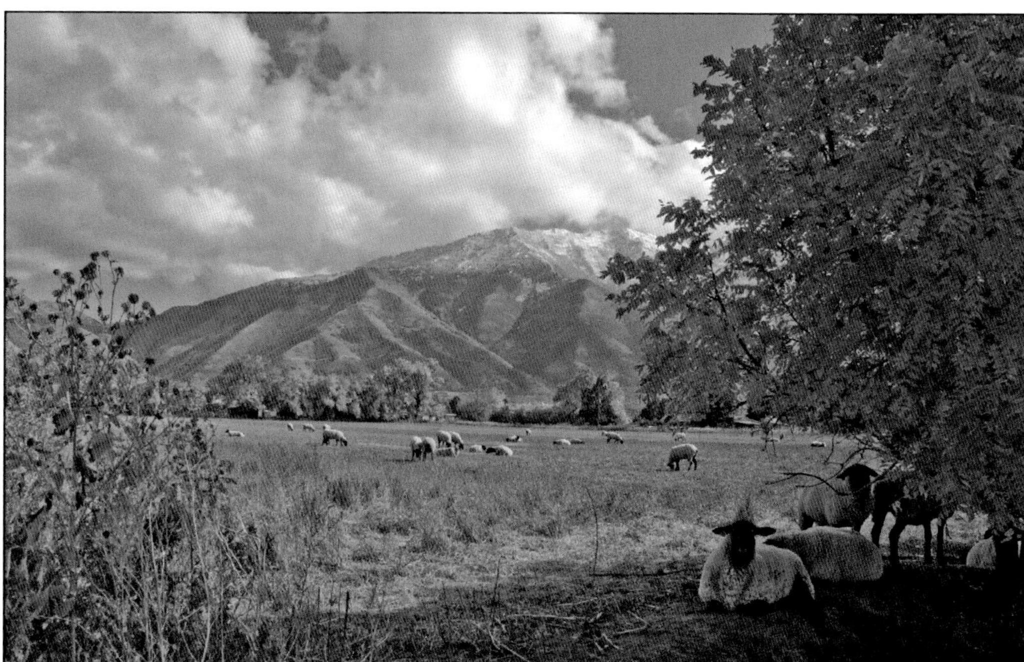

This little lady is casually sitting alongside the bank of an irrigation ditch that no longer exists. This entire field is currently being excavated and paved for a neighborhood of new homes.

Two

Our Development

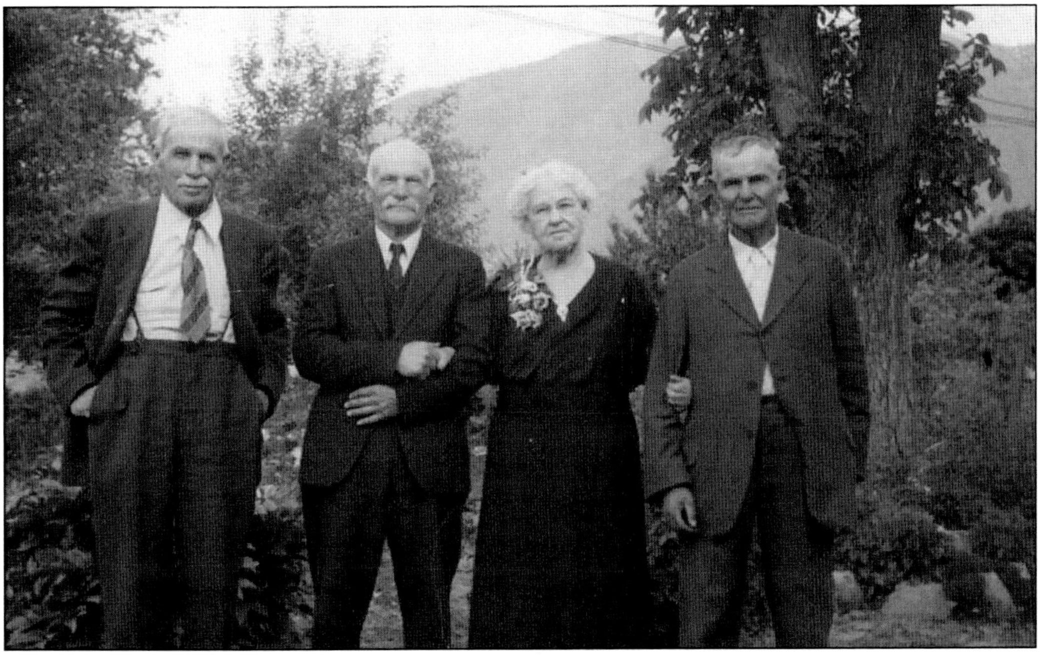

Pictured are, from left to right, Edger, John, Abby Ann, and Monroe Whiting. These are the children of Edwin and Hannah Haines Brown Whiting. In this 1943 photograph, Abby is celebrating her 85th birthday. A designated Mapleton Heritage Tree is in the background. It is an American elm. Heritage Trees are designated by their height, circumference, scientific name, location, and the approximate date they were planted. (Courtesy of Mary Hjorth Fojtek.)

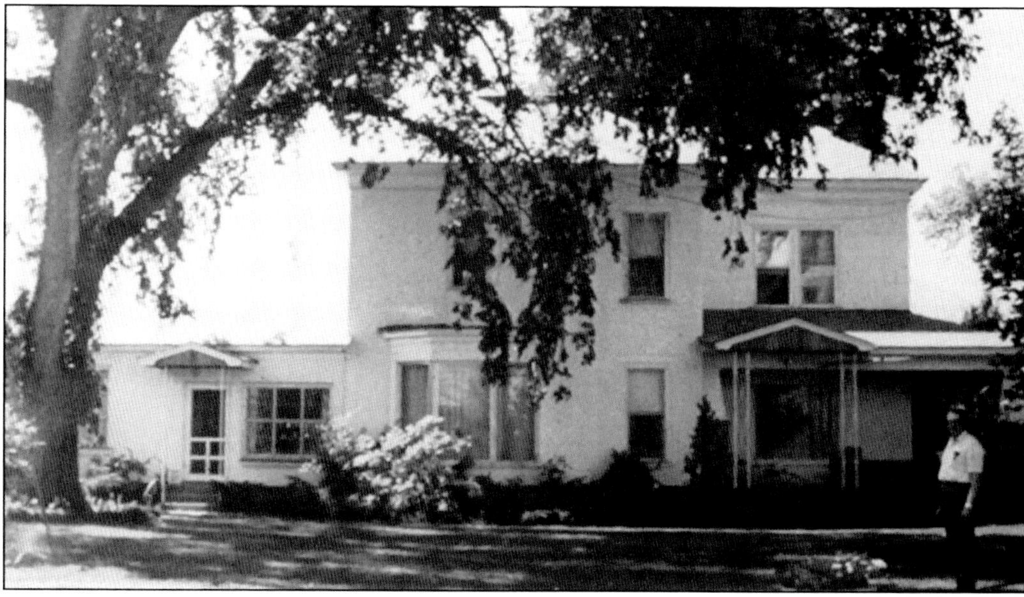

The Mendenhall/Hjorth home is a historic Mapleton home. It was completed in the summer of 1891. The home was made with a rock foundation. Adobe with straw and horsehair plaster formed the walls. Historic homes are designated by who built them, when, where, and what was used in the construction of the home. This picture was taken in 1972. Hugh Hjorth is on the right. There is an American elm Mapleton Heritage Tree on the left, planted by Richard Lovell Mendenhall in 1885. (Courtesy of Mary Hjorth Fojtek.)

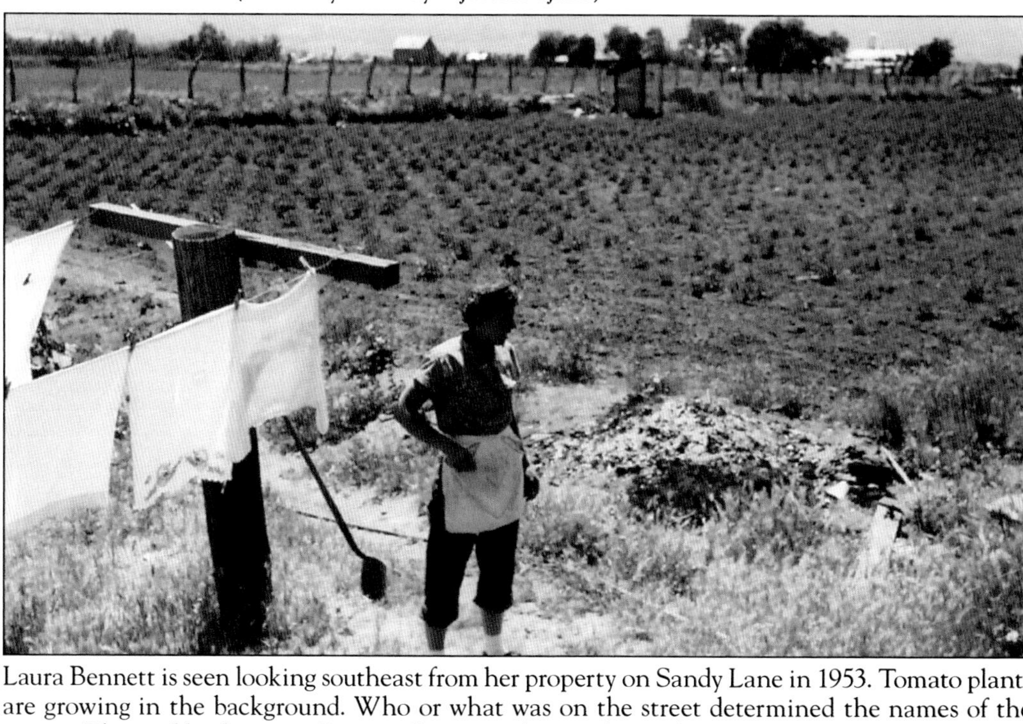

Laura Bennett is seen looking southeast from her property on Sandy Lane in 1953. Tomato plants are growing in the background. Who or what was on the street determined the names of the streets. The road leading into Springville was nicknamed "Sandy Lane" because it was sandy and had many potholes. (Courtesy of Gay Bennett McHargue.)

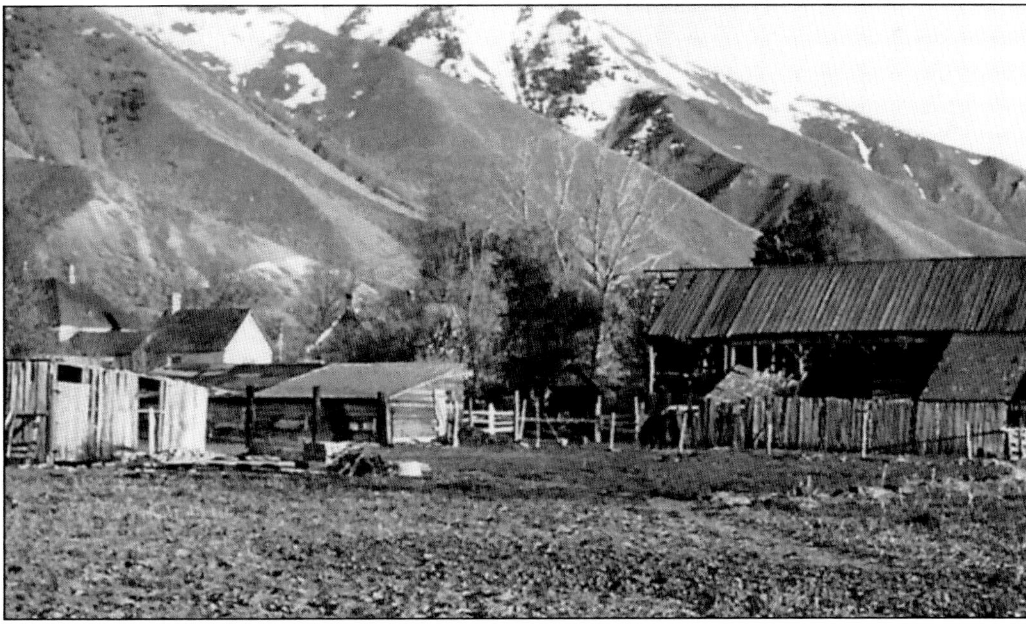

Hyrum Boggs Perry's barn is seen here around 1965. Hyrum was the second son of Stephen Chadwick and Mary Boggs Perry. He built his home at 1184 South Main Street to replace one that burned down. Hyrum, or "Gampy" as everyone called him, loved people. He kept a large garden and served on the Mapleton School Board. He and his wife, Luella, were active in many local service organizations. (Courtesy of Franklin Ole Nielsen.)

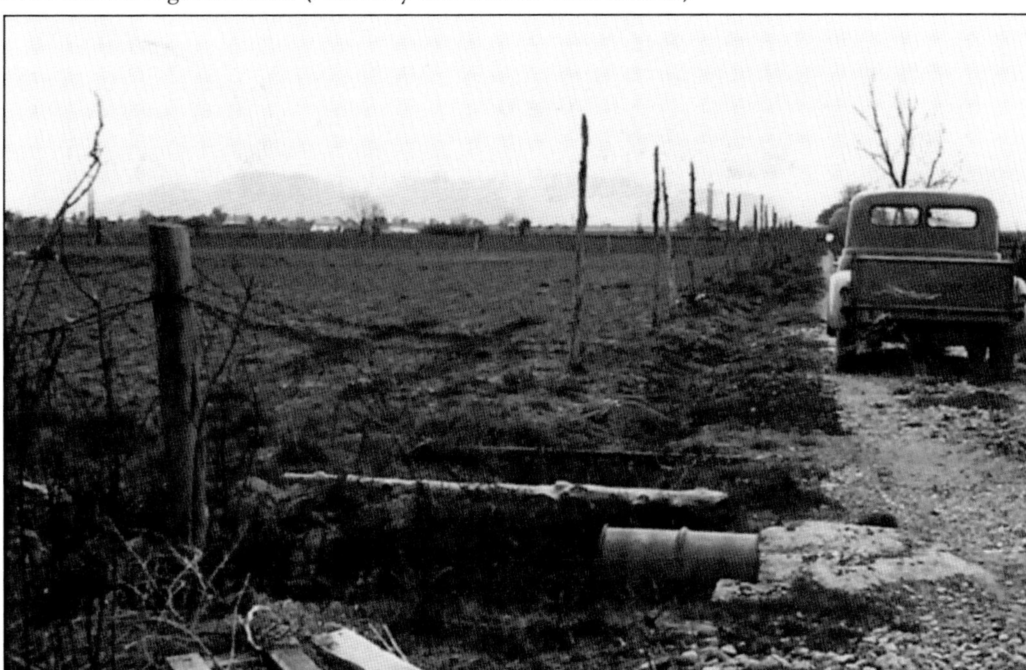

The lane into Hyrum Boggs Perry's property is pictured around 1965. Because of the many Perry families living on South Main Street, the street had the nickname of "Perry Lane." (Courtesy of Franklin Ole Nielsen.)

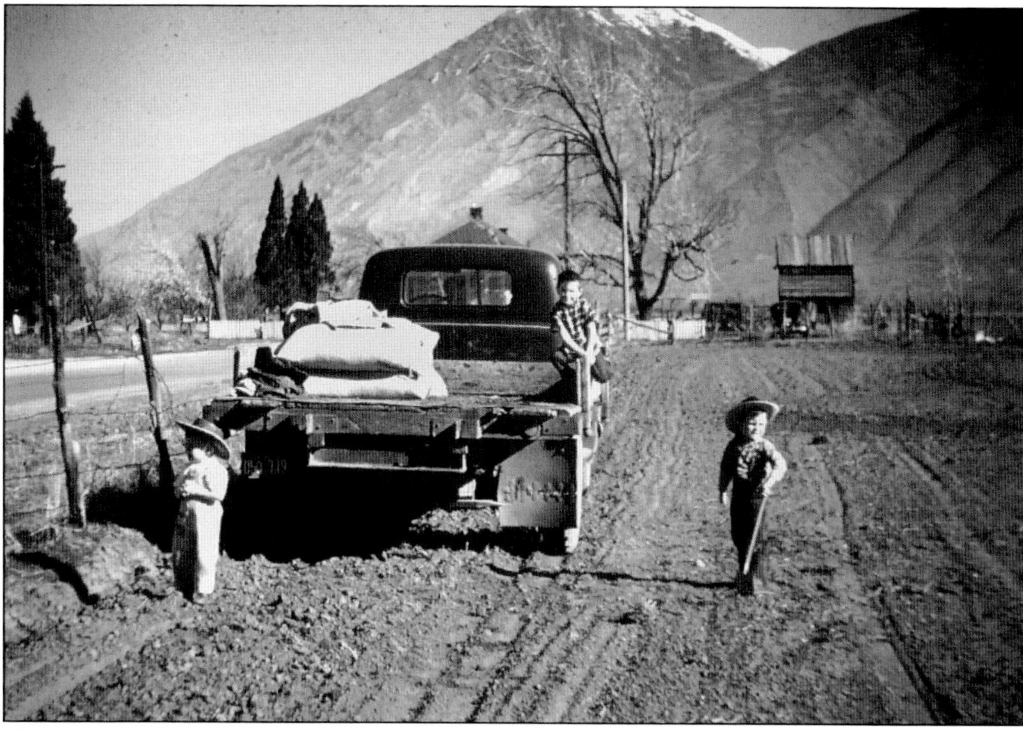

Shown around 1959 on Richard Bills's Main Street property are, (standing) brothers Doug (left) and Stephen Bills and cousin Gordon Bills on the truck. This photograph was taken when Main Street ended right after the Bills home. (Courtesy of Richard Bills.)

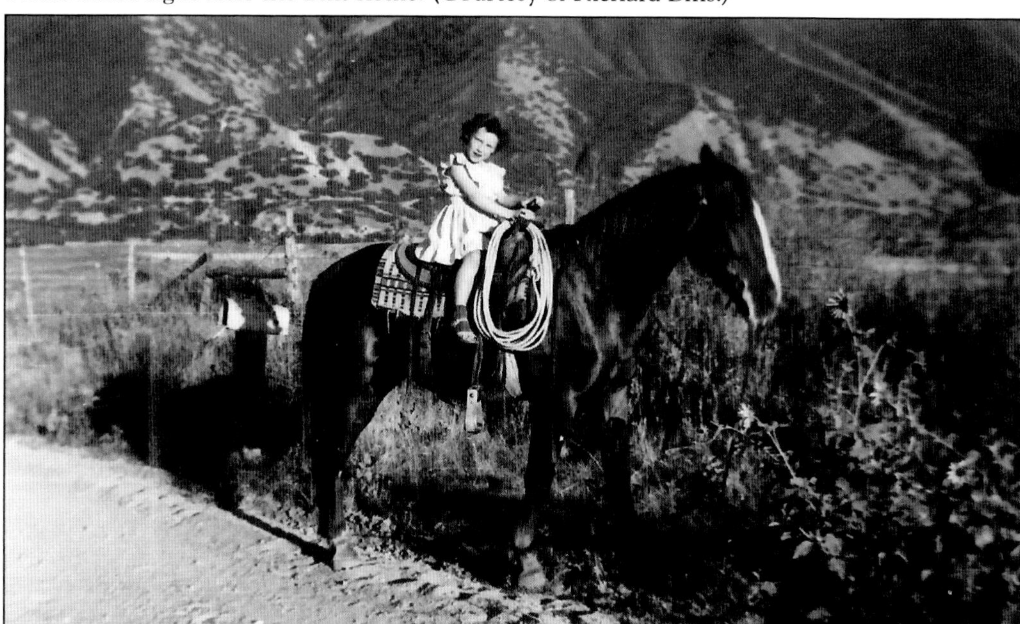

Pictured here is Kerry Lou Hanson, daughter of Oreian and Louise Johnson Hanson. Horses used to be a part of the family, and children learned to ride them as soon as possible. (Courtesy of Kay Bills.)

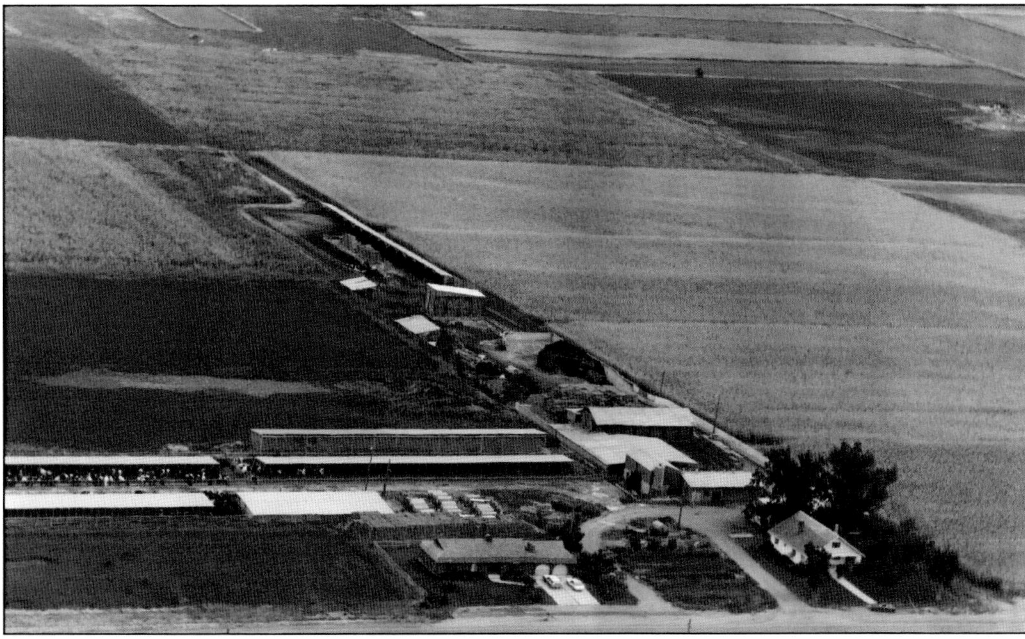

This 1980 aerial view shows the Walpole Dairy Farm, located at 1900 South 1600 West. This dairy milked as many as 320 cows per day. Milk produced here was labeled under the Cream of Weber name. In 2000, the area was developed into the Park Meadows Estates subdivision and the Ira Allan Sports Park. Ira Allan was the previous owner of part of the land. (Courtesy of Rolf and Tangie Walpole.)

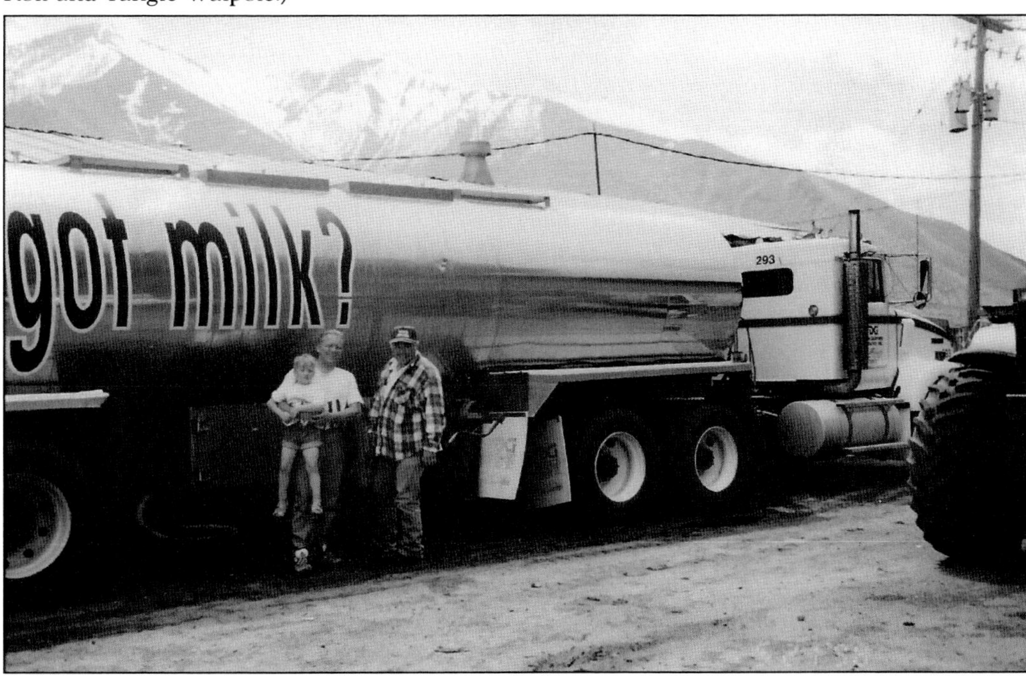

Rolf Walpole (left) is holding his daughter Devonnie Walpole in this 1998 photograph. The man on the right is unidentified. They are standing in front of their milk truck. (Courtesy of Rolf and Tangie Walpole.)

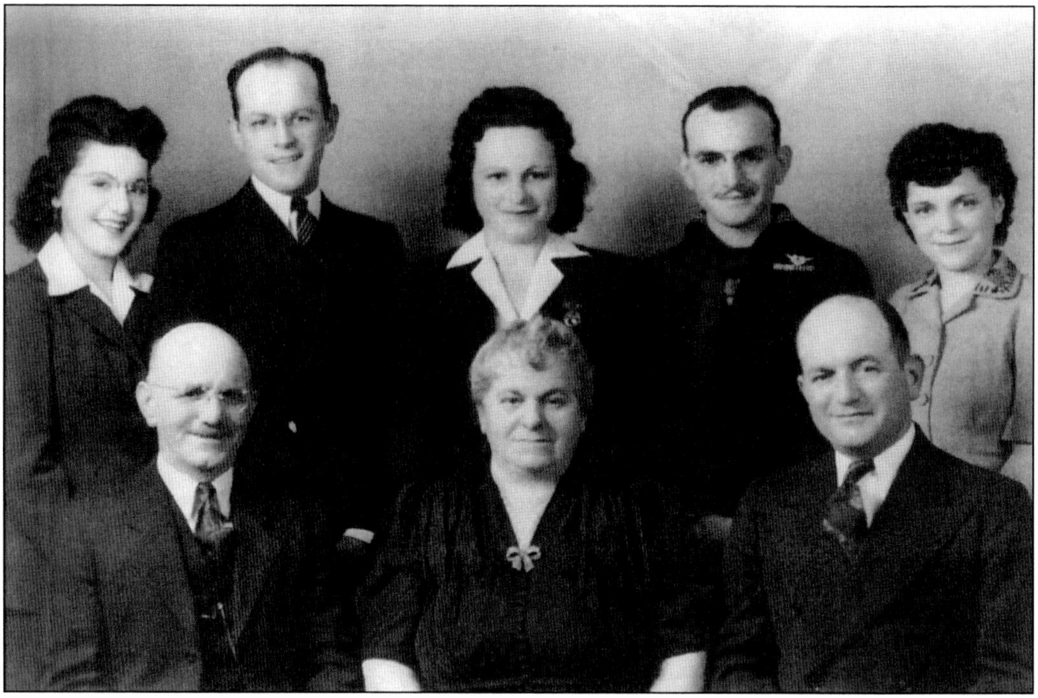

Members of the Carnasecca family pictured here are, from left to right, (first row) Joseph, Clementine, and Egideo "Jim;" (second row) Lena DeRose, Frank, Della Smith, Joseph Jr., and Helen Towers. The Italian Catholic Carnasecca family was a huge asset to Mapleton in the beginning. Clementine Carnasecca, not knowing English, was being swindled when she sold her produce; a neighbor stepped in and helped her understand the economics of America. (Courtesy of the Mapleton Historical Museum.)

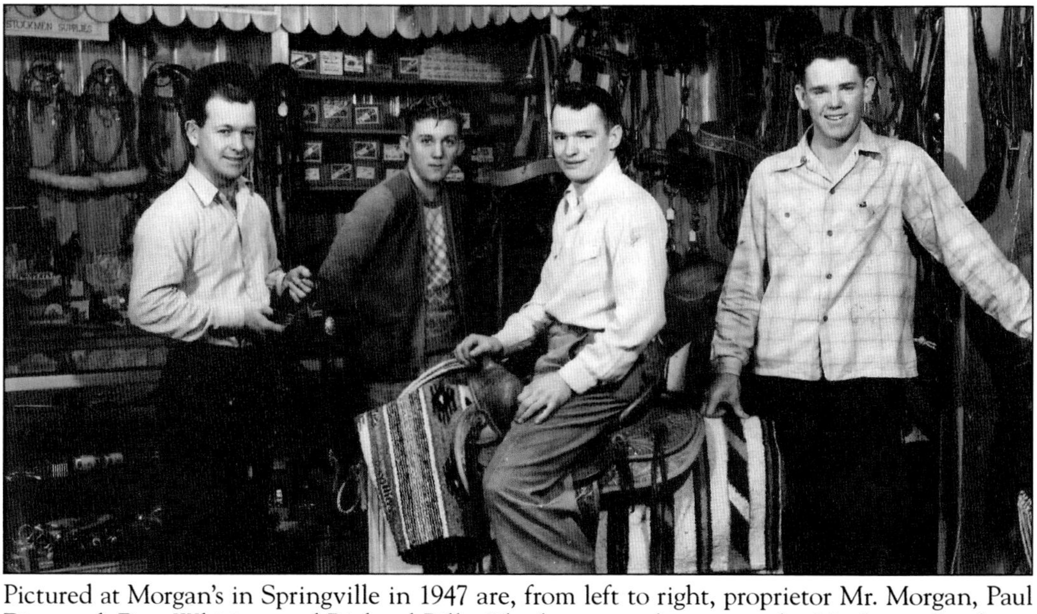

Pictured at Morgan's in Springville in 1947 are, from left to right, proprietor Mr. Morgan, Paul Diamond, Don Whiting, and Richard Bills. The boys were known as the Mapleton Cowboys. (Courtesy of the Mapleton Historical Museum.)

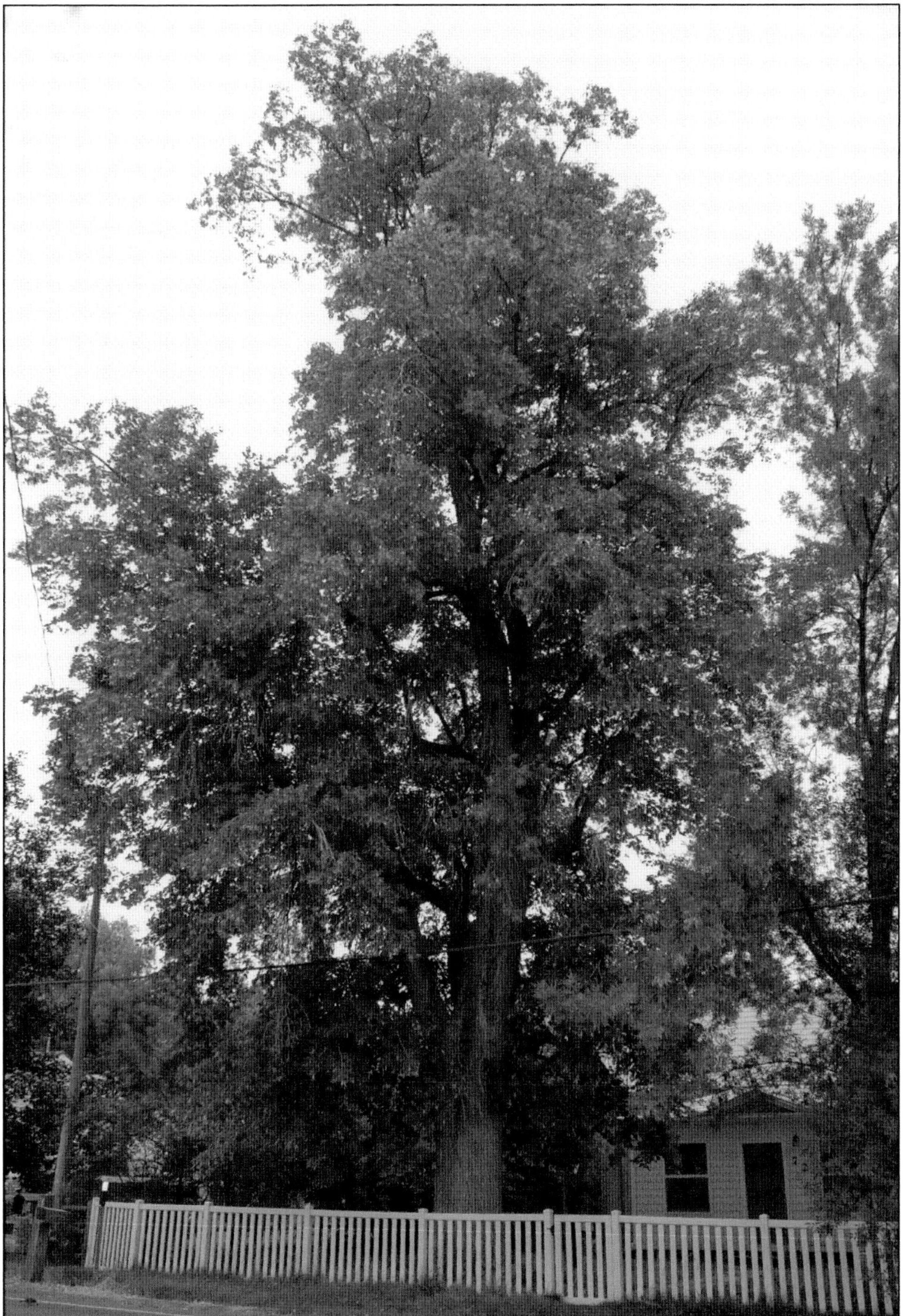

Edwin Whiting planted this linden tree at 727 South Main Street in 1880. It is a designated Heritage Tree in Mapleton. One of Whiting's transplanted trees stands in the southwest front area of the Manti Temple of the Church of Jesus Christ of Latter-day Saints. In the early 1900s, Whiting said, "I brought that in my dinner bucket and I think it was the first evergreen transplanted in Utah."

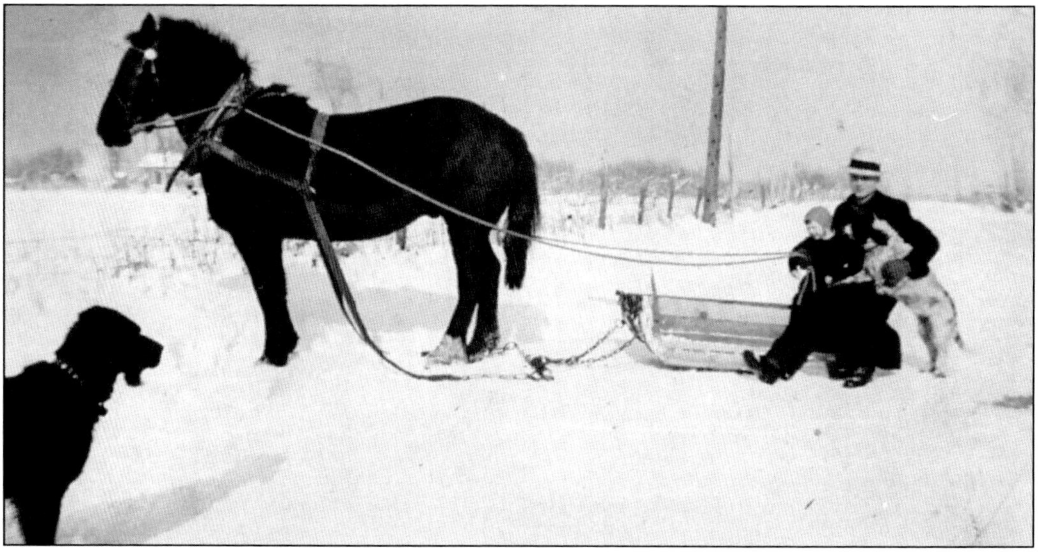

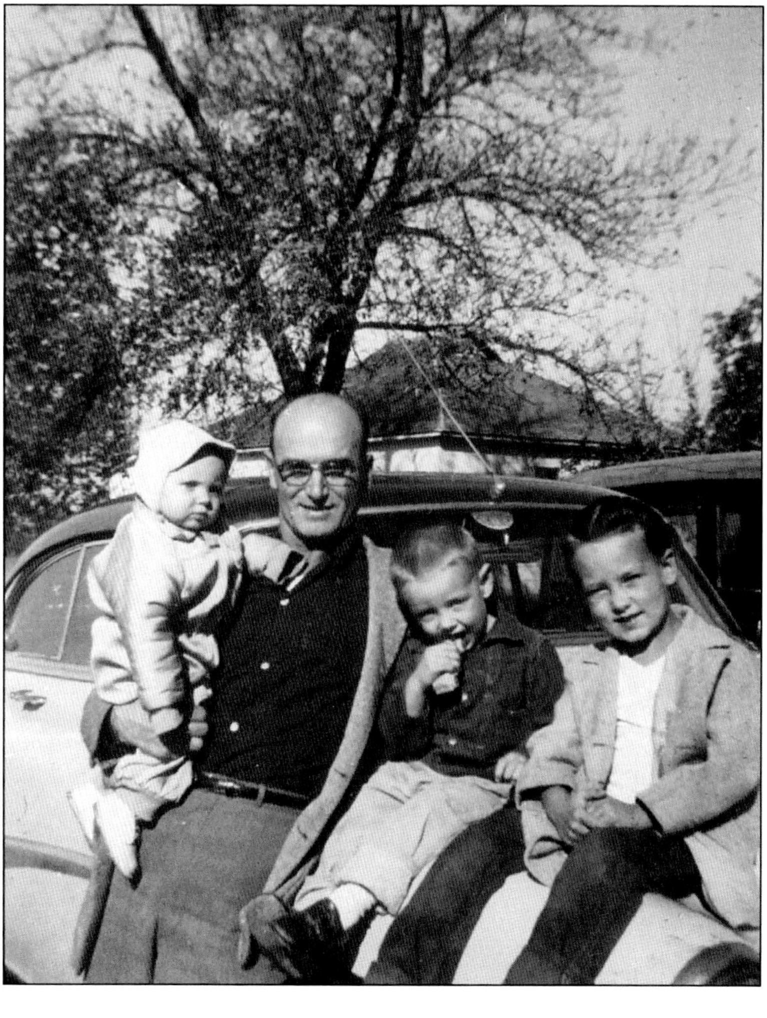

Joe Bleggi is pictured above with his child, their dogs, and Coalie, the horse, and at left with more children. The Bleggi families have always been a big influence within the city, serving in various athletic programs, volunteering with the fire department, and participating in the Jaycees and other service-oriented clubs. (Both courtesy of Angela Bleggi.)

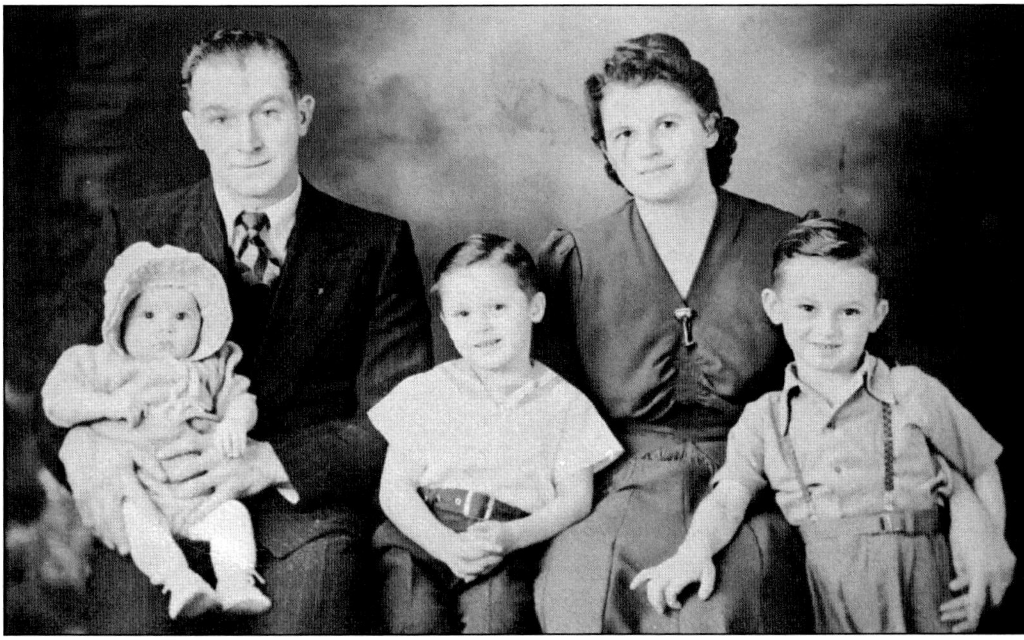

Charlie and Rosie Bleggi are pictured with their children (from left to right) Charlene, Frankie, and Rudy Bleggi. (Courtesy of Angela Bleggi.)

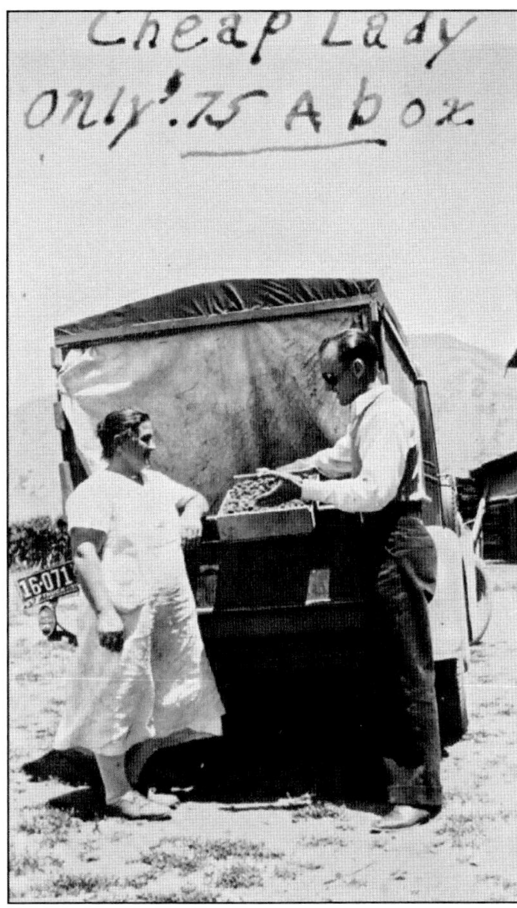

This photograph shows Lewis Bleggi selling fresh produce to a woman in Price, Utah. (Courtesy of Angela Bleggi.)

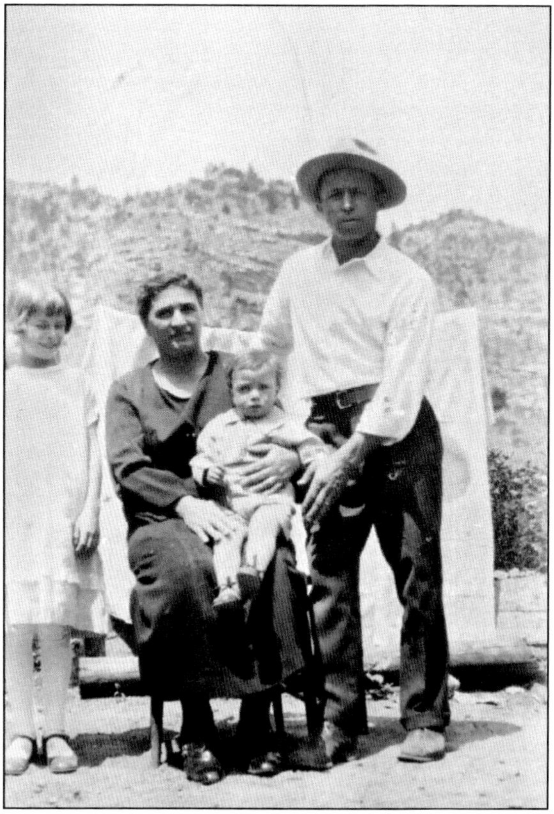

Tony and Anna Bleggi Antonino are seen with their children, from left to right, Rose Bleggi Bona and Nino Antonino. The Italian Catholic Antoninos lived in a predominately Mormon community. They were farmers who also went into the fruit-growing business. The home featured on the cover of this book is where the Antonino family currently resides. (Courtesy of Angela Bleggi.)

Members of the Kolob Stake of the Church of Jesus Christ of Latter-day Saints Young Women's Board are pictured here around 1955. The women who serve on this board organize and prepare events and lessons for all the young women ages 12 to 18 within the stake boundaries. They include all the young women in the eight to ten wards/congregations. (Courtesy of the Mapleton Historical Museum.)

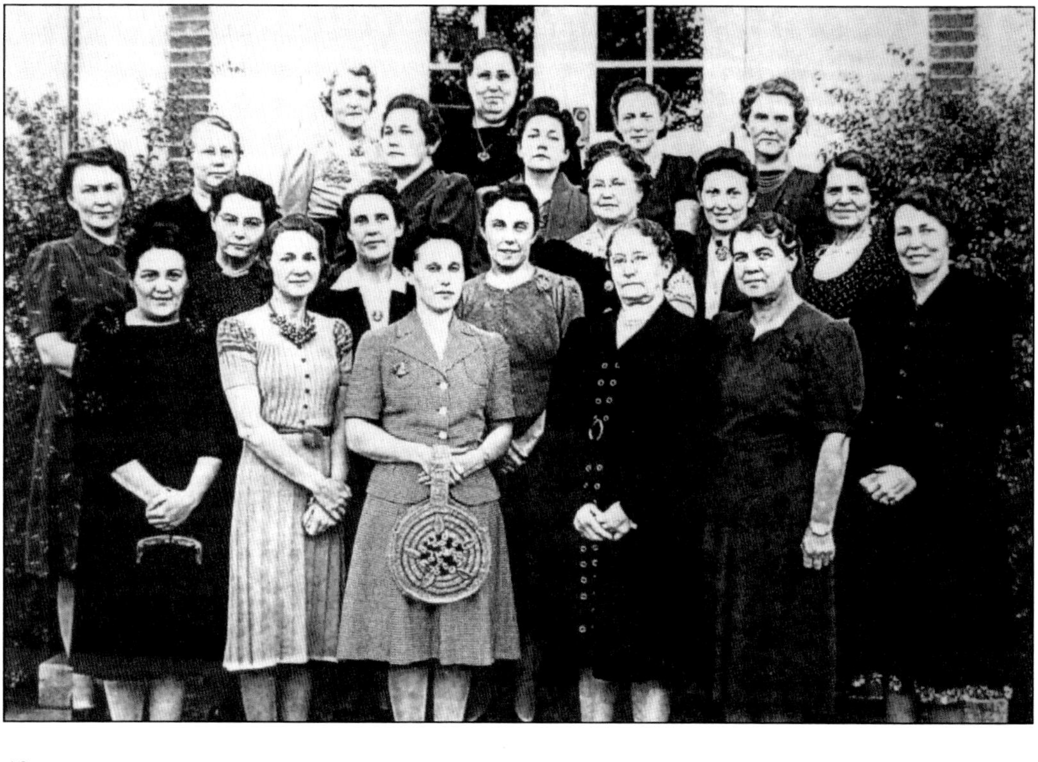

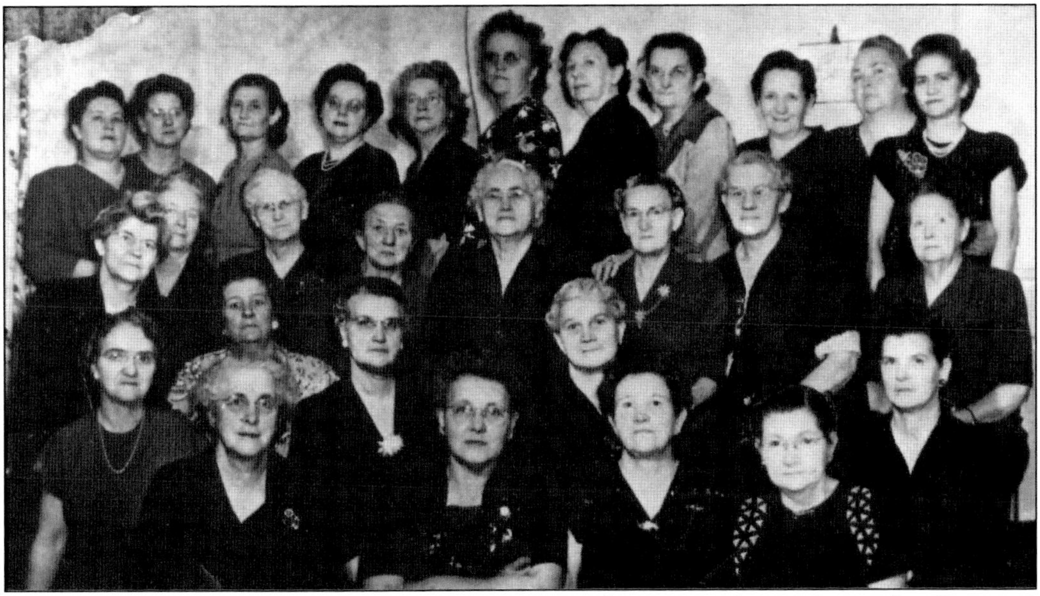

Mapleton Daughters of Utah Pioneers, pictured around 1951, are, from left to right, (first row) Sadie Whiting, Emmeline Bluth, LaVerl Young, and Zina Dibble; (second row) Inez Harmer, Netta Sorensen, Senate Jane Johnson Mendenhall, Martha Houtz, and Norma Adamson; (third row) Eva Bird, Ella Snow Johnson, Ariel Perry, Ruby Jensen, Mary LeRoy, Eenie Perry, Harriett Jensen, and Viola Allen; (fourth row) Pearl Holley, Jessie Beardall, Gladys Perry, Arlena Holley, Nelly Wiscombe, Gen Allen, Ida Whiting, Georgia Plumlee, Milly Bird, Norma Cox, and Blanche Tew. The Daughters of Utah Pioneers preserve all the historical records, data, artifacts, and anything else that applies to the history of the city, state, or nation. (Courtesy of the Mapleton Historical Museum.)

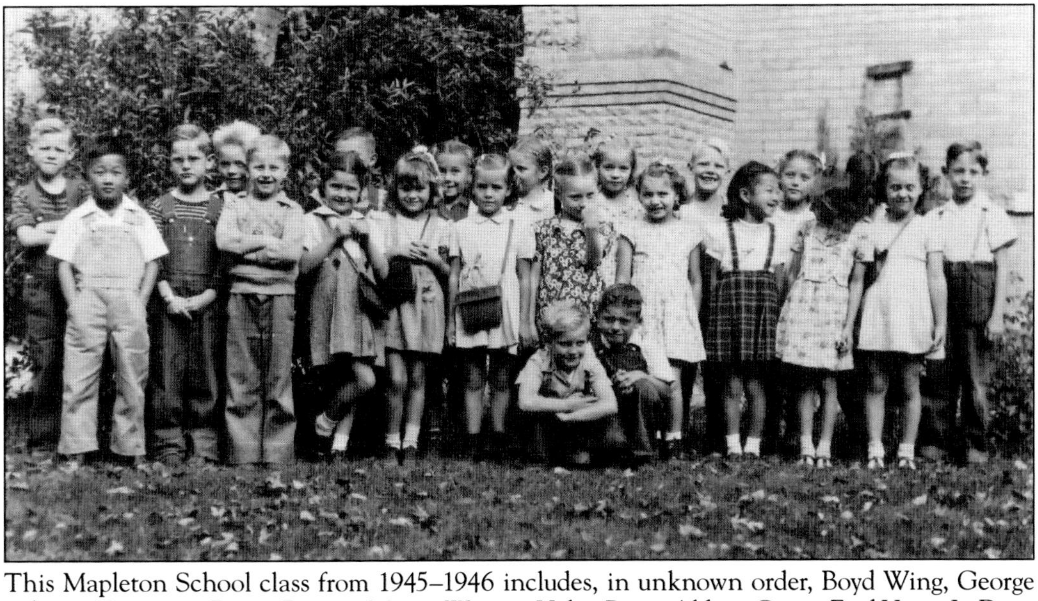

This Mapleton School class from 1945–1946 includes, in unknown order, Boyd Wing, George Lakota, ? Sorenson, Renae Rowan, Morris Warren, Helen Parry, Aldeen Cazier, Fred Hurst, LuDean Jolley, Nancy Dudley, Boyd Halverson, Barbara Hall, Gay Whiting, Ted Robinson, Melvin Hall, and John Beardall. (Courtesy of the Mapleton Historical Museum.)

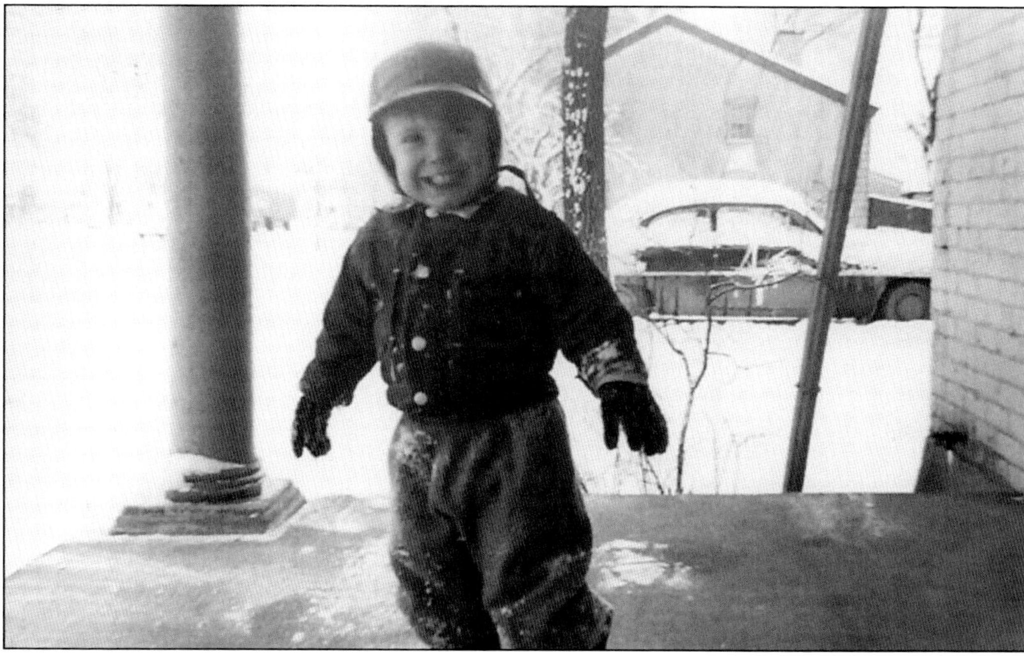

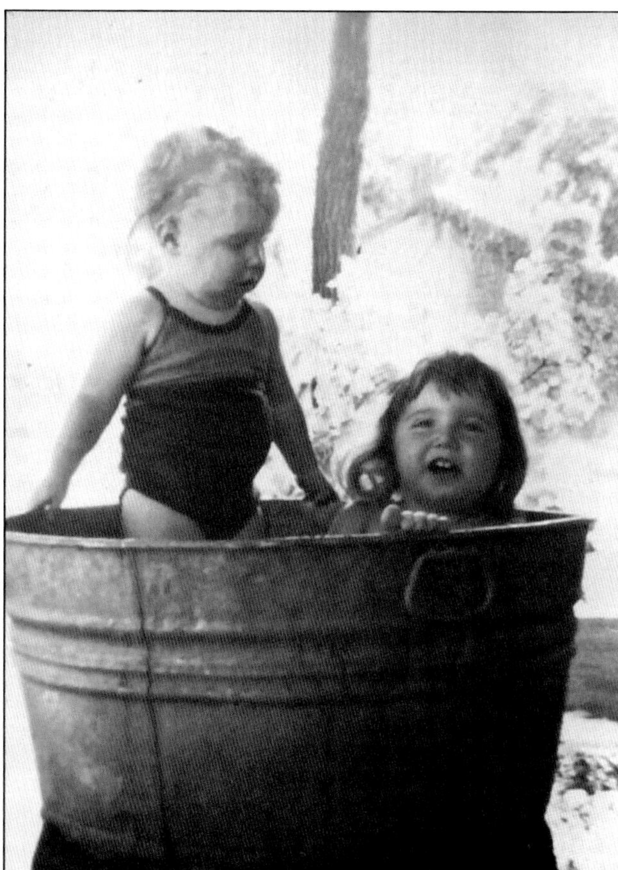

Pictured in the 1950s, Brent Richmond prepares to play some winter baseball, otherwise known as throwing snowballs. The Richmonds were born and raised in Mapleton and can tell the story of when an LDS ward was split into two, meaning the congregation was too big. Members felt like they were losing their best friends. Nowadays, one can live next to a person or across the street from them, and that family could be in a different ward, perhaps even meeting in a different church building. With eight chapels in the area, not everyone in Mapleton knows each other anymore. (Courtesy of Myra Richmond Miller.)

Peggy (left) and Brenda Richmond are seen in their "pool," which also doubled as their bathtub, in the 1950s. (Courtesy of Myra Richmond Miller.)

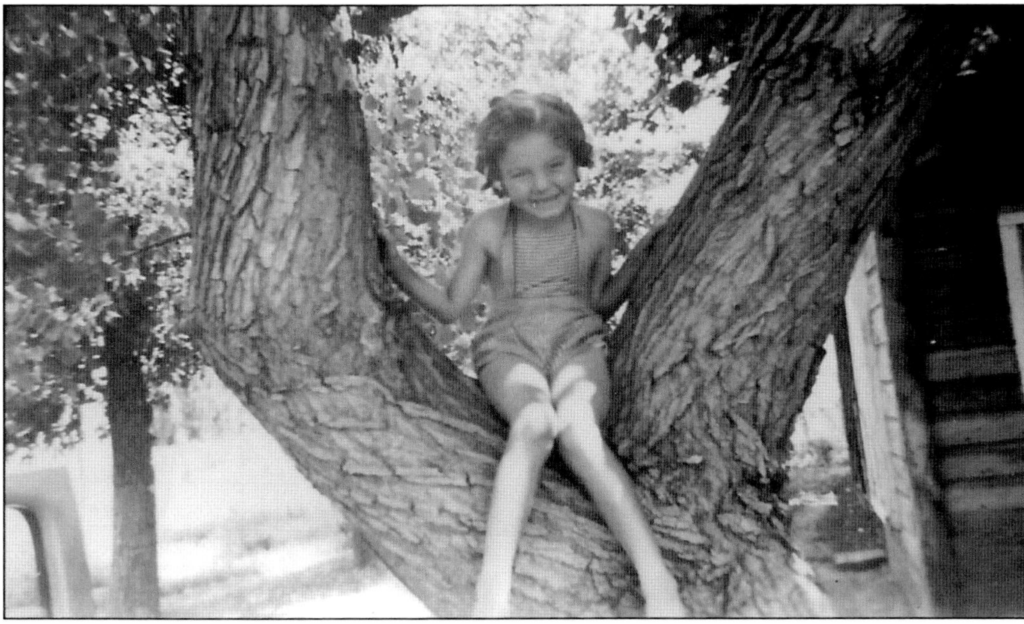

Young Barbara Halverson is playing in a tree at 64 South 1600 West in this photograph, taken in the summer of 1943. Barbara's grandfather Peter Christian Peterson made wooden shoes and Mary Peterson Halverson (Barbara's mother) would go around town selling them in the 1920s and 1930s, $1 for men's and 75¢ for women's. Some residents today still like to wear wooden shoes while working in their yards. (Courtesy of Barbara Halverson Kissel.)

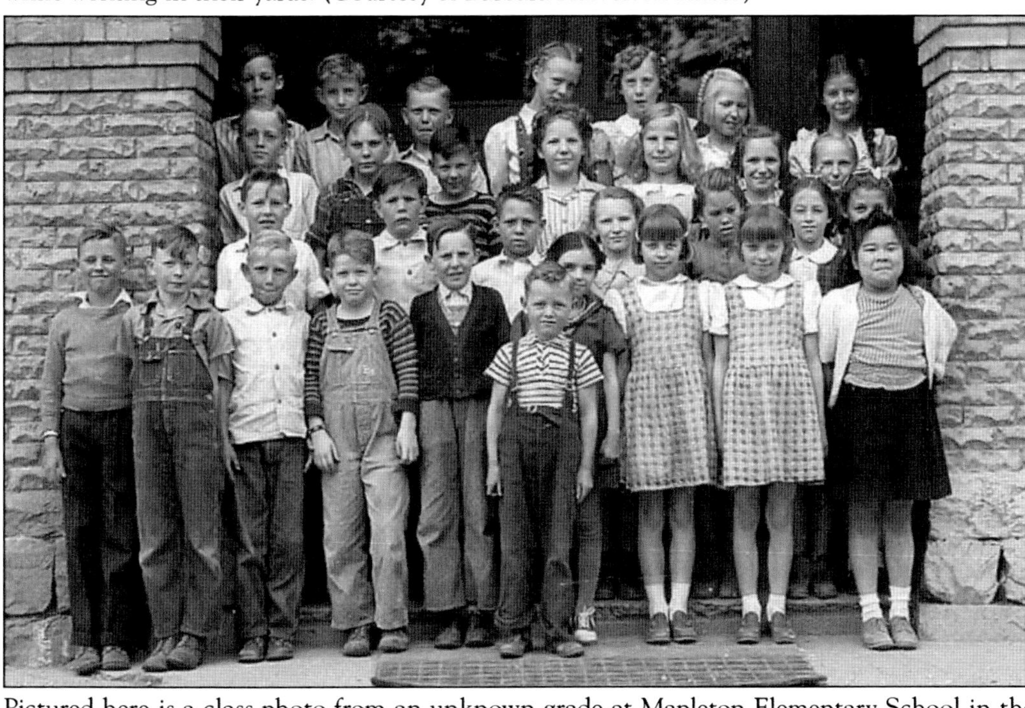

Pictured here is a class photo from an unknown grade at Mapleton Elementary School in the 1940s. Students identified include Duane Binks, Dean Allan, Marilyn Whiting, Bonnie Beardall, and the Medvid twins. (Courtesy of John S. Beardall.)

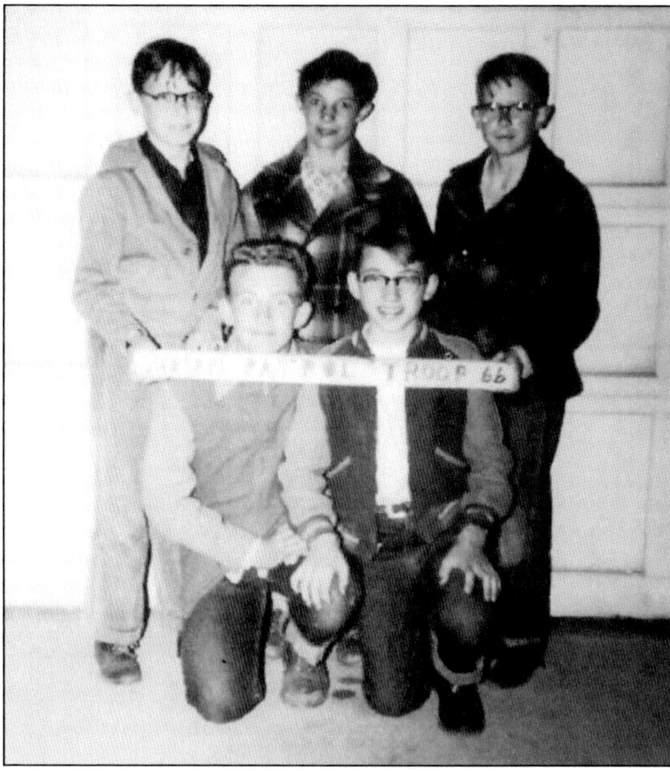

Pictured here from left to right are (first row) Carwin Beardall and Boyd Hales; (second row) John Beardall, Jackie Canto, and Lynn Anderson. They were members of the Indian Patrol of Boy Scout Troop No. 66, Mapleton Ward of the Church of Jesus Christ of Latter-day Saints. The church has embraced the Boy Scouts of America program, and each ward in Mapleton has been registered as a chartered organization within the program. Meetings are held weekly, and awards and recognitions are given out on a quarterly basis to honor the advancements achieved by the boys. (Courtesy of John S. Beardall.)

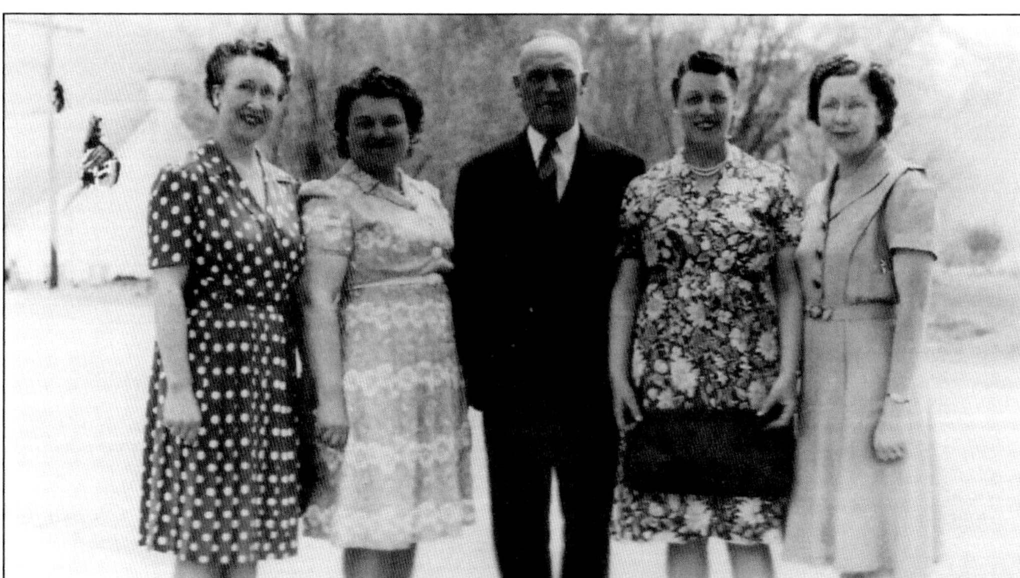

Mapleton Elementary School faculty seen here in 1945 are, from left to right, Mable Hopla, fourth grade; Mary Ann Hansen, third grade; Lester Searle, fifth grade; Ellen Anderson, first grade; and Ruth Anderson, second grade. (Courtesy of John S. Beardall.)

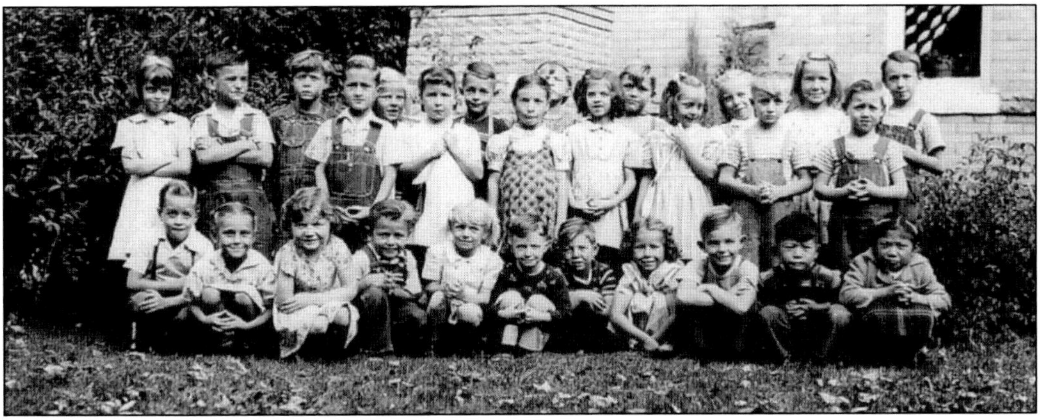

This 1940s Mapleton Elementary School kindergarten class included children from the Jensen, Tew, Wing, and Hjorth families. (Courtesy of John S. Beardall.)

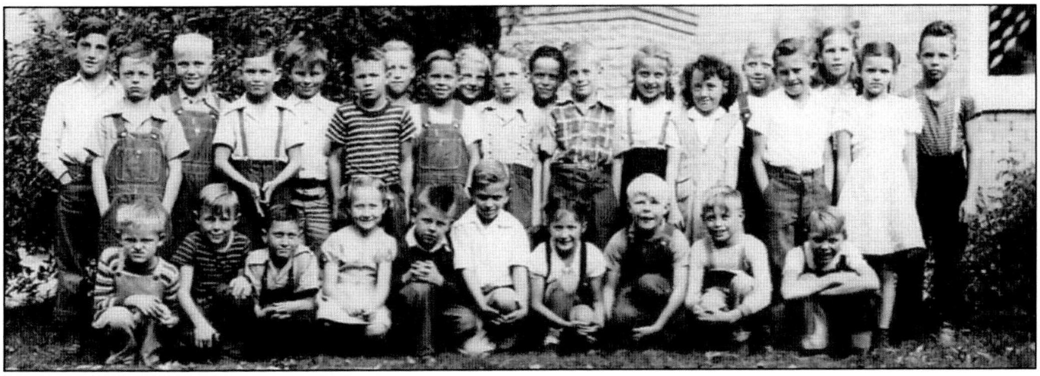

A 1940s Mapleton Elementary School second-grade class is pictured here. Students are, from left to right, (first row) Jerry Shepard, David Cloward, Dowd Dudley, Glenna Warren, Dolan Sorenson, unidentified, Maurine Kennedy, Kay Robinson, Darrel Shepard, and Ted Cox; (second row) Jackie Canto, Raymond Hooper, Rex Jensen, Jimmy Wiscombe, Jack Shepard, Keith Jensen, Jay Wing, Niel Jensen, Colleen Mason, unidentified, Billy Bleggi, Lynn Anderson, Carma Rasmussen, Patty Bleggi, Sammy Fullmer, Jesse Warren, Louise Lessard, Loretta Young, and Sergi Nelson. (Courtesy of John S. Beardall.)

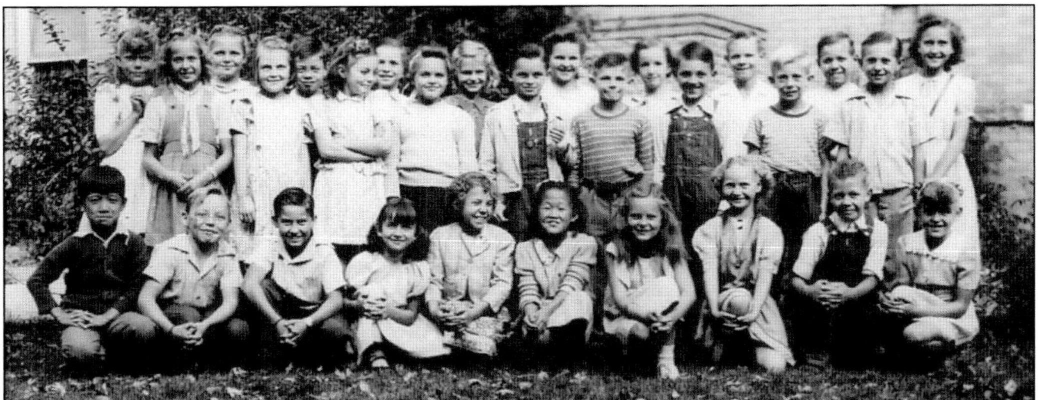

This 1940s Mapleton Elementary School third-grade class included Kay Harmer, Denny Murray, Body Hales, Loris Diamond, and Anne Wiscombe. (Courtesy of John S. Beardall.)

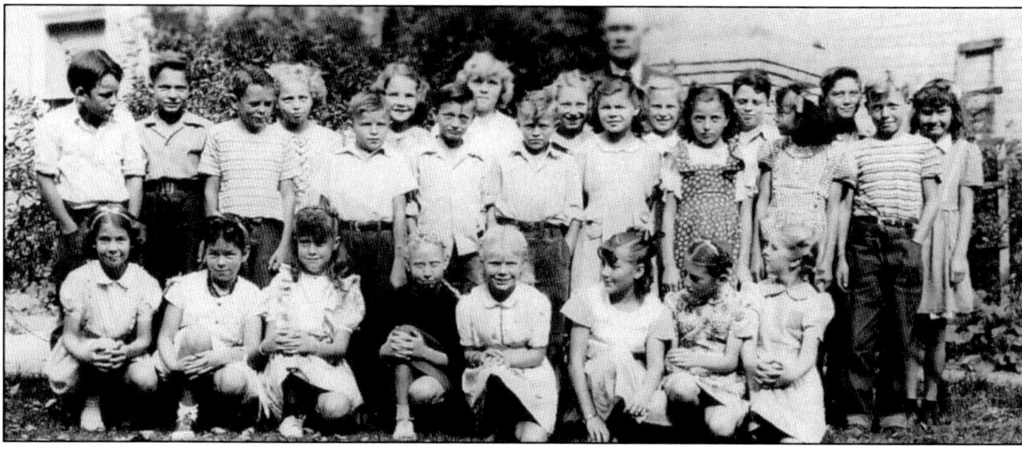

A 1940s Mapleton Elementary School fifth-grade class is pictured here. Teacher Mr. Searle had in his class Mary Ann Bird, Doris Hales, and David Allen, among other students. (Courtesy of John S. Beardall.)

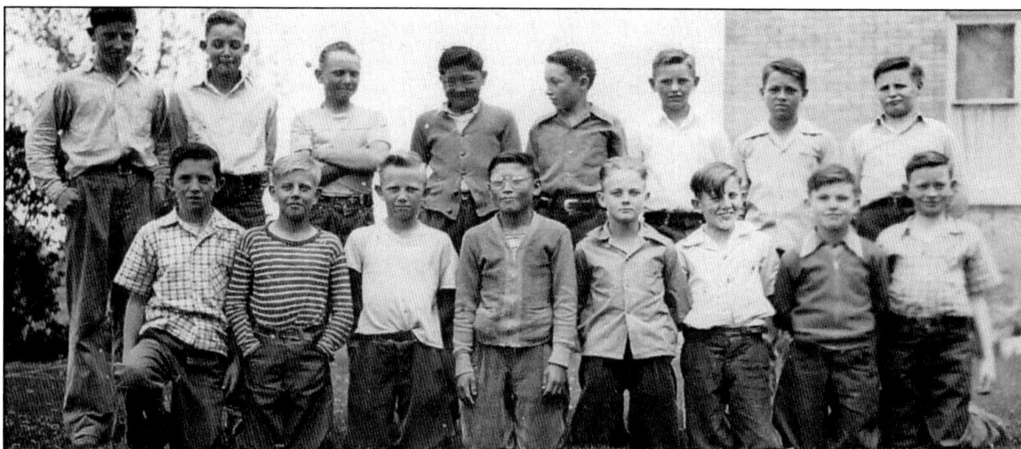

Pictured here in the 1940s are the boys of Mapleton Elementary School's sixth-grade class; included are Bliss Harmer and Darrel Warren. (Courtesy of John S. Beardall.)

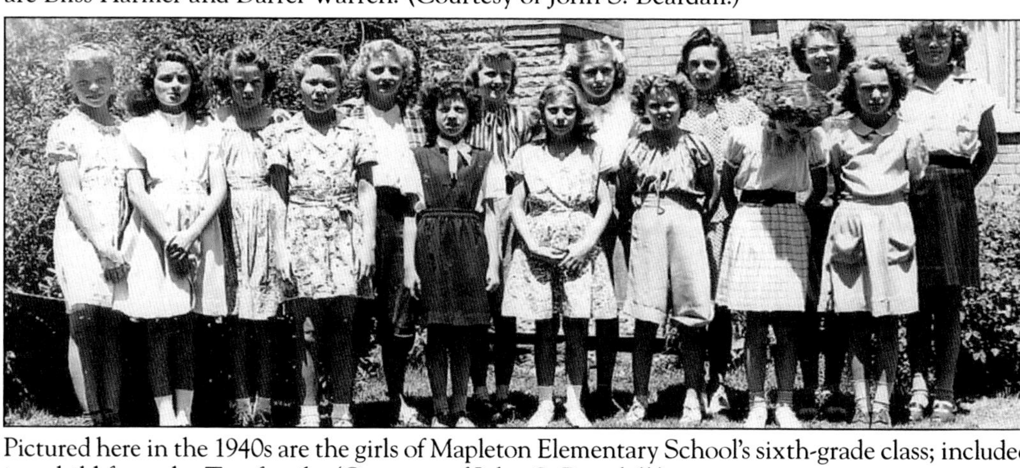

Pictured here in the 1940s are the girls of Mapleton Elementary School's sixth-grade class; included is a child from the Tew family. (Courtesy of John S. Beardall.)

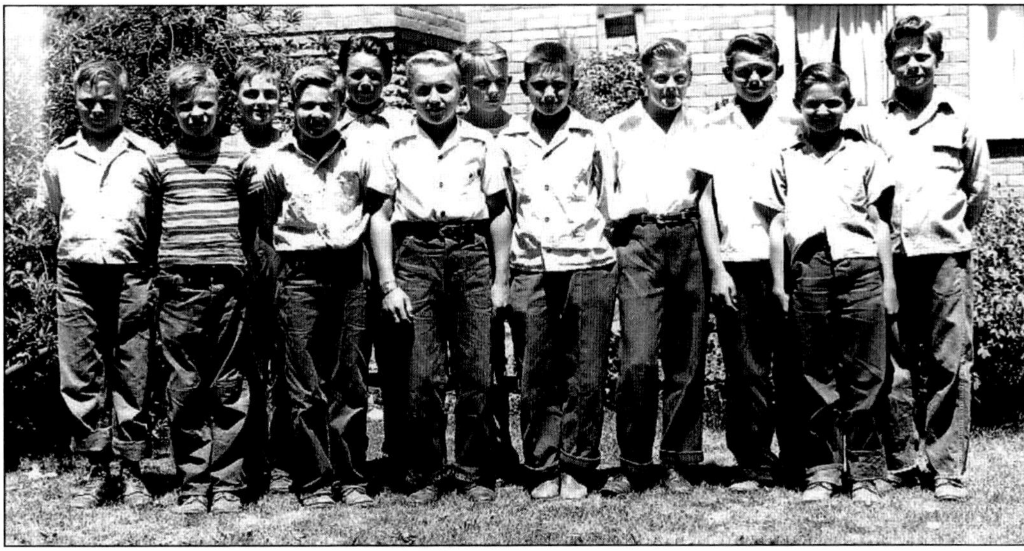

This unknown grade from Mapleton Elementary School in the 1940s includes Kent Jensen and children from the Sorenson and Allan families. (Courtesy of John S. Beardall.)

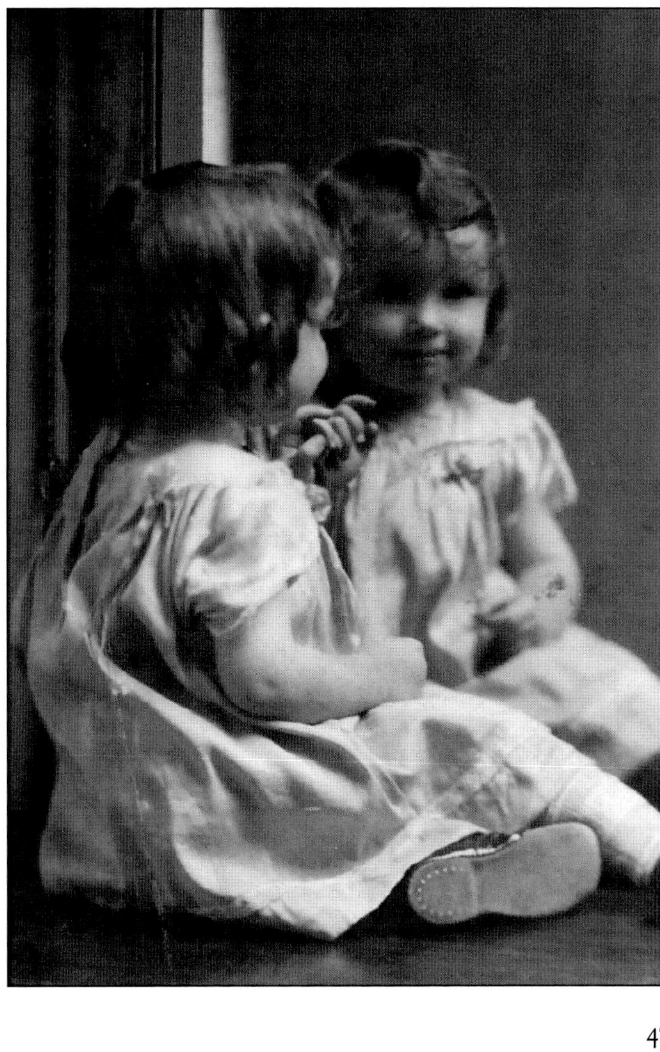

Pictured is four-year-old Louise Johnson. Louise's mother, Luella Snow Johnson, was the daughter of Edwin Marion and Frances Evaline Perry Snow. Luella was born in Mapleton on September 10, 1890, and married Elmer Johnson in 1911. When their children were growing up, they had a phonograph and recordings of music. All the children developed a love of music. The children raised in the city were Lenore J. Bills, Donald Snow Johnson, Verl Elmer Johnson, Edda Frances J. Heaton, Louise Johnson Hanson, Ralph Aaron Johnson, Welburn "K" Johnson, and Merilyn J. Tuttle. (Courtesy of Kay Bills.)

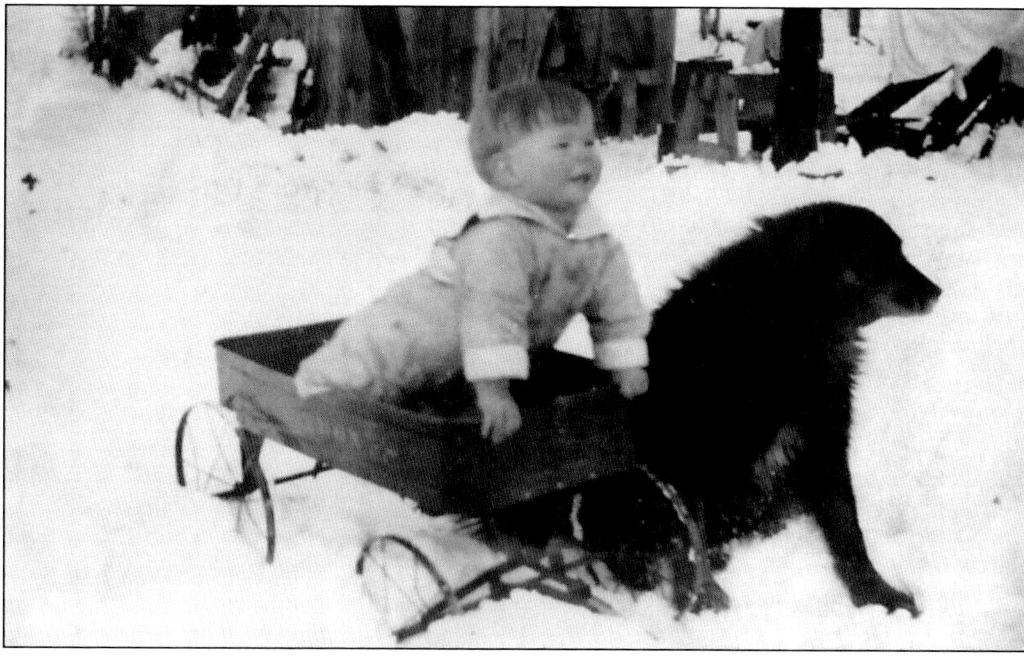

Welburn "K" Johnson is seen in a wagon with his dog. (Courtesy of Kay Bills.)

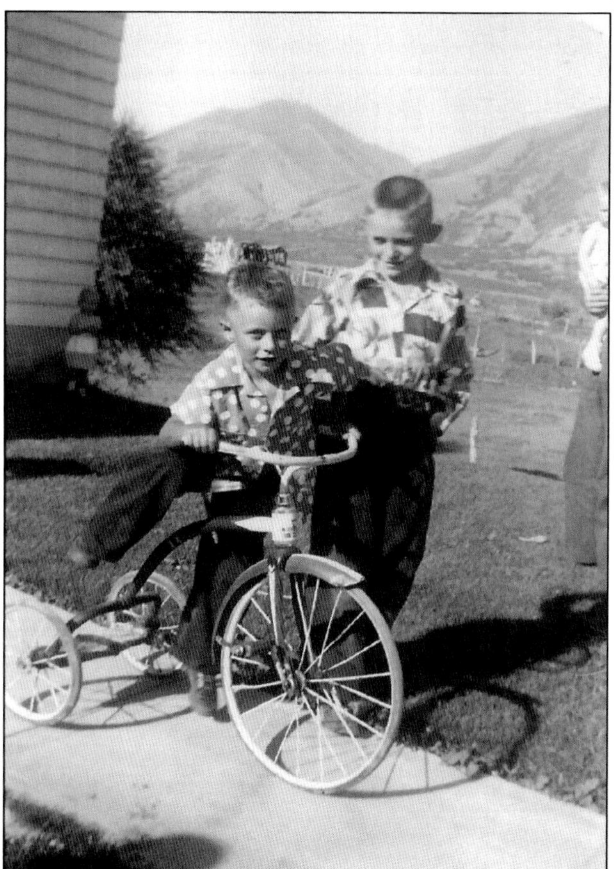

Carl (on the bike) and Ronald "Ronnie," sons of Verl and Idonna Johnson, are seen playing with their bicycle. (Courtesy of Kay Bills.)

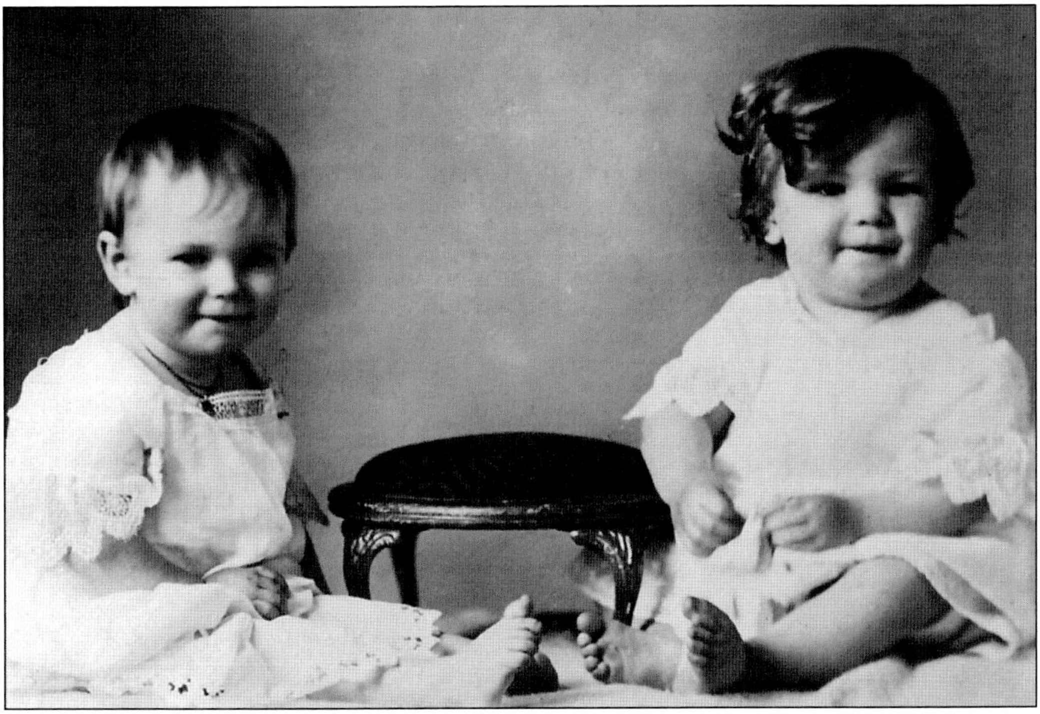

Posing for a picture are cousins Lenore (left) and Hugh Johnson. (Courtesy of Kay Bills.)

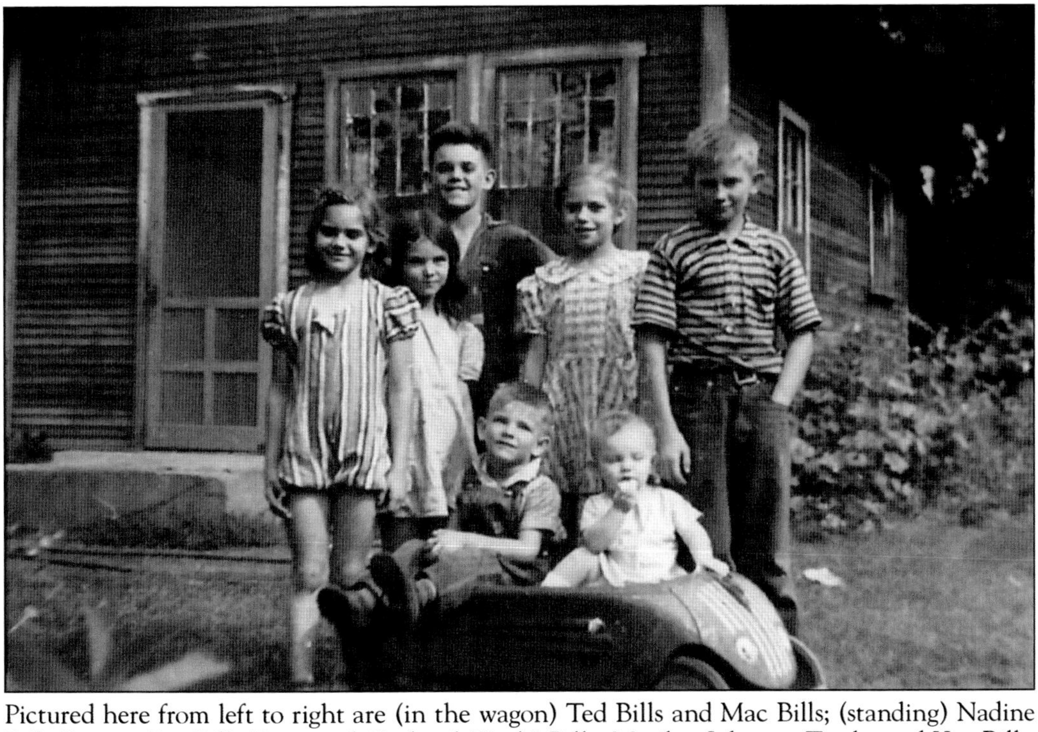

Pictured here from left to right are (in the wagon) Ted Bills and Mac Bills; (standing) Nadine Bills Barnes, Pat Bills Haymond, Richard "Dick" Bills, Merilyn Johnson Tuttle, and Kay Bills. (Courtesy of Kay Bills.)

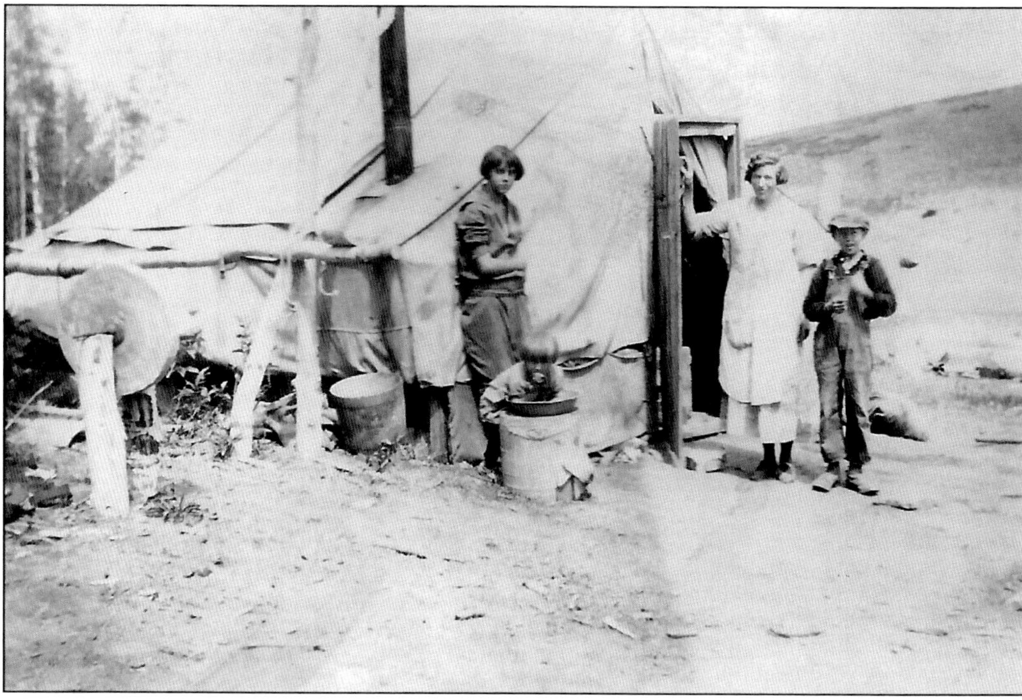

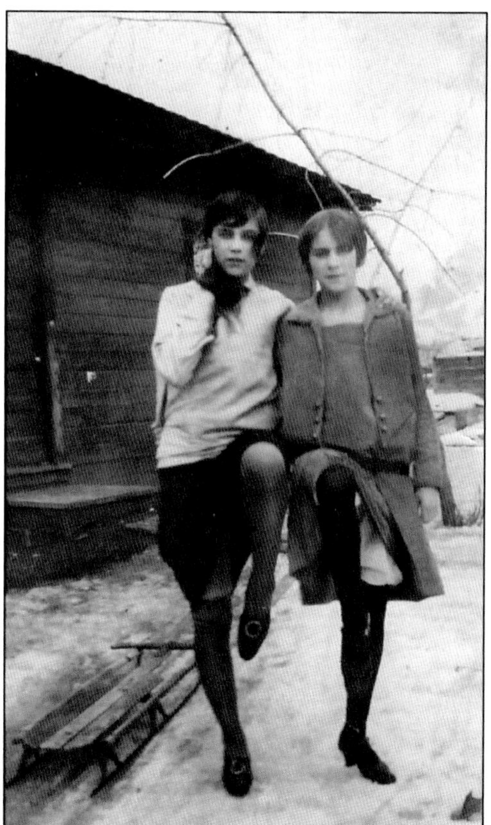

Edda Johnson Heaton is seen here on the left crouching by the wash basin on top of a barrel. Lenore Johnson Bills is behind her, leaning on the tent. Ella Snow Johnson is in the doorway, and Donald Johnson is at right. This photograph was taken in the Skyline Drive area, where they were camping while their families worked in the timber. A hand grinder is visible on the left by the tent. (Courtesy of Kay Bills.)

Lenore Johnson (left) and her friend Evelyn are off to an event. (Courtesy of Kay Bills.)

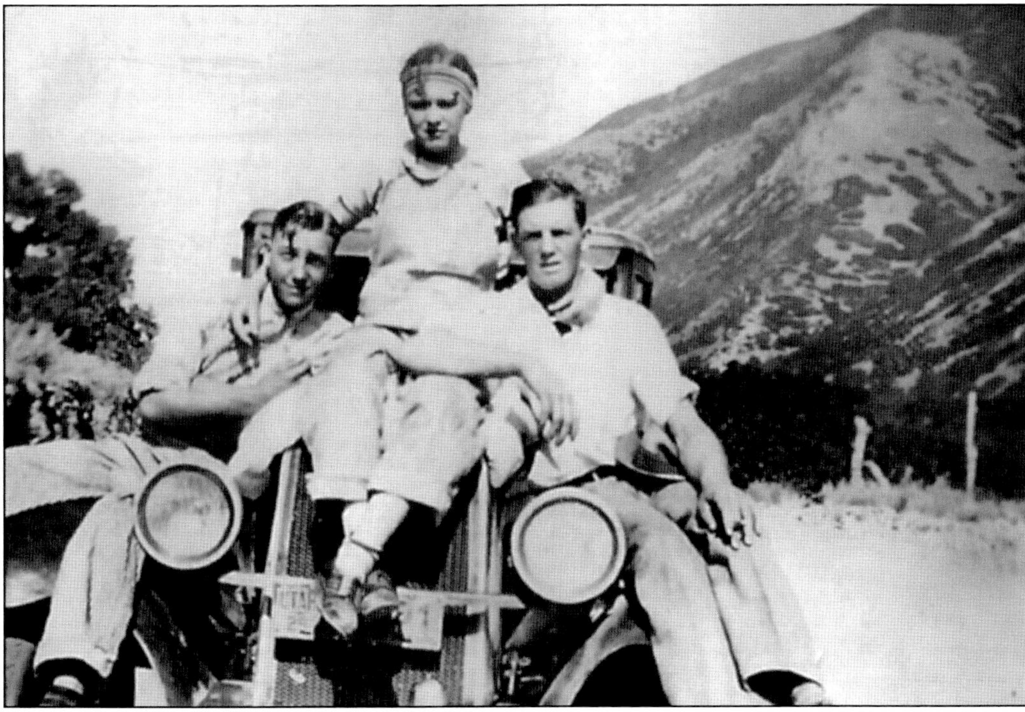

Relaxing on top of a car are, from left to right, Donald Hall, Elaine Bird, and Doug Bills, who served as the mayor from 1962 to 1969. (Courtesy of Kay Bills.)

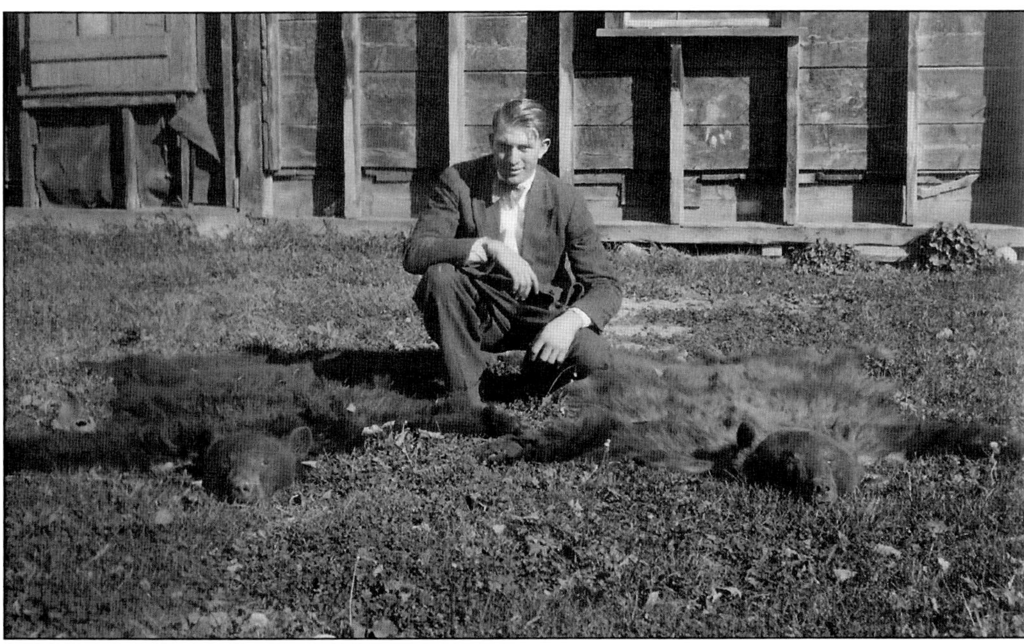

Here, Welby Warren shows off the bears he hunted. Welby owned a blacksmith shop in town for a few years. He also served as a bishop in the Church of Jesus Christ of Latter-day Saints in the mid-1950s. (Courtesy of Kay Bills.)

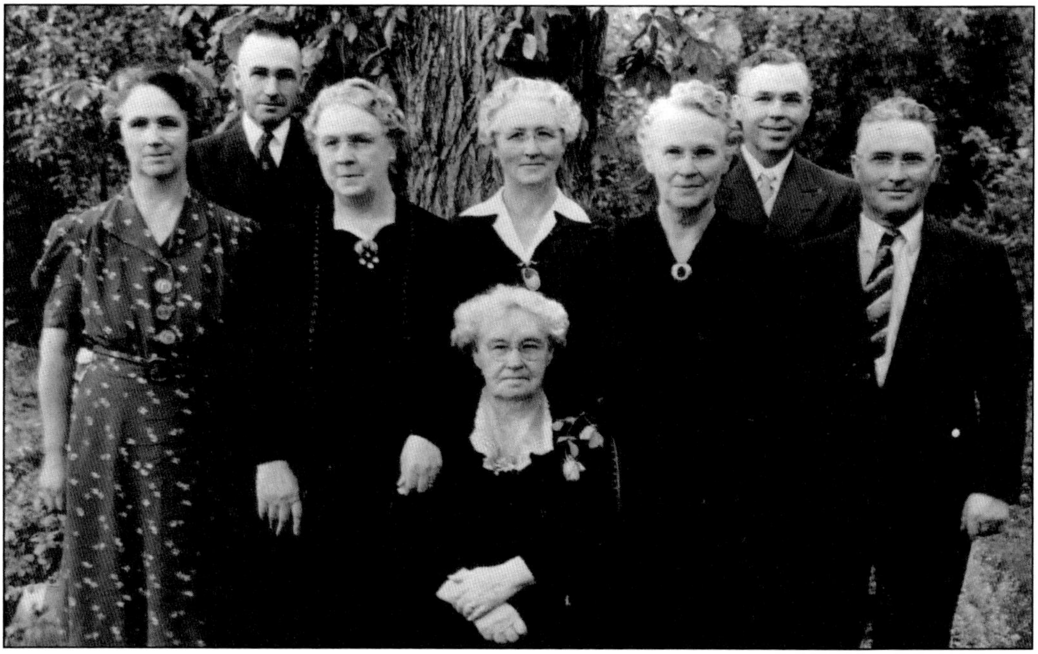

This is Abby Ann Whiting Bird's 80th birthday party in June 1938. Abby Ann is sitting, and behind her are seven of her eight children. They are, from left to right, (first row) Bessie, Emogene, Hannah, and Elmer; (second row) Freeman, Jennie, and Merrill. Abby was the first child of Edwin Whiting and his fourth wife, Hannah Haines Brown. Mary Cox Whiting, Edwin's third wife, educated her. On special evenings, the family would sing, pull taffy, tell stories, play games, and listen to Abby play a Jew's harp. (Courtesy of Mary Hjorth Fojtek.)

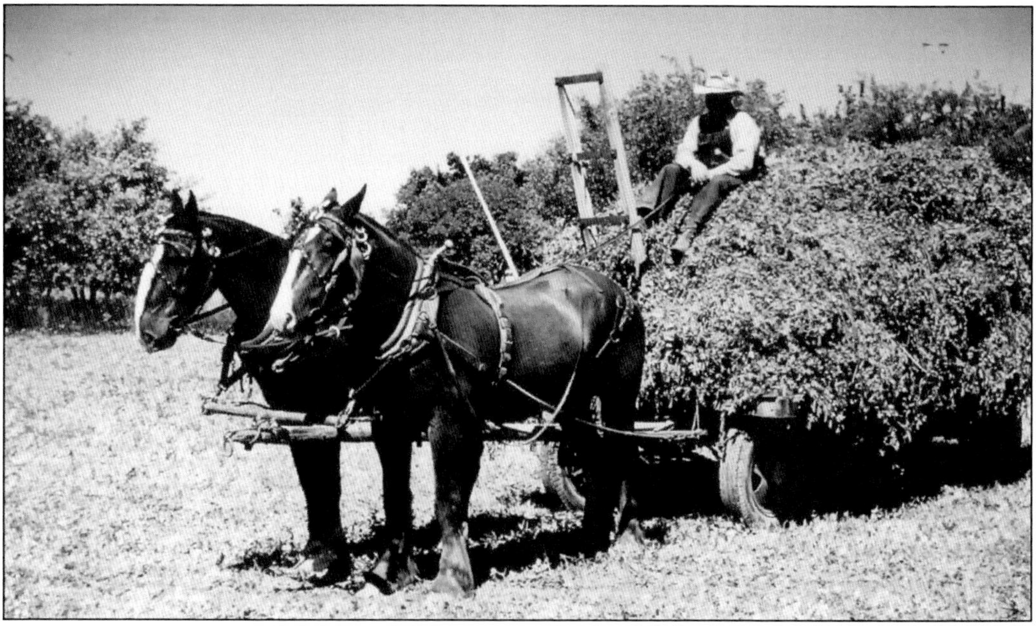

Joe Wiscombe is shown here harvesting peas grown on his farm in 1958. The Del Monte Cannery in Spanish Fork canned crops grown in Mapleton, including green beans, cream-style corn, diced tomatoes, and sweet peas. (Courtesy of the Mapleton Historical Museum.)

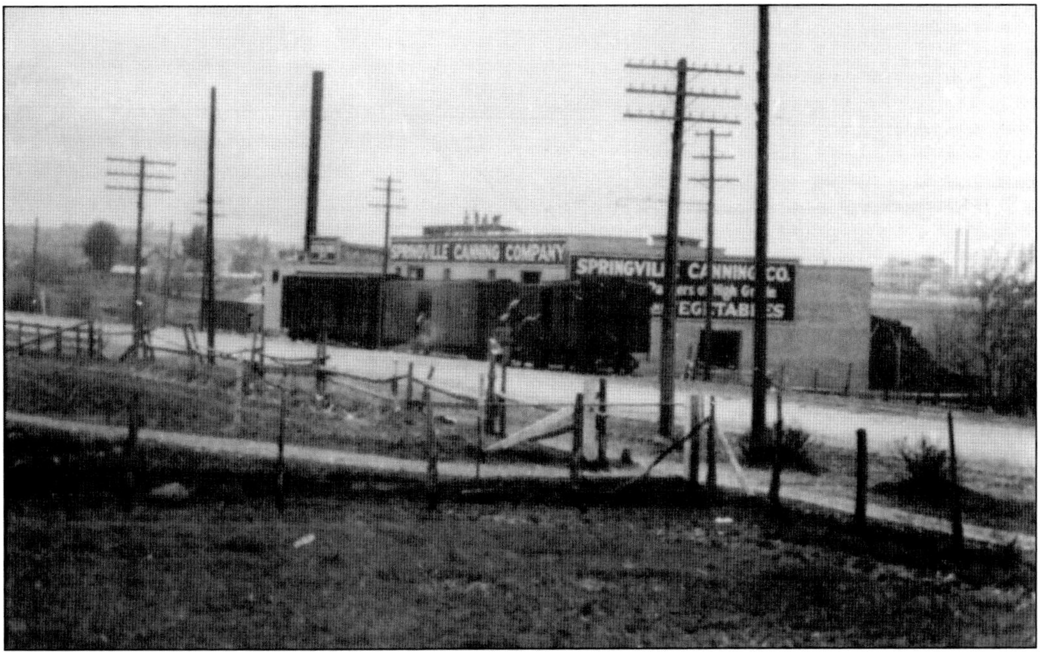

This c. 1918 photograph taken by George Edward Anderson shows the Eddington Canning Company, located along the Straightline in Springville, which processed the row crops that were grown in Mapleton. (Courtesy of the Mapleton Historical Museum.)

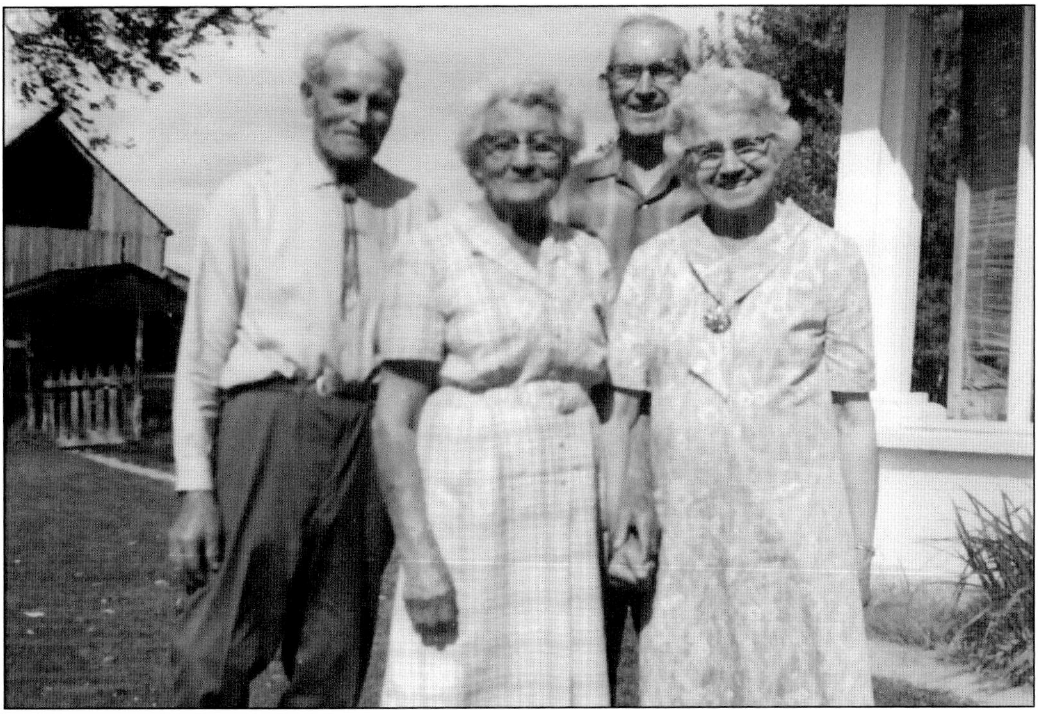

Pictured here from left to right are (first row) Rebecca Allan Twede and Martha Allan Houtz; (second row) Henry and James G. Allan. The original Allan family settlers had the first self-tying grain binder on the bench (Mapleton). (Courtesy of Collin Allan.)

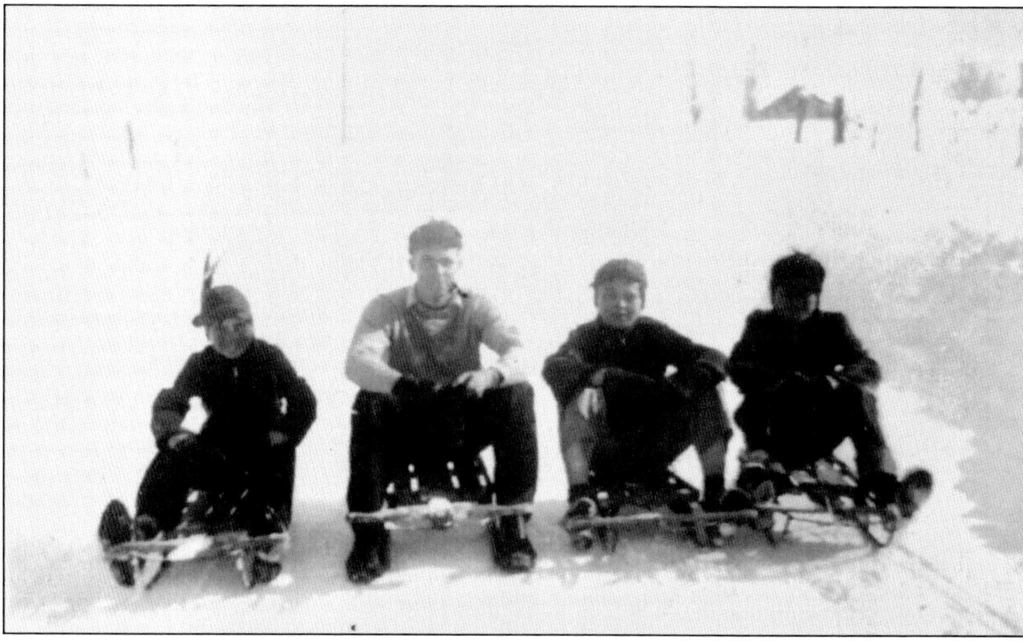

This photograph was taken in January 1944 on 1600 South. Sleigh riding was done in the road in front of the house, and very few cars ever interrupted the fun. From left to right are Collin, Evan, Neal, and Dean Allan. (Courtesy of Collin Allan.)

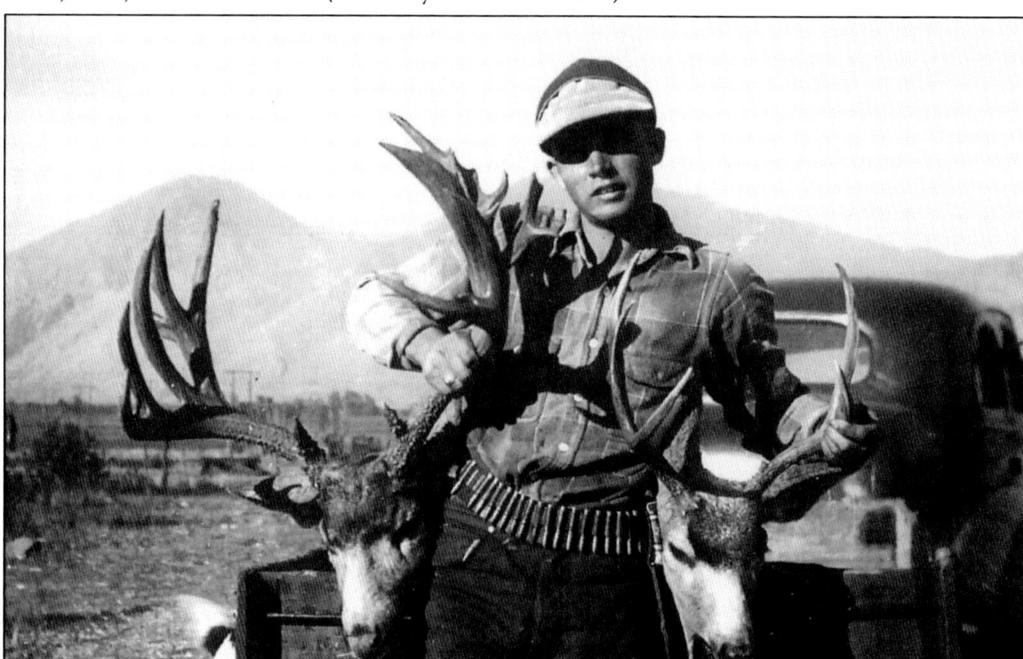

Evan Allan is seen with his deer, which he took down on the face of Maple Mountain. Evan was a lieutenant and a pilot in the Army Air Corps. He was only 19 when Pearl Harbor was bombed and the United States entered World War II. While serving in England, he was killed in action on September 18, 1944. His B-24 Liberator bomber was shot down over Germany. (Courtesy of Collin Allan.)

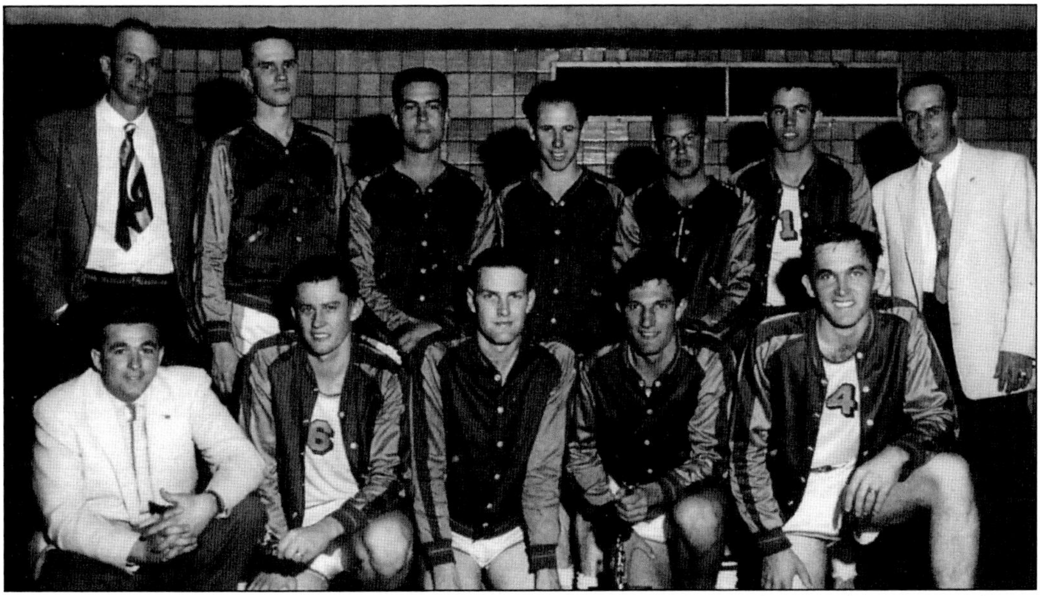

Pictured are Kolob Stake champions for the Church of Jesus Christ of Latter-day Saints. Players for the Mapleton First Ward men's basketball team in 1960 are, from left to right, (first row) coach Wave Miguel, Glade Binks, Kay Tew, Jackie Canto, and Collin Allan; (second row) coach "Doc" Snow, Alma Jansen, Lynn Bird, Dean Binks, Denny Murray, Keith Jensen, and coach Nino Antonino. Young women and men as well as the adults in the church play basketball. A stage at the rear of the buildings is used for theatrical productions, too. (Courtesy of Collin Allan.)

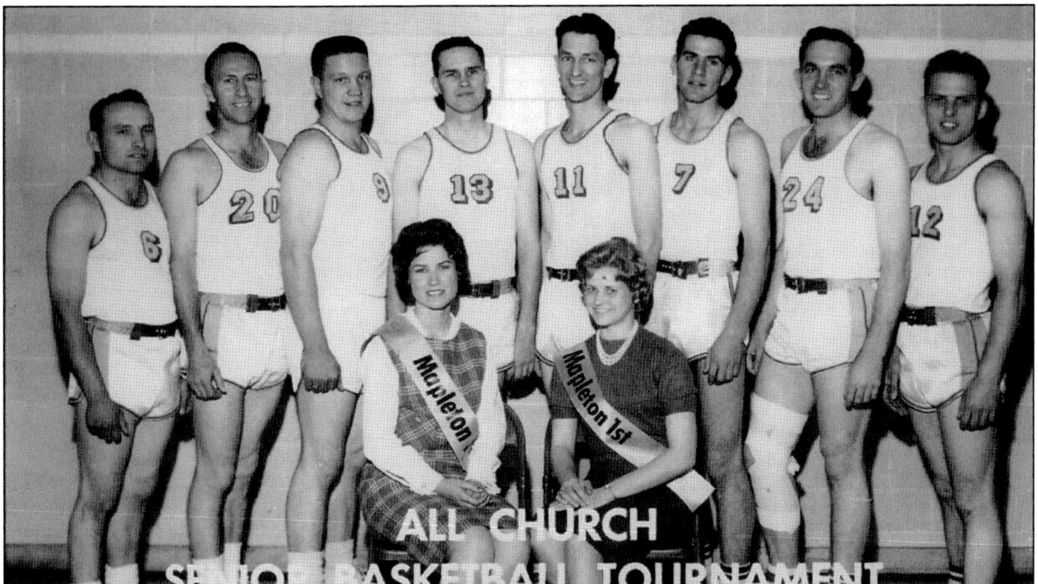

Winners of the All-Church Tournament in 1961 are, from left to right, Clyde Mortensen, Wayne Haws, Ron Graves, Alma Jensen, Elwood Jones, Jay Jensen, Collin Allan, and Morris Warren. Jay Jensen, No. 7, became a general authority in the Church of Jesus Christ of Latter-day Saints. He also served as president of the Seventies Quorum, overseeing church members throughout the world. (Courtesy of Collin Allan.)

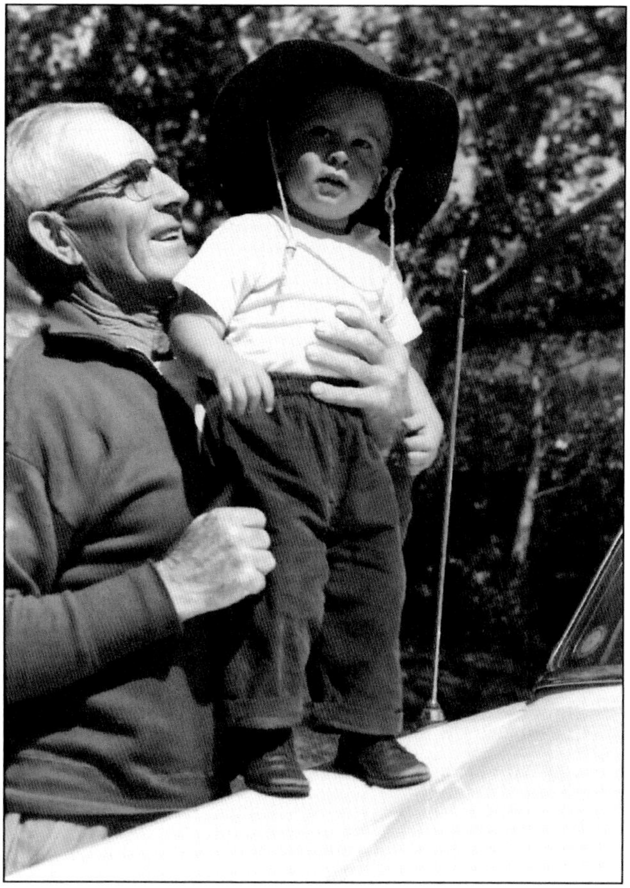

James G. Allan and his grandson Scott E. Allan are descendants of Charles Edward and Elizabeth Watkins Allan, who had 12 children. Charles Edward's greatest contribution to Mapleton was bringing the purebred Hereford stock here in 1904 after he bought a bull and three heifers in Chicago at the World's Fair. (Courtesy of Collin Allan.)

The "School Wagon" was used to transport Mapleton students into Springville. This photograph was taken in 1915 and shows some of the sophomore class at Springville High School. From left to right are (first row) Eliza Holley, Fern Hurst, Delphia Jolley, Catherine Whiting, Flora Gardner, Grace Gallup, and Alta Law; (second row) Bird Tew, Victor Whiting, Harvey Whitney, S. LaVell Bird, Mack Whitney, and Raymond Dibble. Walter Frederick Hurst is in the background. He was the driver of this horse-drawn bus. (Courtesy of the Mapleton Historical Museum.)

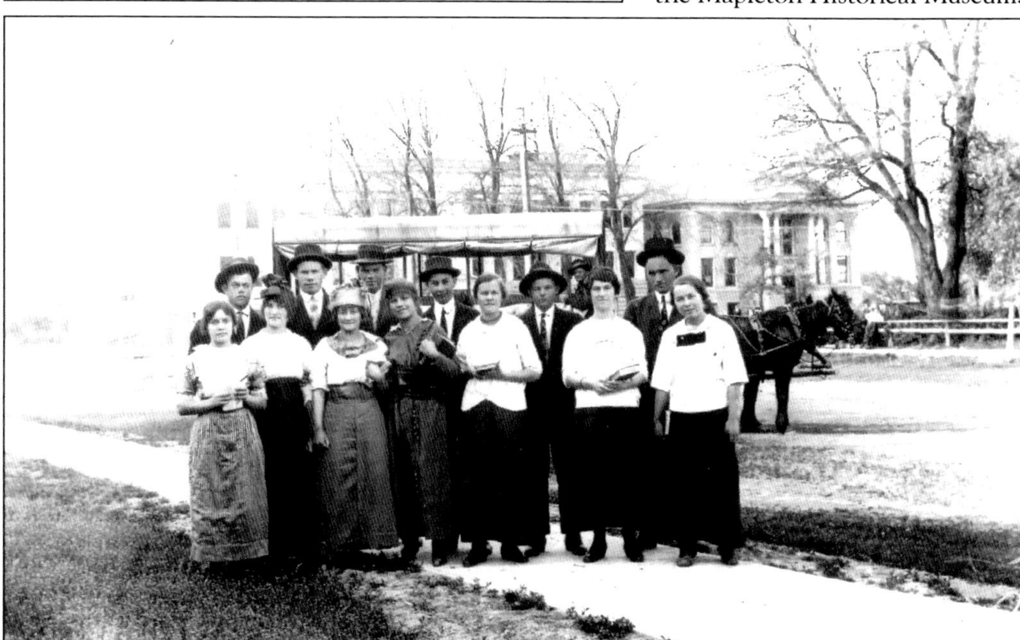

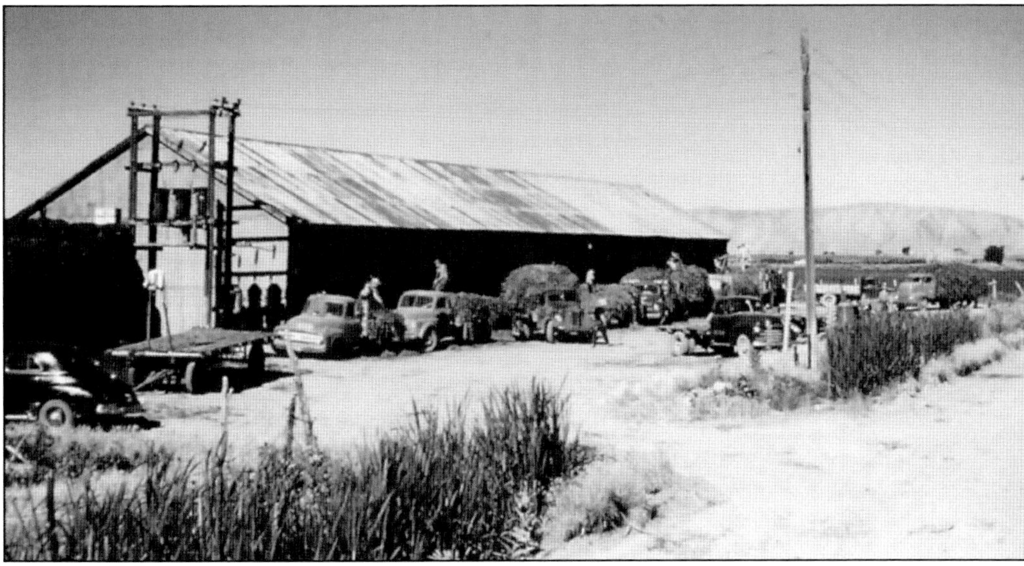

The Del Monte pea viner, one of four in the city, was located near 1100 West and 800 South. The trucks belonged to Joe, Jim, and Elmer Wiscombe in the 1960s. Jim Wiscombe served on the town board and was also the marshal. He served as president of the Mapleton Irrigation and Canal Company. (Courtesy of the Mapleton Historical Museum.)

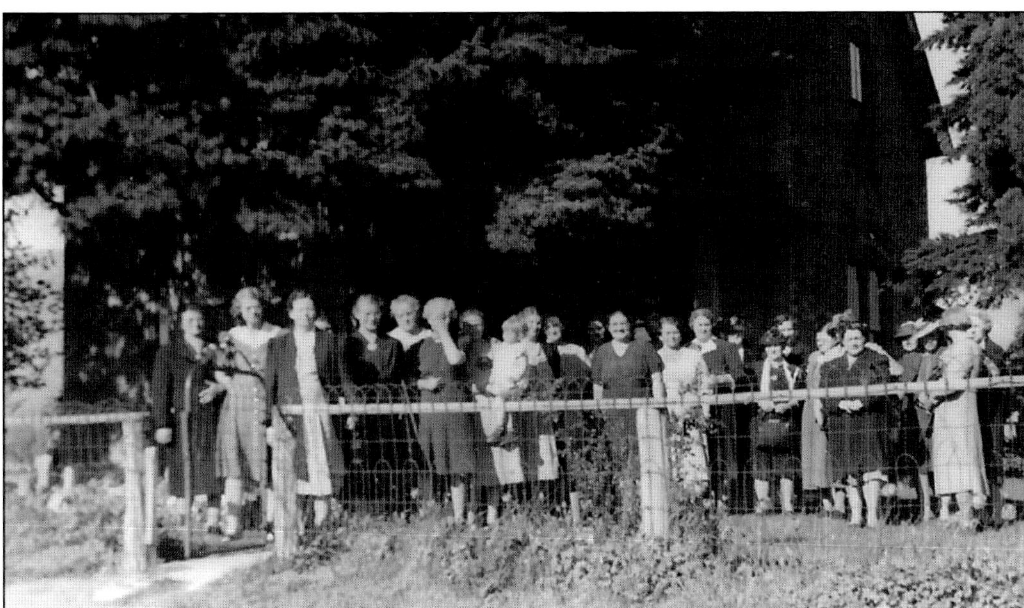

Standing by the Albert Milton Whiting tree, the Daughters of Utah Pioneers placed a marker here in 1940. Albert Milton Whiting has a special way with animals and was often called upon to cure them. He was appointed the town marshal because of his kind and gentle ways. He and his wife, Harriet Susanna Perry, were the parents of 16 children. (Courtesy of the Mapleton Historical Museum.)

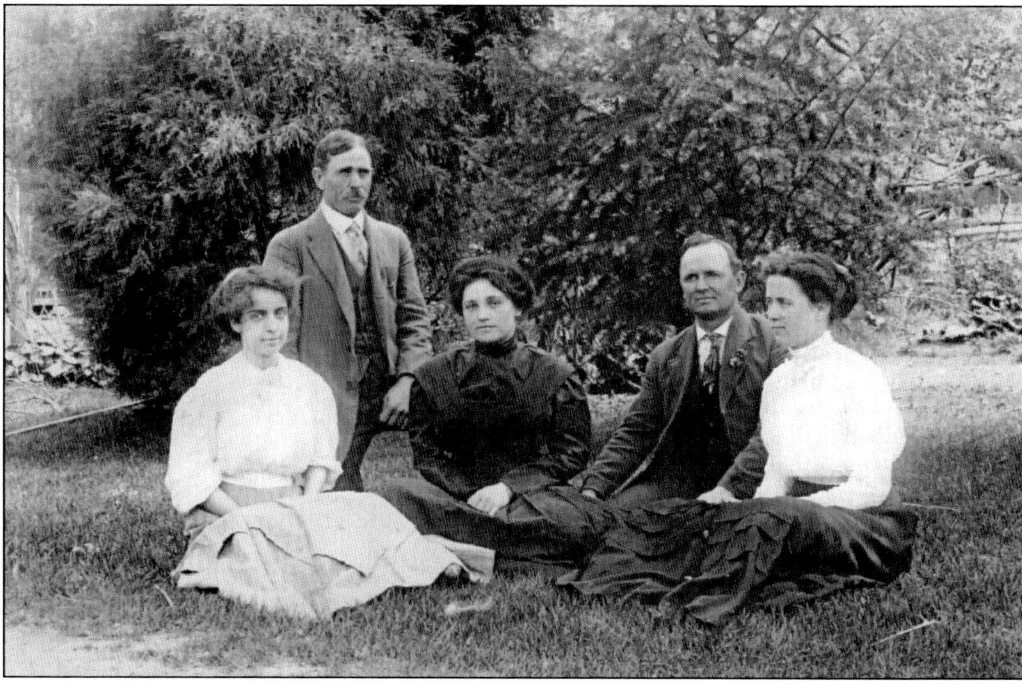

Mapleton school teachers gather on the lawn. On the left in front is Olive Carlton Whiting, and the rest are unidentified. (Courtesy of the Mapleton Historical Museum.)

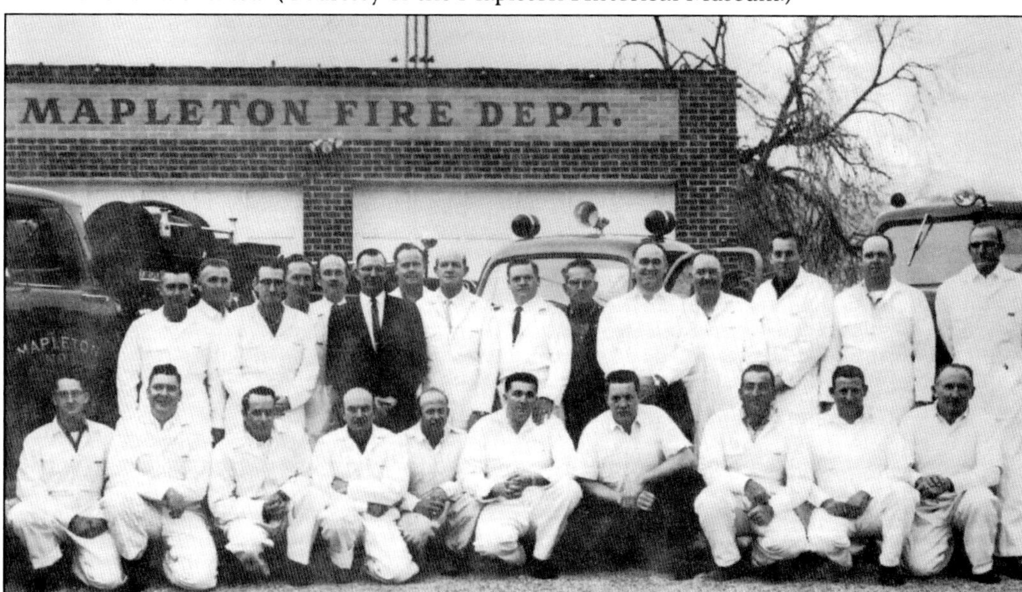

Members of the Mapleton City Volunteer Fire Department pictured here are, from left to right, (first row) Roger Evans, Ned Poulsen, Nino Antonino, Joe Carnasecca, Stan Jensen, Wave Miguel, Ron Graves, Johnny Bleggi, Herbert Miner, and Ralph Harmer; (second row) Leonard Mason, Lyle Paulson, Quinton Lowe, Norman Barker, Doug Brown, Welby Warren, Ned Lee, Doug Bills, Norman Graves, Cecil Dickerson, LaVere Tippetts, Fay Jensen, Lynn Bjarnson, Dick Bills, and Neil Steiner. (Courtesy of the Mapleton Historical Museum.)

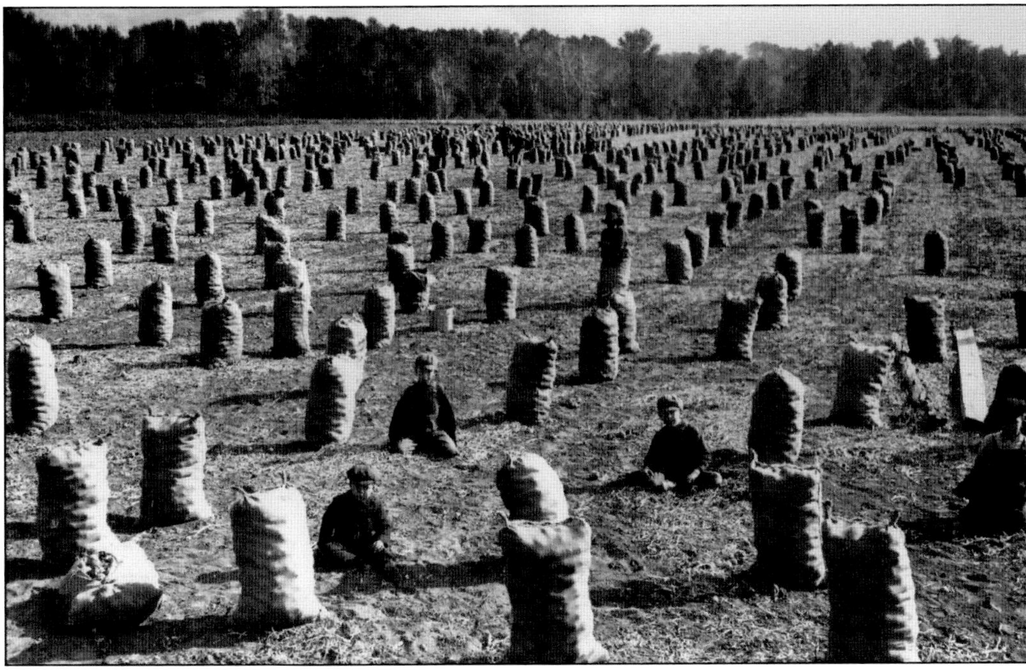

Hyrum S. Clyde's c. 1906 onion crop was located in the Hobble Creek area in Springville, on the north side of Mapleton. Second from right, taking a break from working the field with Wilford and his brothers, was George Dewey Clyde, Utah's governor from 1957 to 1965. This print was displayed at the San Francisco World's Fair in 1939 as part of the Utah exhibit, demonstrating the state's agricultural productivity. It also shows the state's other bumper crop—its children. George Edward Anderson took this photograph, and Rell G. Francis preserved it. (Courtesy of the Springville-Mapleton Pioneer Museum.)

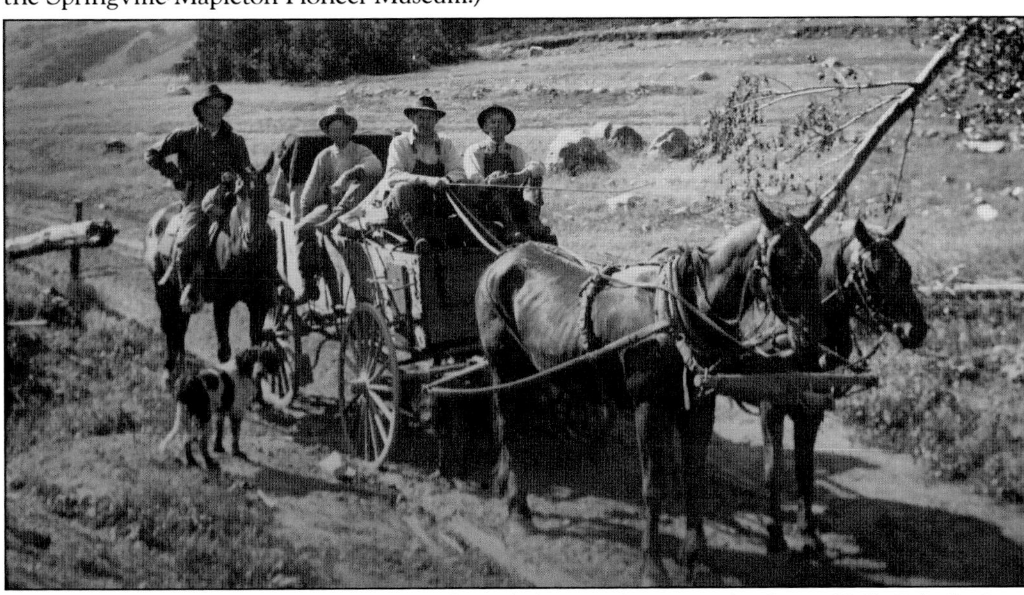

Members of this c. 1914 Thorn fishing outfit include, in unknown order, Jasper Hall, Othello, Ivan, and Newton. The Thorn families helped to establish both Springville and Mapleton. (Courtesy of the Springville-Mapleton Pioneer Museum.)

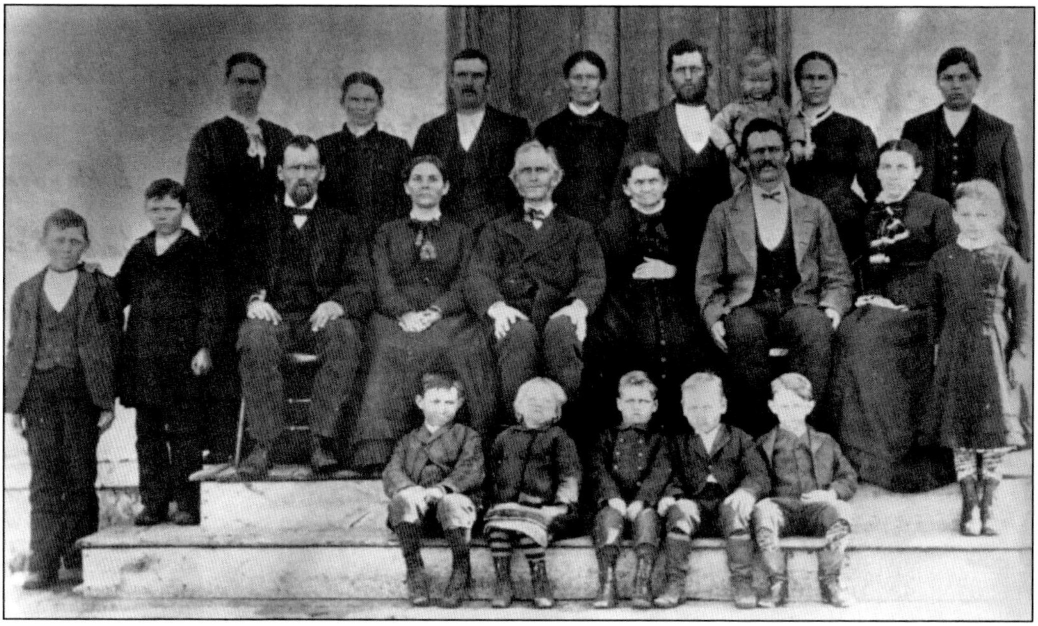

Here is a photograph from the c. 1878 William and Sarah Mendenhall family reunion. This is the first known Mendenhall family photograph since they crossed the plains in 1852. Sitting in the center are William Mendenhall (hands on legs) and his wife, Sarah Lovell Mendenhall (hand on stomach); on the right of Sarah is their son Richard Lovell Mendenhall and his wife, Mariah Catherine Houtz Mendenhall. Standing next to her is their daughter Irena Boyer Mendenhall, and the little boy sitting on the far right, on the steps, is the younger Richard Lovell Mendenhall. (Courtesy of Mary Hjorth Fojtek.)

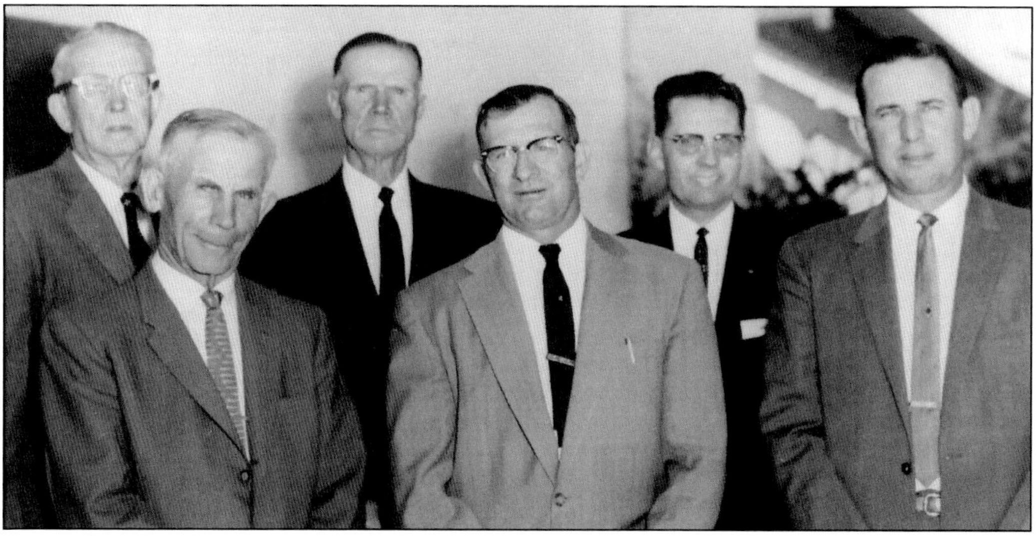

Pictured in the 1980s are past bishops for the Church of Jesus Christ of Latter-day Saints in Mapleton. From left to right are Loren Nielsen, Oscar Whiting, Frank Jensen, Welby Warren, Reed Bennett, and Stewart Whiting. Bishops serve the congregation in many ways, like a father figure. Members remember the bishops they have had throughout their lifetimes like a person remembers his schoolteachers or principals. Bishops serve without any pay. This volunteer time takes up many hours of their day for quite a few years. (Courtesy of the Mapleton Historical Museum.)

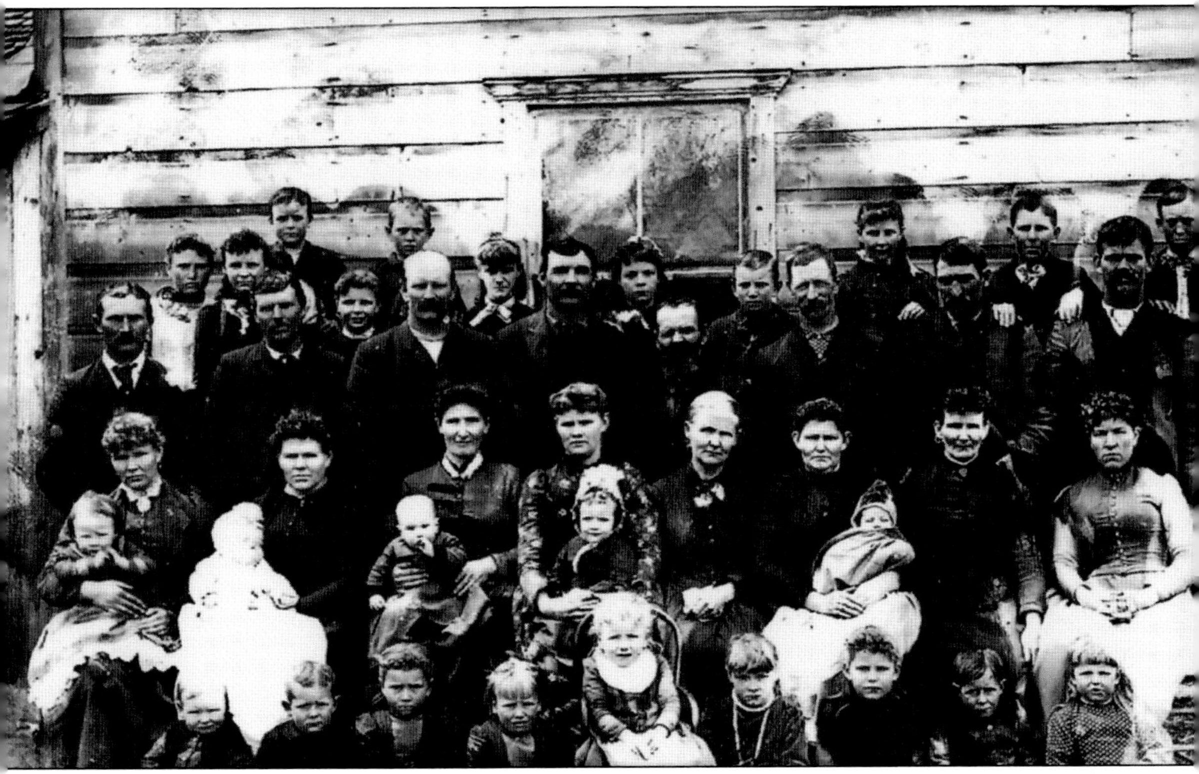

The family of Amos Sweet and Abigail Ardilla Childs Warren is pictured here around 1892. The children are, from left to right, (first row) Mark Dallin, Amos Luke Gallup, Belva Gallup, Lucy Warren, Altha Warren (seated), Louie Hinch, Augusta Gallup, Earl Vance Wordsworth, and Myrtle Ann Warren. The remaining family members are, from left to right, Franklin and Altha "Althea" Warren Fullmer with baby Elden Fullmer, Stephen and Polly Warren Dallin with baby Maude Dallin, Amos Benoni and Caroline Lucy Fullmer Warren with baby Theodore Warren, William and Millie Warren Hinch with baby Millie Odessa Gallup, Amos Sweet and Abigail Ardilla Childs Warren, James and Eleanor Warren Gallup with baby Persenda Gallup, John and Sarah Ardilla "Sadie" Warren Wordsworth, John Riley, and Hannah Davis Warren. Pictured in the back from left to right are Ariel Warren, May Hinch, Jesse Benoni Warren, Malinda Gallup, Amos Wellington Warren, Ardilla Gallup, Maggie Hinch, Billie Hinch, Abbie Wordsworth, James Alva Gallup, and Bassett Smith. (Courtesy of M. Lee Taylor.)

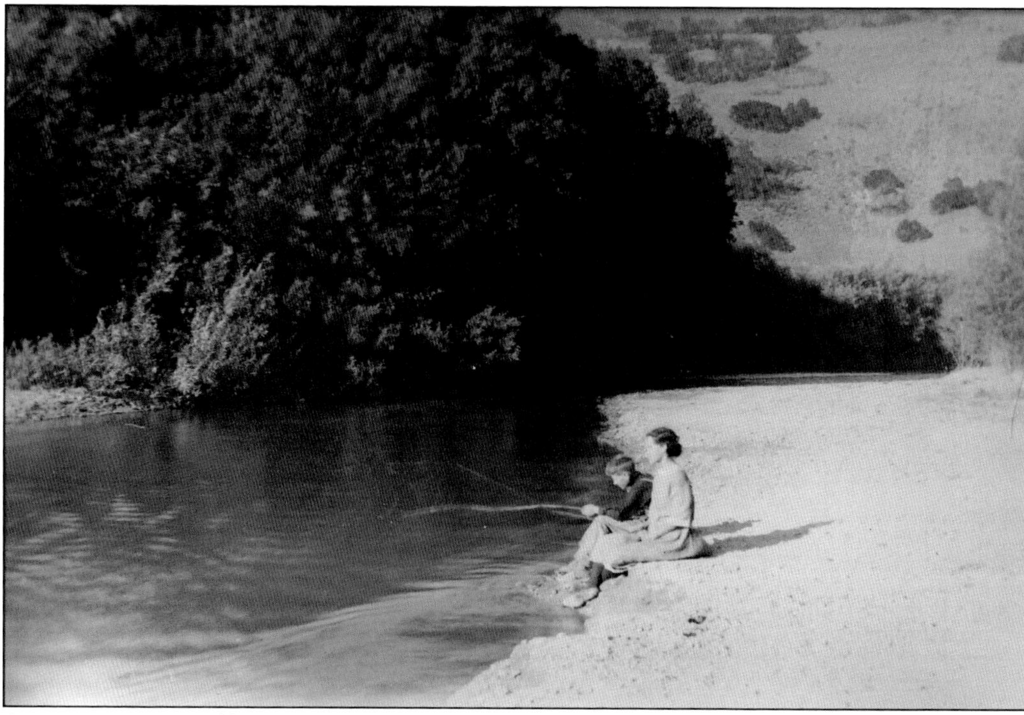

A young woman and boy are seen here on a relaxing fishing trip. The area around Mapleton has always had beautiful scenery. (Courtesy of the Mapleton Historical Museum.)

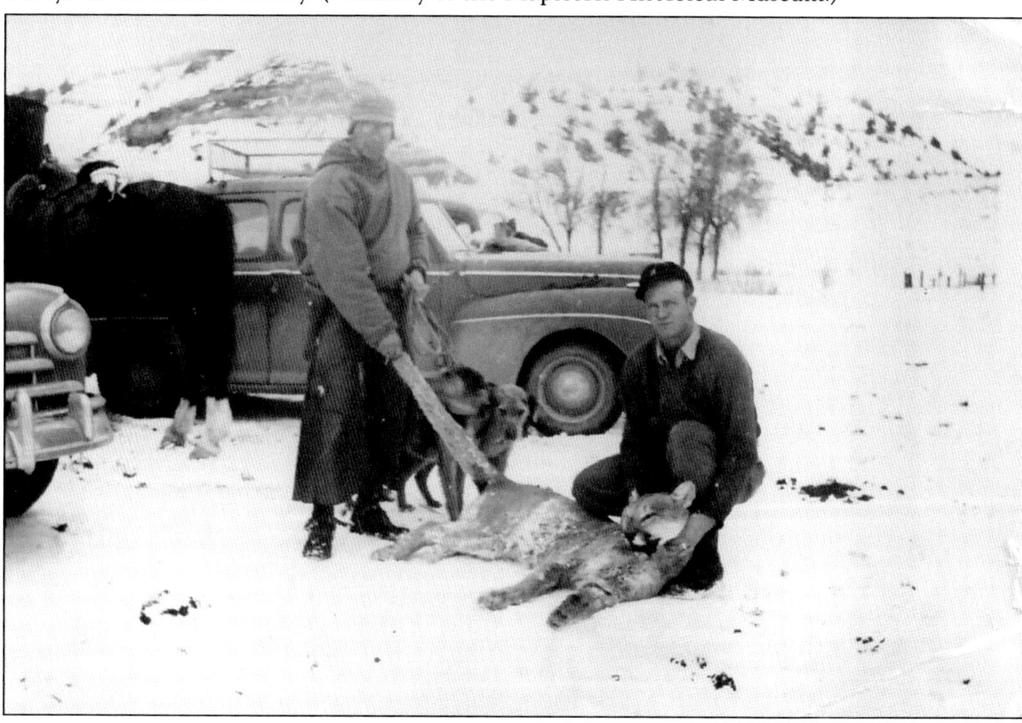

Doug Bills is pictured here on the right after a cat hunt with his hunting buddy. (Courtesy of Kay Bills.)

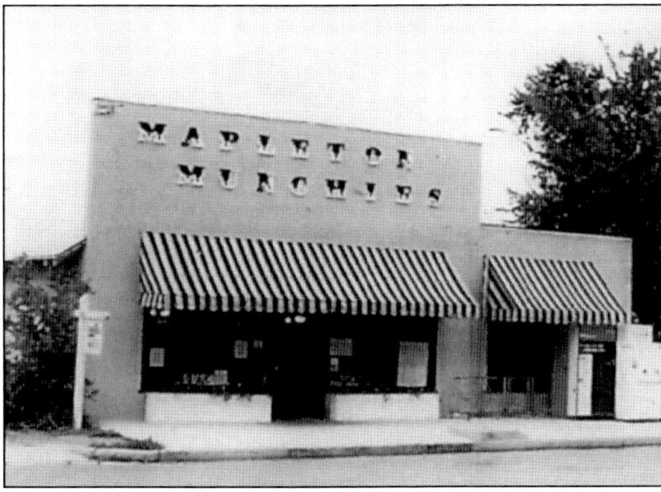

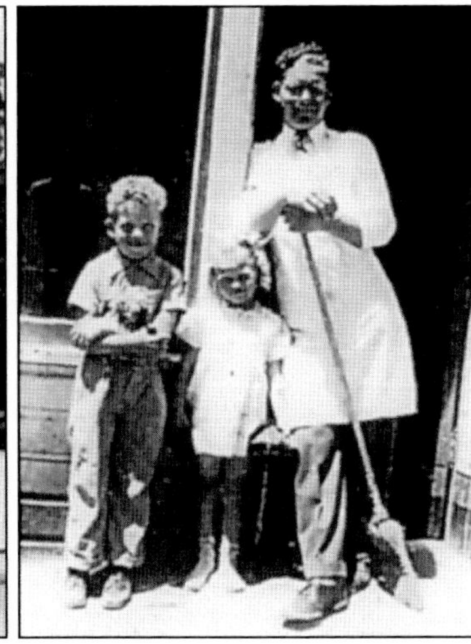

The Mapleton Munchies store is pictured here on the left before it was torn down. From left to right on the right are Bert, Georgene, and Harold Gividen, store proprietor. A memorial plaque located at the pavilion by the "White Church" honors the Gividen family and all they did for the residents of the city. (Courtesy of the Mapleton Historical Museum.)

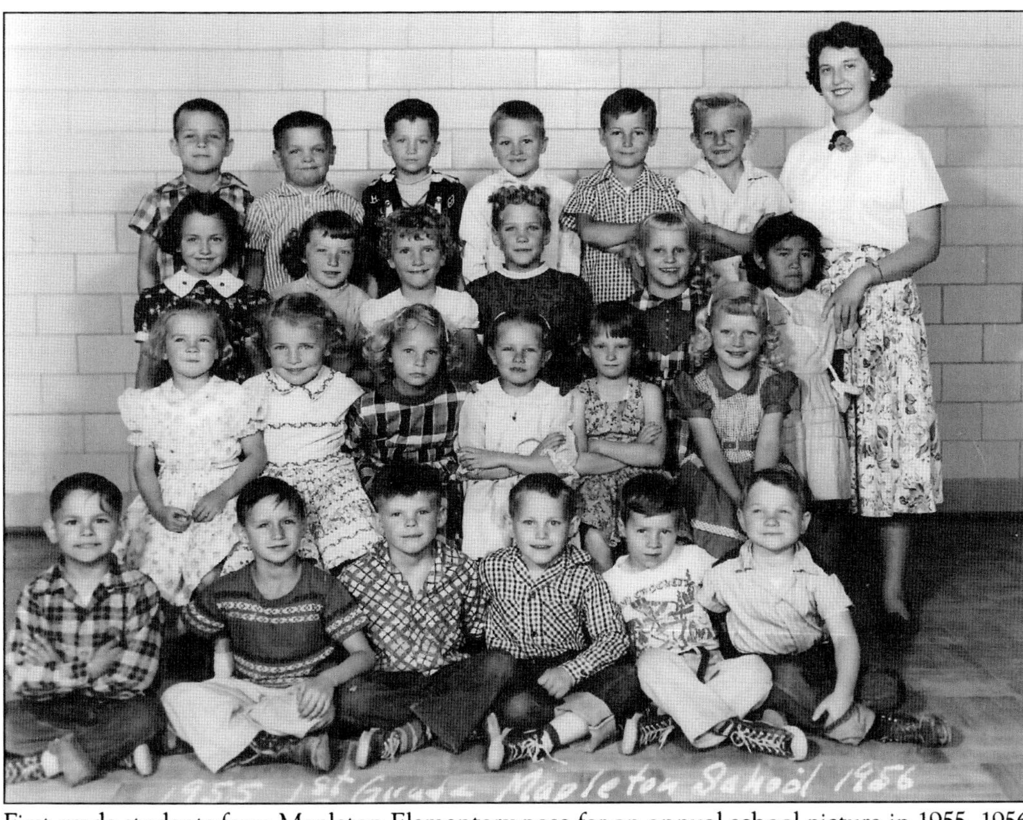

First-grade students from Mapleton Elementary pose for an annual school picture in 1955–1956. (Courtesy of the Mapleton Historical Museum.)

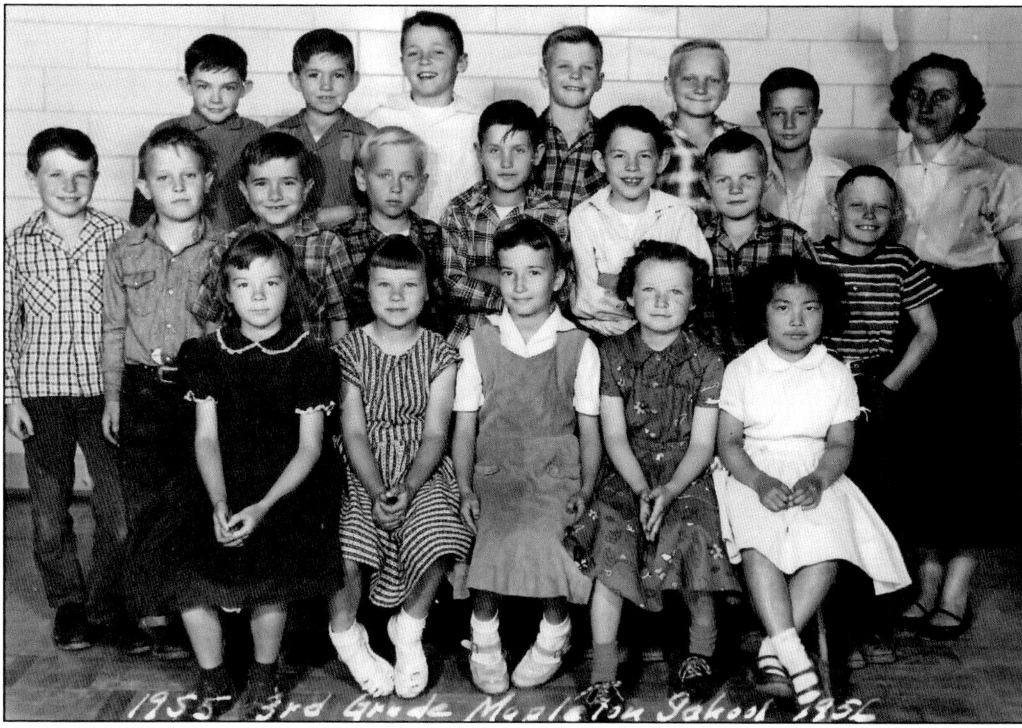

Above, third-grade students at Mapleton Elementary assemble in rows for a class photograph in 1955, while a fourth-grade class from the same school year is seen below. (Both courtesy of the Mapleton Historical Museum.)

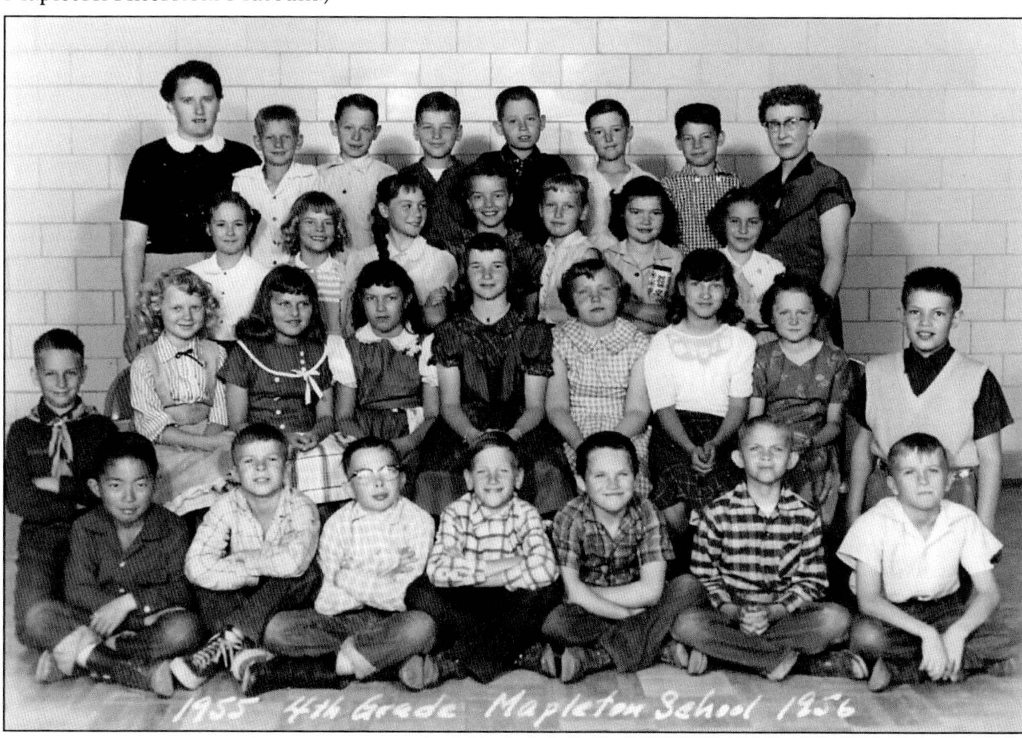

Three

THE BEGINNING

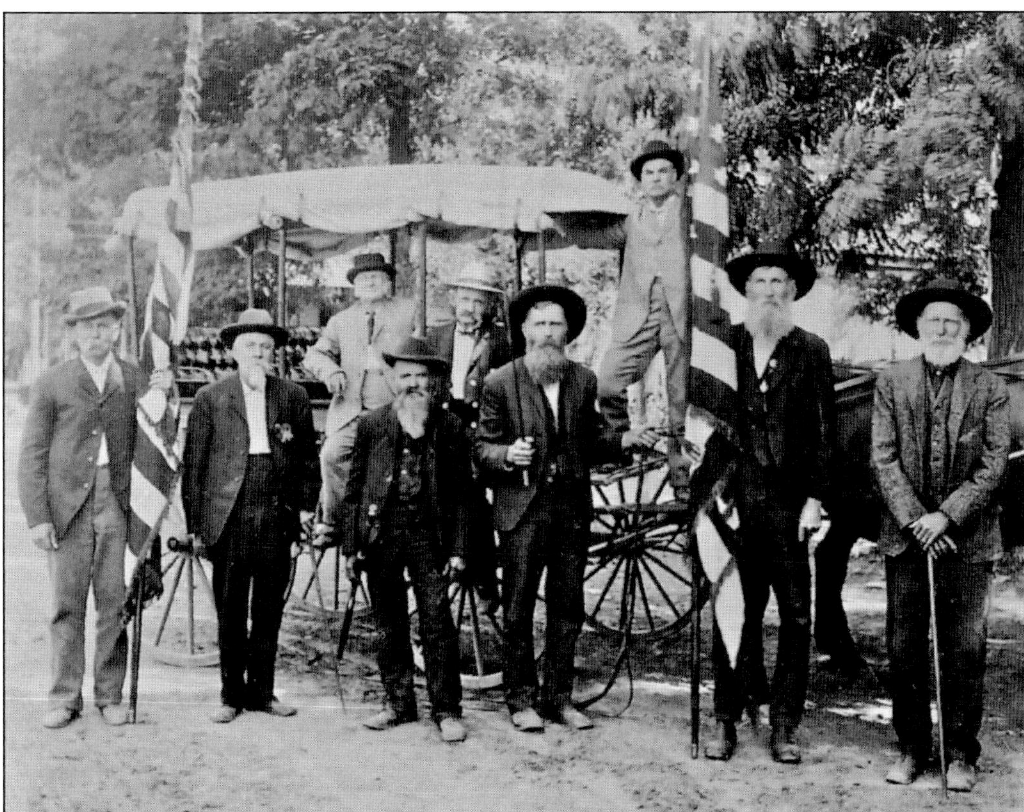

Black Hawk War veterans pictured here are, from left to right, Moses DeVere Childs, Henry Roylance, Edwin Lee (in buggy), Amos Sweet Warren, Walter Wheeler (in buggy), Albert Harmer, Joseph Westwood (on wagon), John Hubbard Noakes, and William Morgan Clyde. (Courtesy of M. Lee Taylor.)

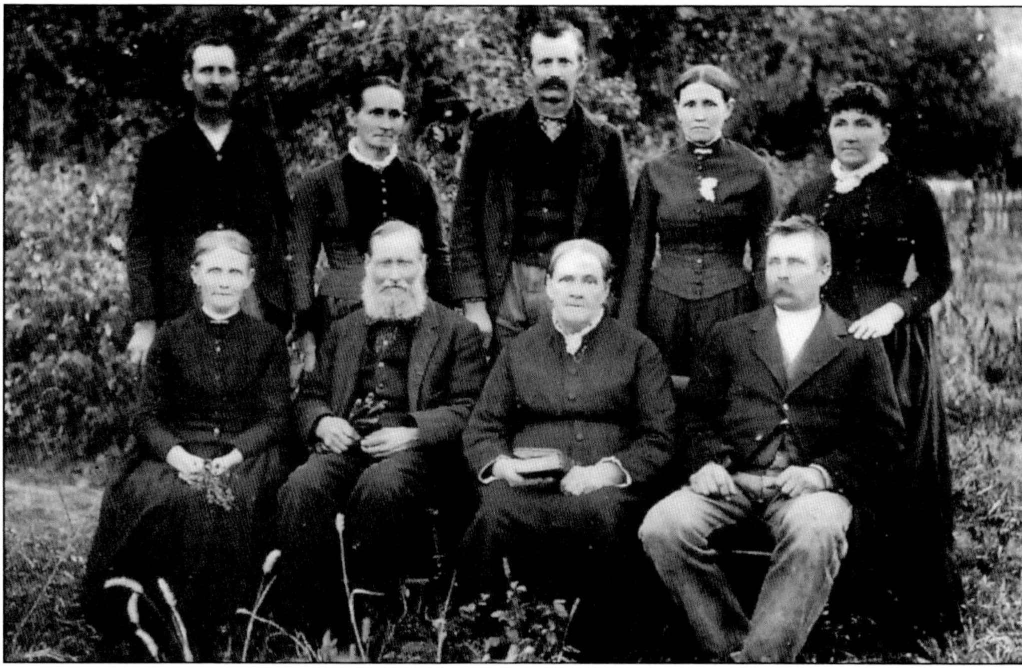

Here is Moses Child's family photograph. Abigail Ardilla, who married Amos Sweet Warren, is in the first row at far left. M. Lee Taylor's great grandfather, Moses DeVere Childs, is in the first row at far right. Amos Sweet's son Amos B. was the supervisor for the deacon's quorum in the Church of Jesus Christ of Latter-day Saints. The deacons would vie with each other to see which ones might care for the meetinghouse during the coming week. The young men would scrub the floors, fill the kerosene lamps, wash the lamp chimneys, polish the stove, chop wood, and get coal. There was always a hope that a show or a dance would happen during the week, and they wanted everything to be ready if something occurred. (Courtesy of M. Lee Taylor.)

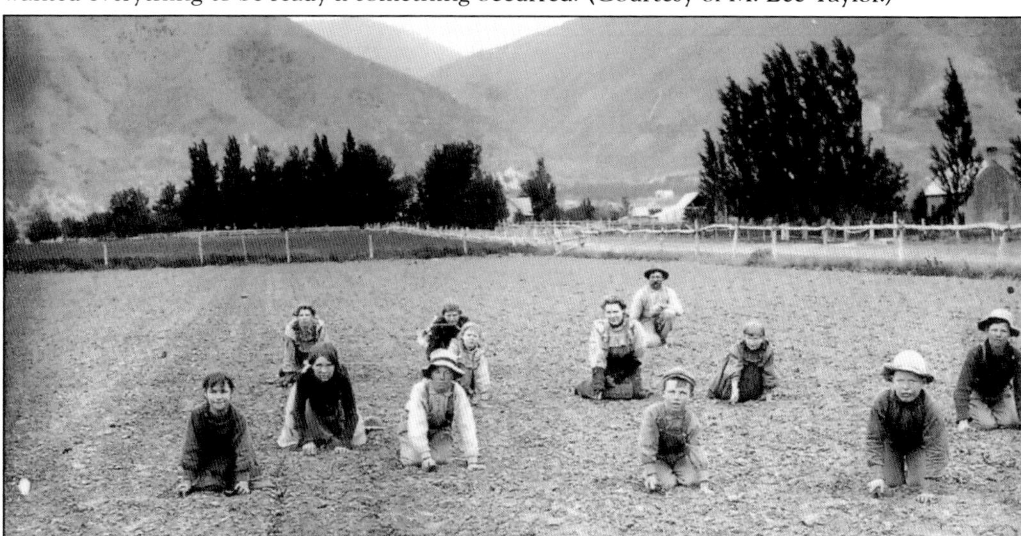

Ed Snow's family and friends are thinning beets in their Mapleton field in this George Edward Anderson photograph; some of Edwin Marion and Frances Evaline Perry Snow's children at this time were Ruby, Edwin Marion, and Luella Snow. (Courtesy of M. Lee Taylor.)

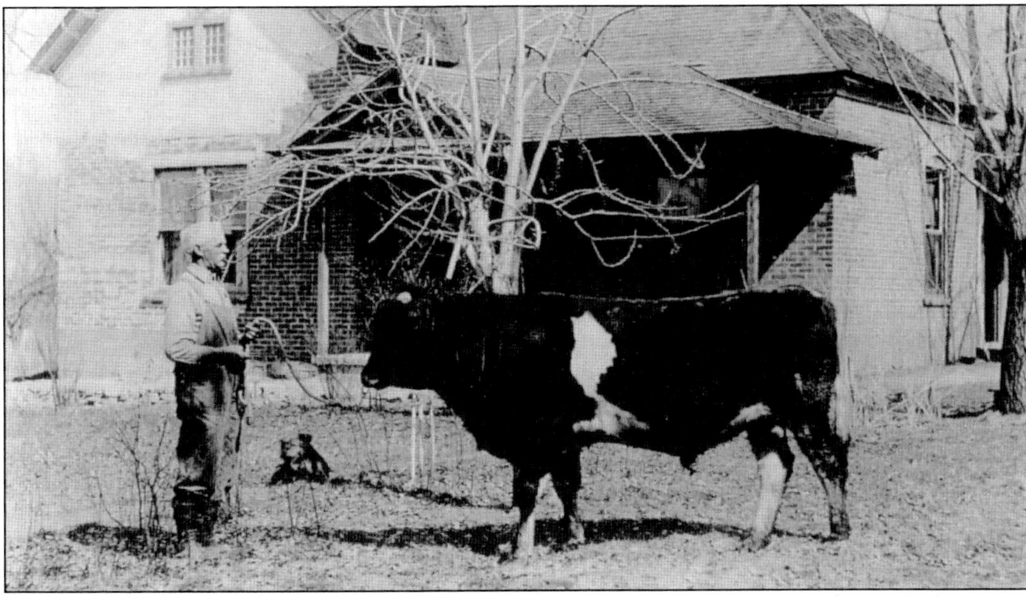

Edwin Joshua Marchbanks is seen with his prized bull. The original farm consisted of 60 acres, and the land had to be cleared in order for buildings to be built. This home at 435 West 1600 South has since been razed, but there are still a number of old trees on the property. (Courtesy of J. Brent Haymond.)

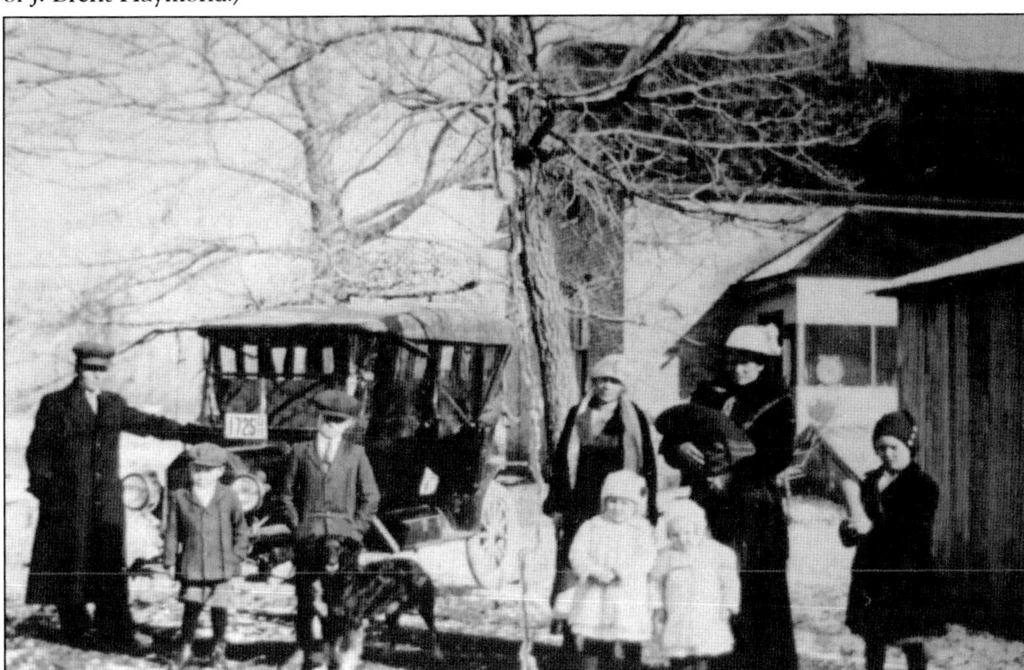

Leo Harmer's family, home, and Model T are seen around 1913. From left to right are Angus Leo, Ralph, Arthur, Elva, Erma, Jonina holding Harold, and Helen. At age 16, with only a few semesters of education completed, Leo was working away from home hauling lumber for contractors. He was paid $1 a day for his efforts. George Edward Anderson took this photograph, and Rell G. Francis preserved it. (Courtesy of J. Brent Haymond.)

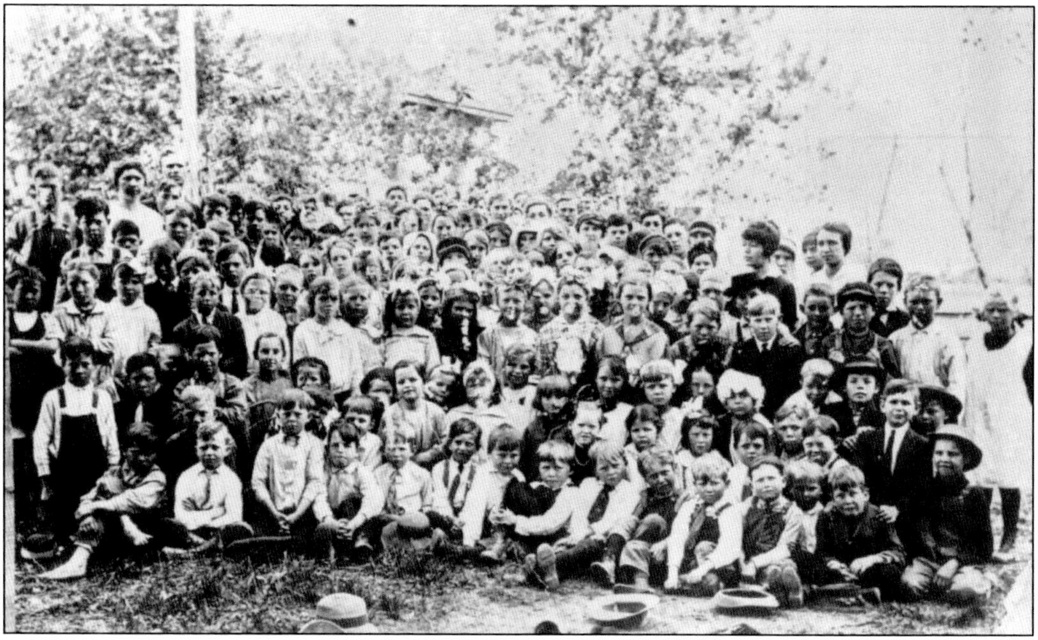

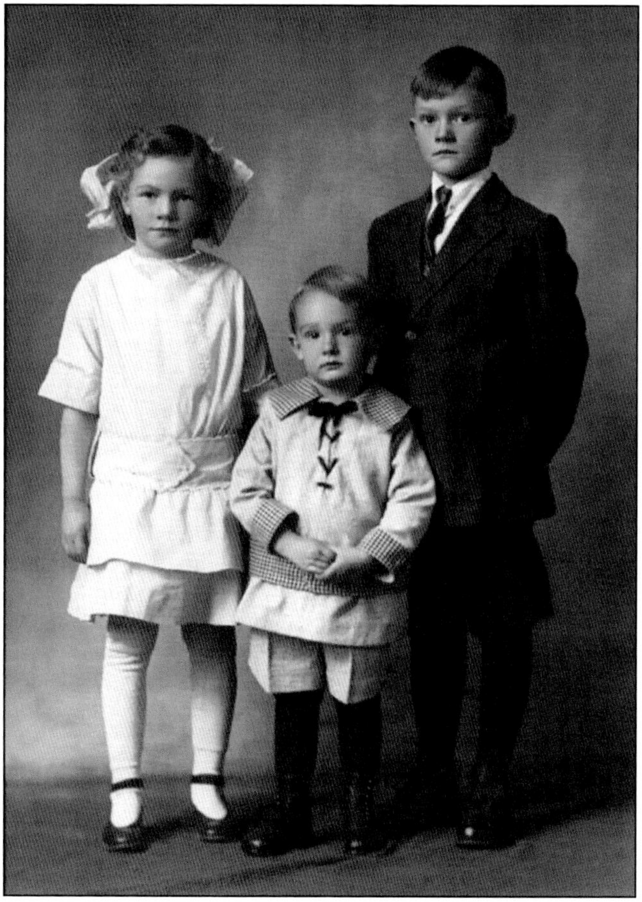

Here is the 1913 Mapleton School second-grade class. Helen Mendenhall is in the picture, and J. Brent Haymond's grandfather Ted Haymond is in the first row at far right. Others identified by the Mapleton Historical Museum are Bernice Haymond, Madge Johnson, Ivy Larson, Ellis Murray, Frank Snow, and Ernest Binks. (Courtesy of J. Brent Haymond.)

Pictured here from left to right are Louise, Art, and Wendell Mendenhall in 1916. They are the children of R. Lovell and Hannah Bird Mendenhall. R. Lovell rode a horse into Springville to attend school. At that time, there was no organized school for him to attend in Mapleton. He eventually attended Brigham Young University in Provo. He served a term as Mapleton's town board president. (Courtesy of Elfie Huntington.)

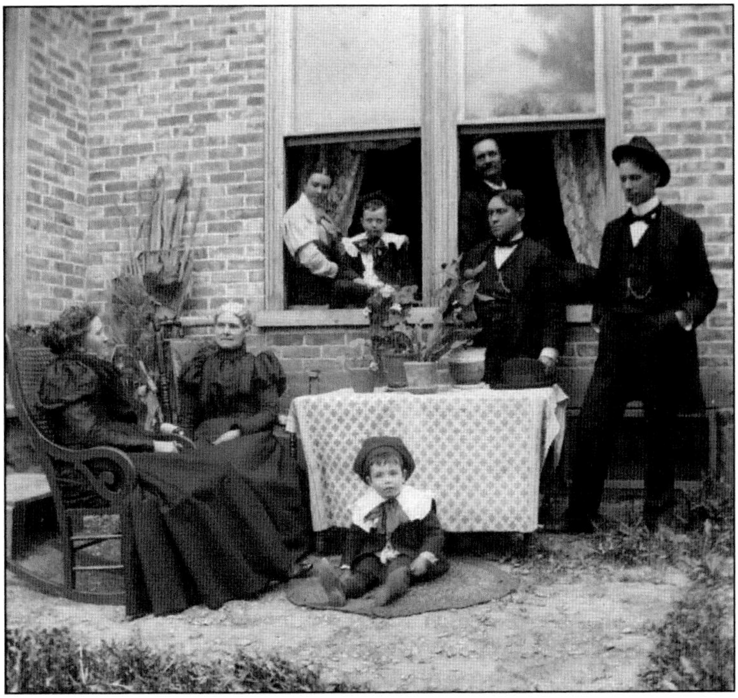

Here is a c. 1892 family gathering at the new home of Richard and Mariah Catherine Mendenhall, located at 1365 West 800 North. (Courtesy of Mary Hjorth Fojtek.)

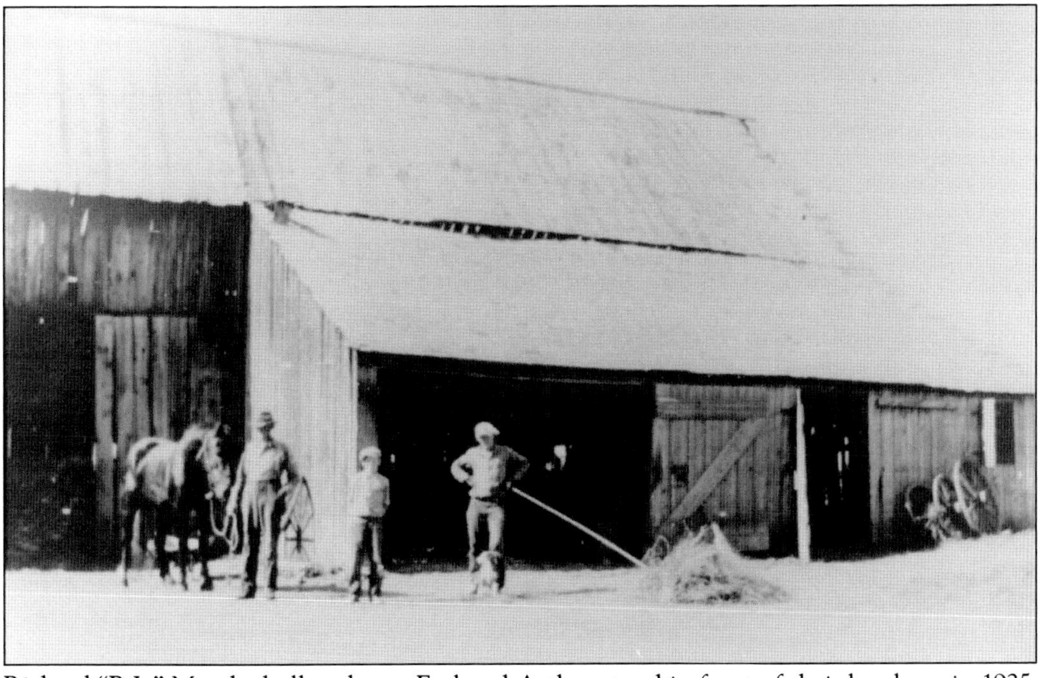

Richard "R.L." Mendenhall and sons Earl and Arthur stand in front of their hay barn in 1925. Mendenhall was a very successful farmer and sheep rancher. He operated 70 acres of farmland and several hundred head of sheep. R.L. and Mariah had twins (a boy and a girl), and when asked what he thought about his twins, he replied, "I think they are wonderful, but I wouldn't take a million dollars for the pair that I have and I wouldn't give a dime for another pair." (Courtesy of Mary Hjorth Fojtek.)

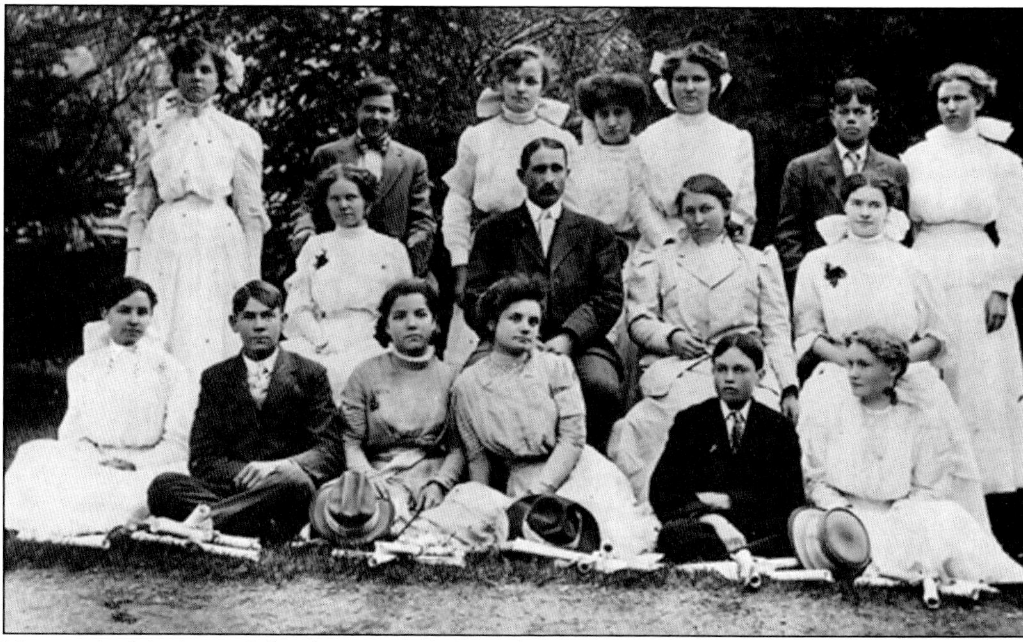

Here is the Mapleton School's 1904 eighth-grade graduating class. From left to right are, (first row) unidentified, Ruel Jensen, unidentified, Edna Whiting Mills, unidentified, and Rose Snyder Curtis; (second row) Jenny Houtz Tew, Clara Larsen Perry, the principal, and Suzy Whiting Fuller; (third row) unidentified, Burton Tew, unidentified, Violet Moore (Floyd Miner's grandmother, also pictured on the cover as a child), Mary Ellen Larsen (Miller), Brian Tew, and Kate Hopler. (Courtesy of Floyd Miner.)

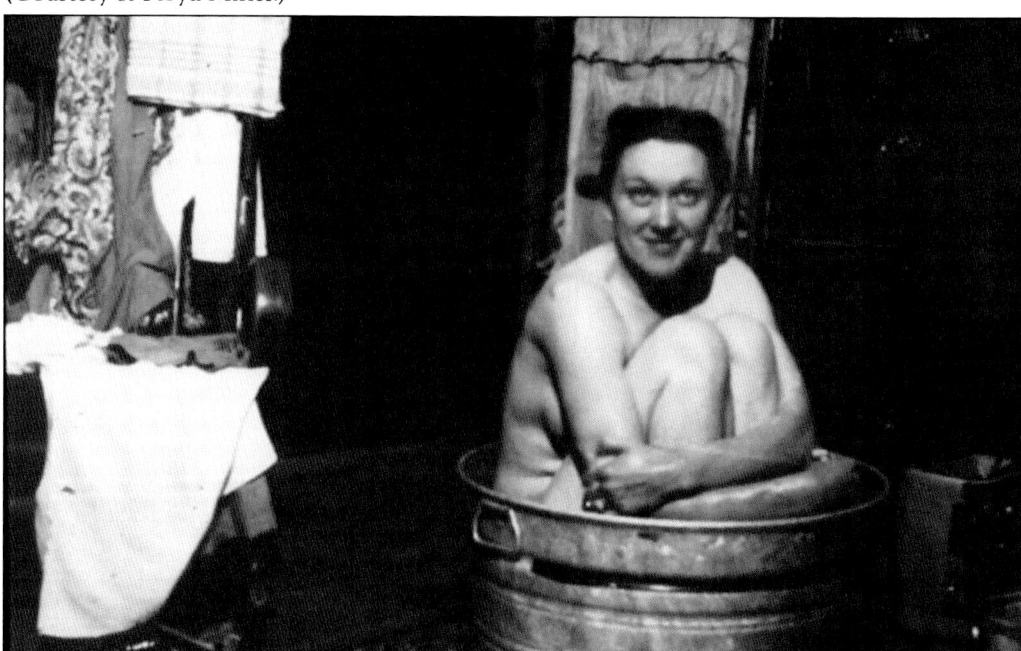

Erma Mendenhall is seen enjoying the modern conveniences of 1939 in her new home. It had a "bath and a path" to the outhouse. (Courtesy of Mary Hjorth Fojtek.)

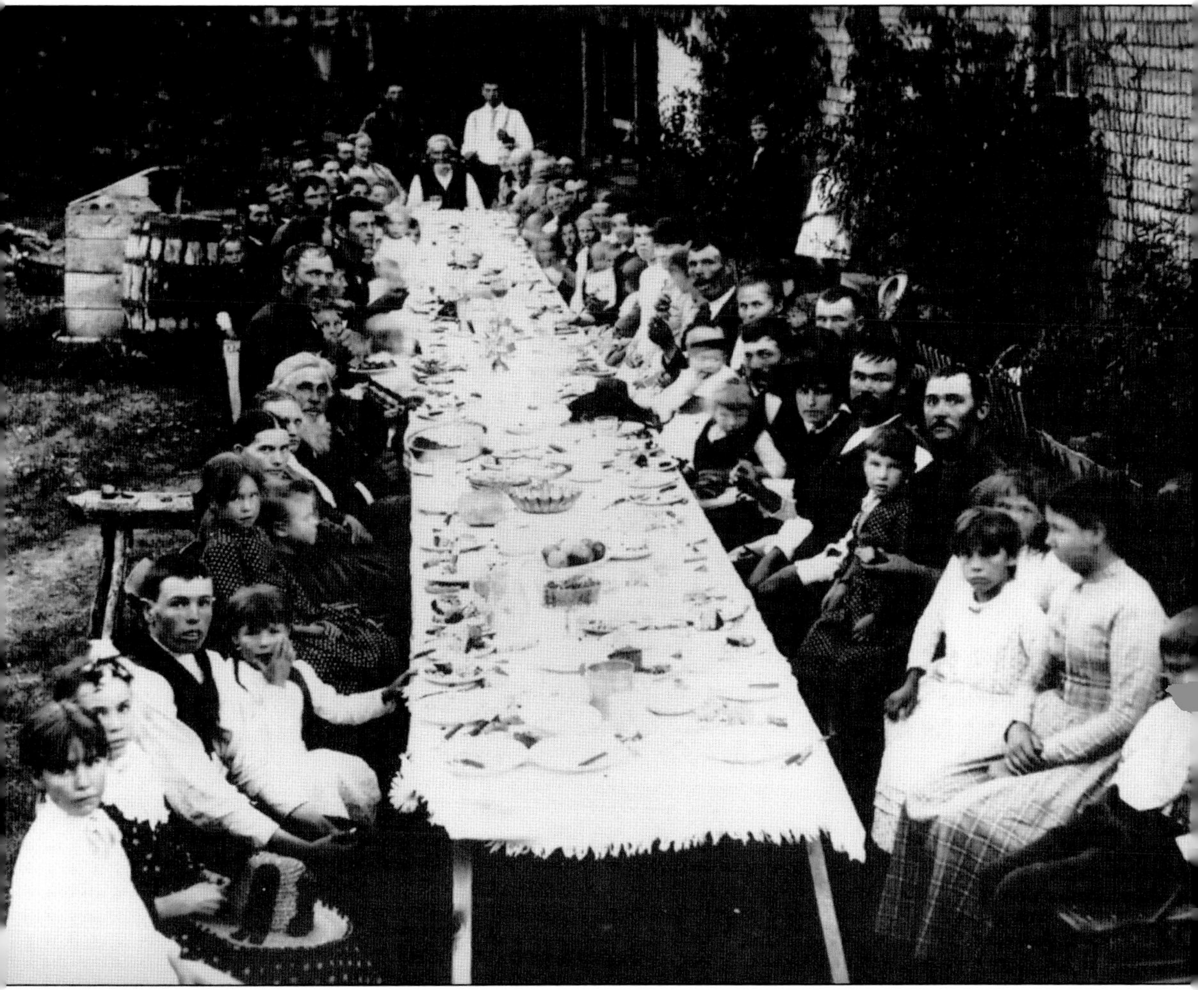

An Edwin Whiting family reunion was held in Springville in the mid-1900s. Harriet Jensen tells this story about going up Hobble Creek during the summers to help at her grandfather Edwin Whiting's sawmill. She would watch for leaks around the dam with her uncle Fred. She hauled water and sprinkled it in the dust by the front door to make it hard, and occasionally, it grew some grass to make the area by the front door look nice. She said her grandmother would save up newspapers all winter, and in the spring, she used them to paper over the logs inside the cabin. That was the first time she had ever heard of wallpaper. Among those pictured here are Edwin, Elizabeth Tillotson, Mary E. Cox (wife), Hannah Brown (wife), Albert, Harriet Perry, Monroe, Bell Whiting Manwaring, Fanny, John Edwin (Jack), Sara, Gertrude Perry Killpack, Hattie Curtis Evans, Dora Curtis, Edger, Frances Perry Snow, Eddie Snow, Edward Snow, Ruby Snow, John, Kit Waterman, Lorenzo, Charles M. Bird, Hannah Bird Mendenhall, Fannie Whiting Fullmer, Hattie Whiting Jensen, Verna, Charley Bird, Mary Curtis, Madge, Frederick, Clara Curtis, Bessie Bird, Libby Bromley, Caroline Whiting Bromley, Mary Perry, Stephen C. Perry, Aaron Johnson, Louisa Whiting Johnson, William T. Tew, Clara Snow Tew, Leon Perry, Ernst Perry, Lewis R. Perry, Lizzie Alveman, Lucius, Willis Perry, Wells Snow, Arthur, Daniel, Wilford Woodruff, Joe Curtis, Harold C., and Mary Emily. (Courtesy of the Mapleton Historical Museum.)

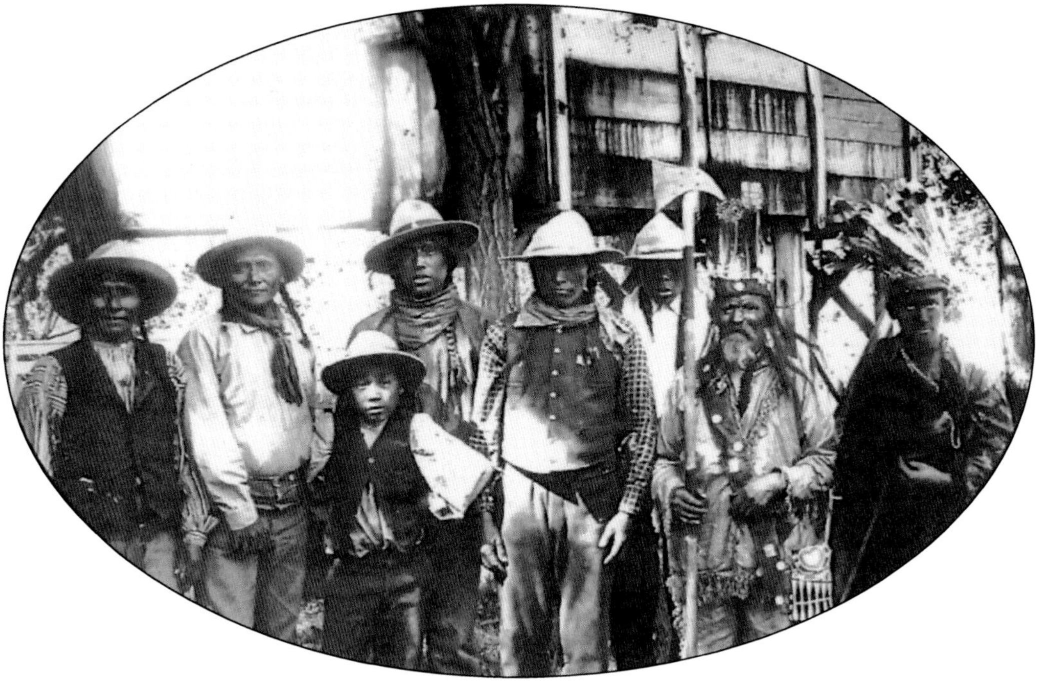

Amos Sweet Warren is pictured second from right with his son Benoni (far right), at a celebration in Springville in July 1900. Shown here in costume, the white people dressed up as Indians. The Indians dressed up as white men. Warren was one of the first settlers in the area in 1850, and worked as a blacksmith and beekeeper. George Edward Anderson took this photograph, and Rell G. Francis preserved it. (Courtesy of M. Lee Taylor.)

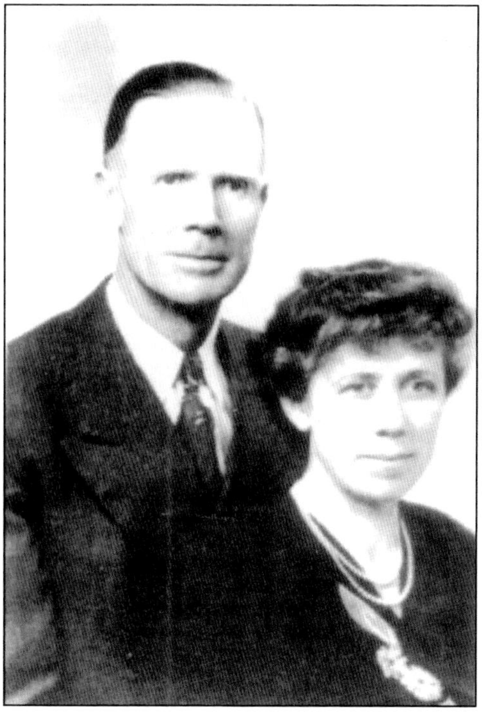

Frank and Vanda Jensen are pictured here. Grandson Ron Jensen tells of fun times in the 1950s and 1960s when his father, Paul Minor Jensen (one of Frank and Vanda's sons), would weld and bolt an extra support to the classic Flexible Flyer sleds to make them stronger for kids in Mapleton. A large "Sled Hill" was graded from the Whitings' property and ran all the way down to where Central Bank stands today. Children enjoyed this hill for many winters. (Courtesy of the Mapleton Historical Museum.)

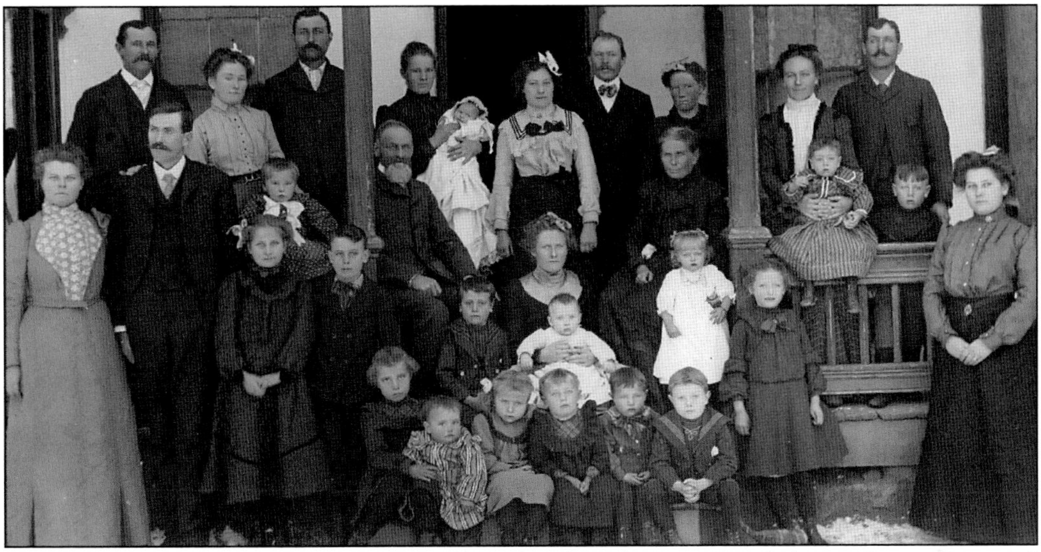

Here is a scene from the William Price Fullmer family gathering. From left to right are (first row) Beatrice, Ross, Margaret, Maude, Dick, and David John; (second row) Elizabeth Bromley, Samuel C., Eva, Joseph (seated), Elmer, Phoebe Perry (holding Fern Perry), Lula Jensen, Mina Johnson (leaning on railing), Ammon Johnson, Earl Johnson (in front of railing), and Amy; (third row) Harvey Perry, Mary Fullmer Perry (with Edward Perry on lap), William P. Jr., William Price Sr. (seated), Fannie and baby, Gertrude, Maria Jane Curtis (seated), Erastus Jensen, Addie Jensen, Lutitia Fullmer Johnson, and Silas Johnson. William says that the greatest comfort was when water was piped into the house. Water had to be carried from the canyons in barrels during the droughts, so this one luxury was marvelous. George Edward Anderson took this photograph, and Rell G. Francis preserved it. (Courtesy of M. Lee Taylor.)

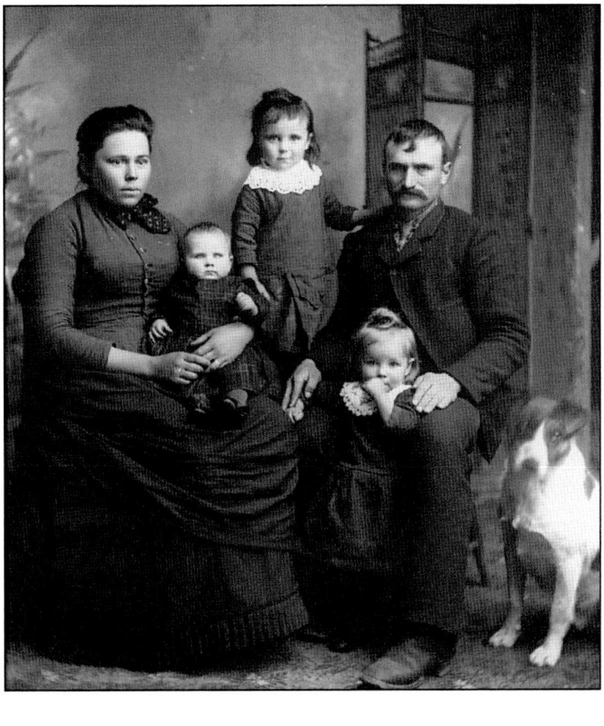

These are M. Lee Taylor's great-grandparents Alonzo Smith Fullmer and his wife Luella Estella Perry with their family and dog. Alonzo was a partner in the first brickyard in Mapleton, which was conveniently located on the corner of his property. (Courtesy of M. Lee Taylor.)

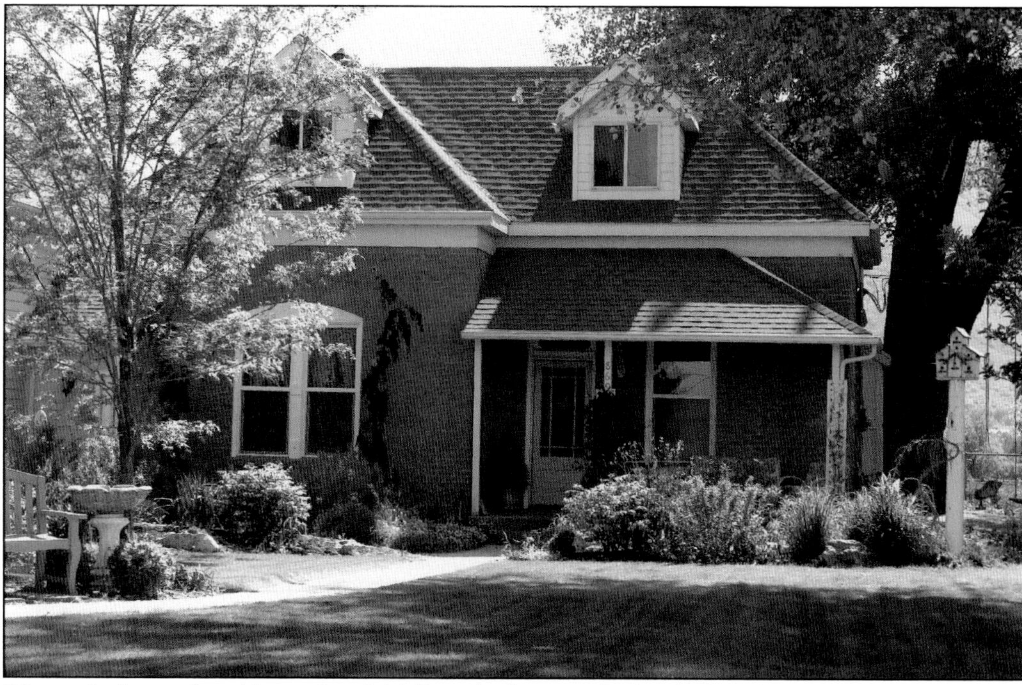

This is the home that Alonzo Smith Fullmer built using the bricks from his brickyard. The address is 869 South 800 West, Mapleton. (Courtesy of M. Lee Taylor.)

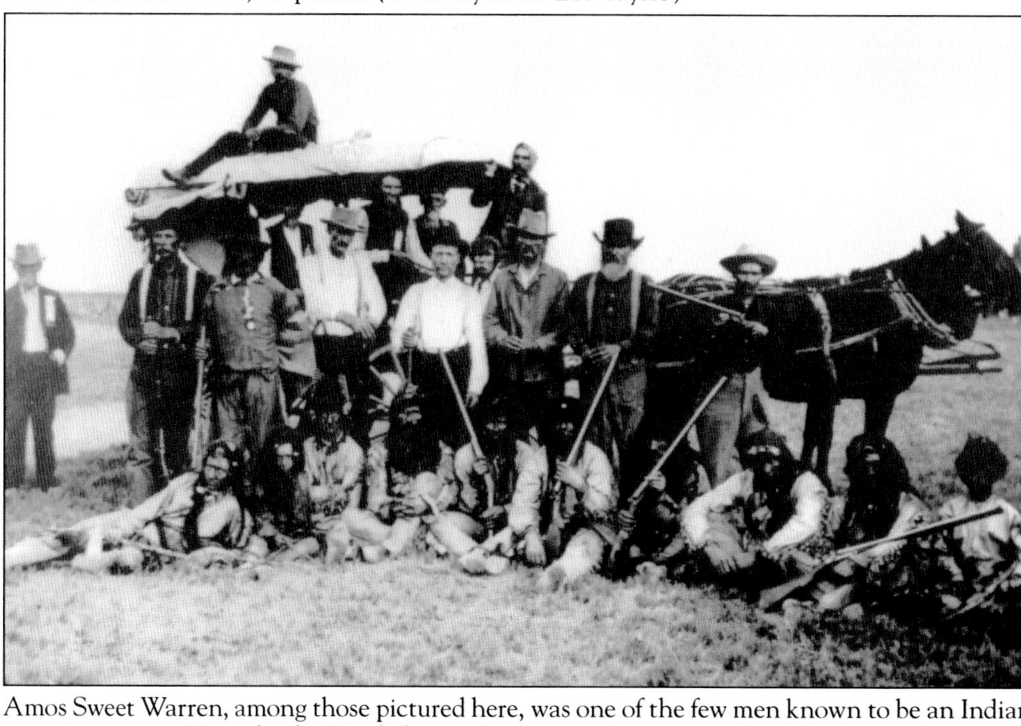

Amos Sweet Warren, among those pictured here, was one of the few men known to be an Indian scout interpreter. He spoke the Ute dialect and kept many hostilities at bay. The Native Americans often camped on his lot in Springville. This George Edward Anderson photograph was preserved by Rell G. Francis. (Courtesy of the Mapleton Historical Museum.)

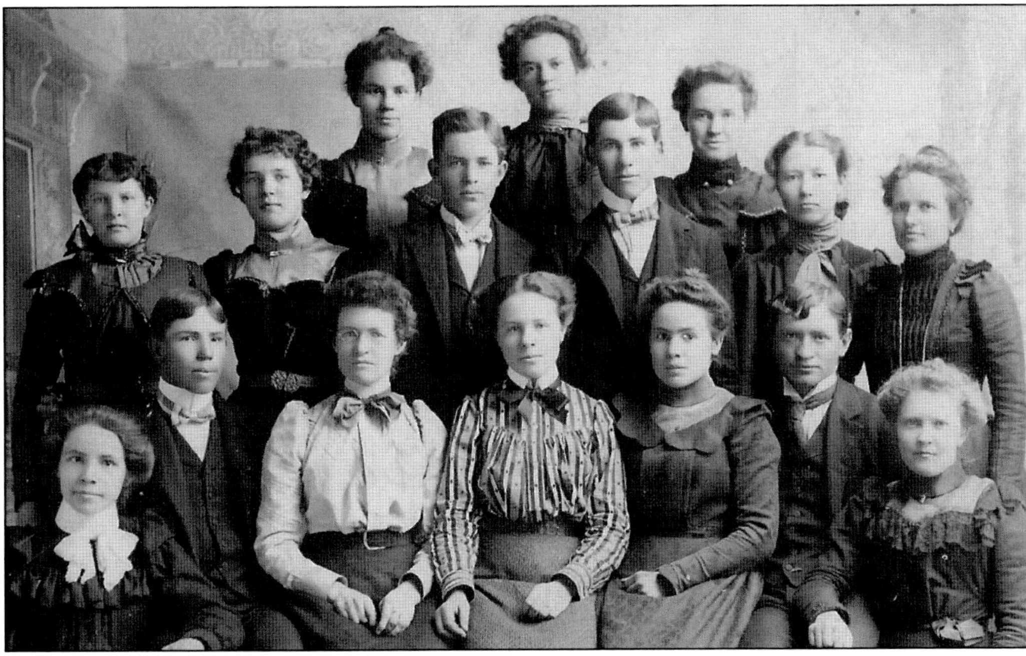

This is a George Edward Anderson photograph of the Whiting cousins. From left to right are (first row) Ethel Whiting, Bert Whiting, Dora Curtis, Bessie Bird, Madge Whiting, Burr Whiting, and Bell Whiting; (second row) Jessie Whitney, May Whiting, Eddie Whiting, Ray Whiting, Jennie Bird, and Pearl Whiting; (third row) Hattie Whiting, Erma Perry, and Hannah Bird. (Courtesy of the Springville-Mapleton Pioneer Museum.)

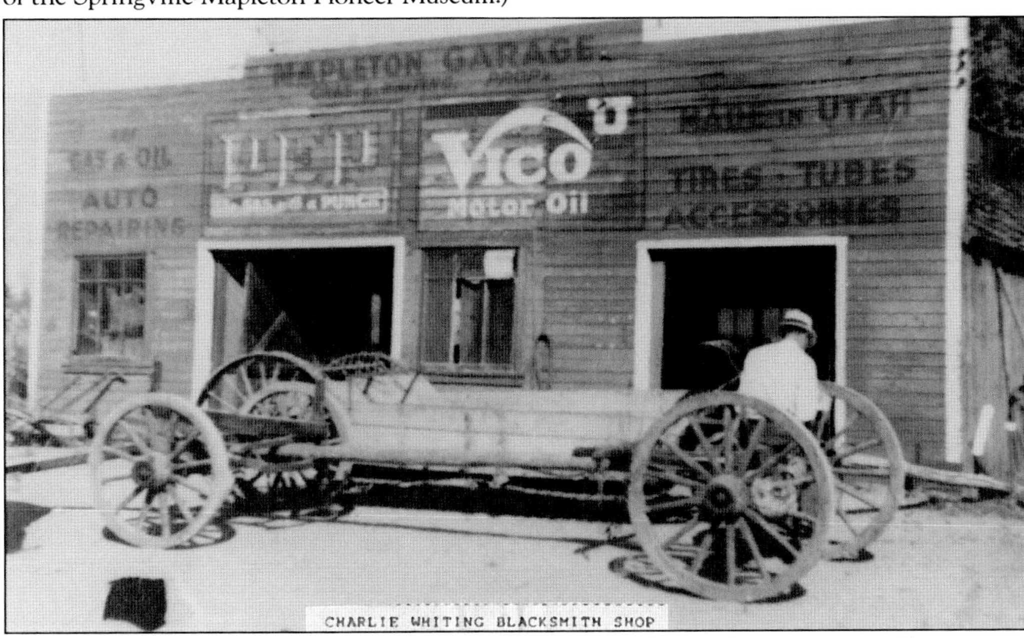

Charlie's Blacksmith Shop on the north side of Charles L. Whiting's home is pictured here around 1914. Charles operated this business from 1912 to 1936. The shop was a vital presence in the community offering repair work to farmers' equipment, and he also shod the horses. (Courtesy of the Mapleton Historical Museum.)

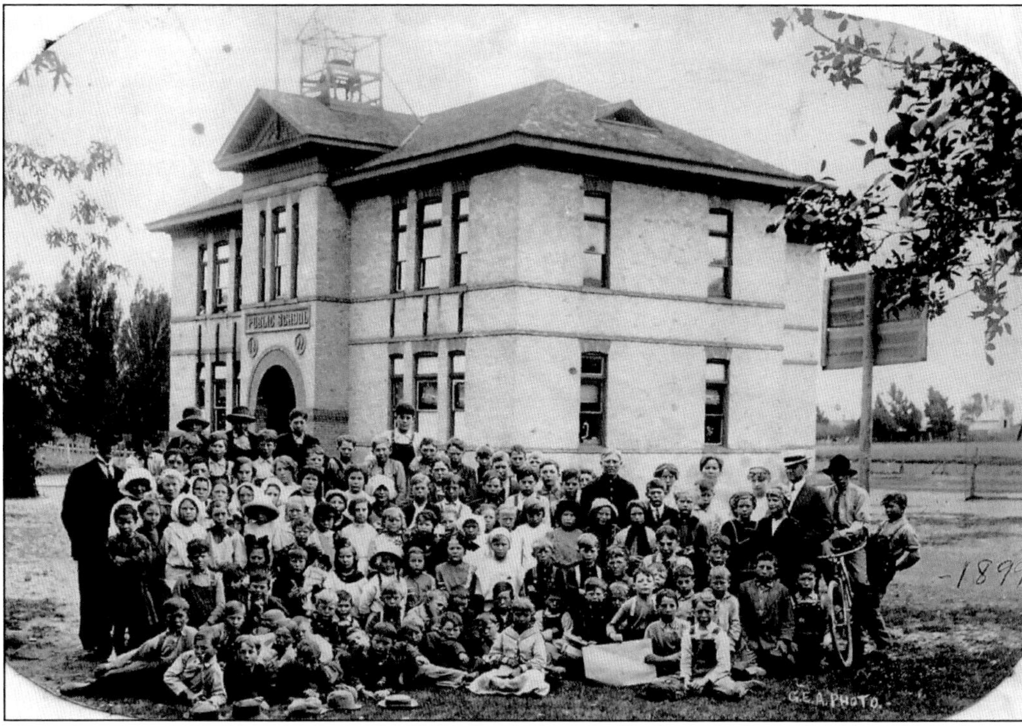

The First Central School in Mapleton is pictured here in 1899 at 120 West Maple Street. George Edward Anderson took this photograph. (Courtesy of the Mapleton Historical Museum.)

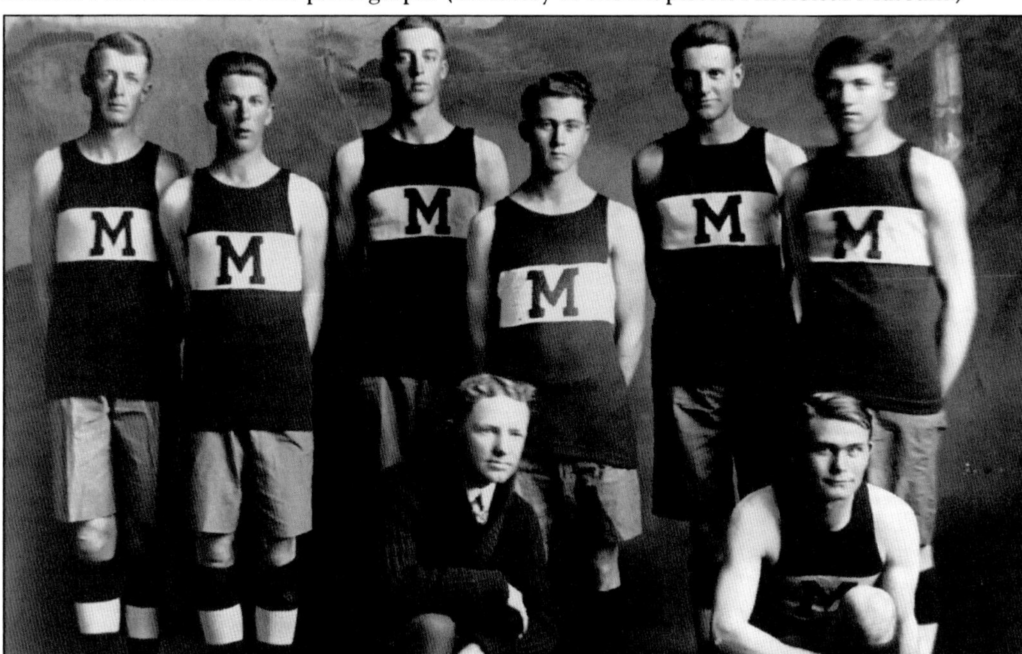

Members of this Mapleton men's basketball team pose for the camera in 1920. Basketball was a favorite pastime for many residents. All the residents would pack the gym to cheer on the players. (Courtesy of the Mapleton Historical Museum.)

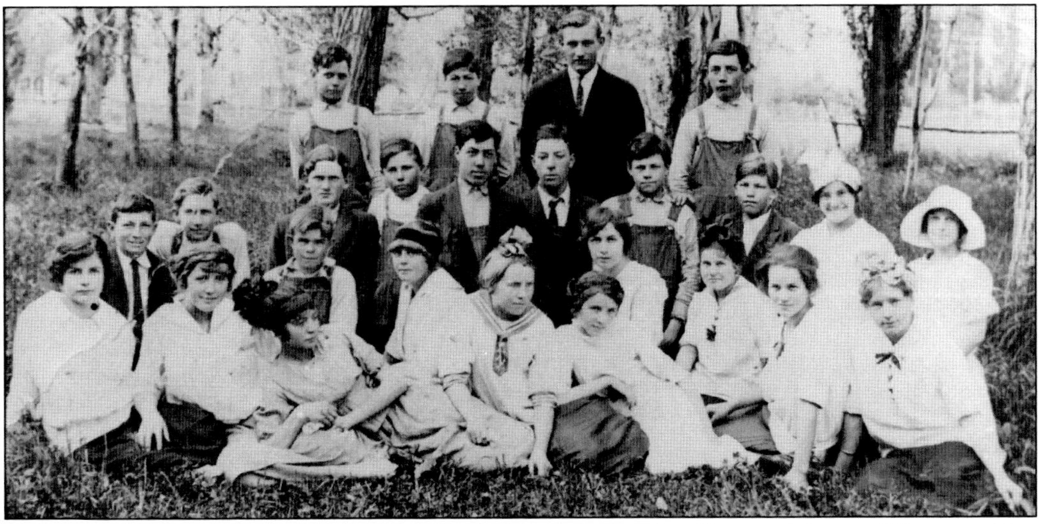

Mapleton eighth-grade graduates of 1915 are, from left to right, (first row) Bessie Whitney, Alga Harmer, Velma Hales, Stella Otteson, Lorna Whiting, Irene Roundy, Helen Carrick, Meribah Bird, Eva Llewellyn, and Thelma Lee; (second row) Willis Bird, George Murray, Bill Bromley, Jay Stone, Edward Perry, Carrel Waters, Hugh Law, Burton Tew, Tom Carrick, Norma Holley, and Lula Evans; (third row) Barney Mendenhall, Clarence Roundy, Wallace Brockbank (teacher), and Roland Hill. George Edward Anderson took this photograph, and Rell G. Francis preserved it. (Courtesy of the Mapleton Historical Museum.)

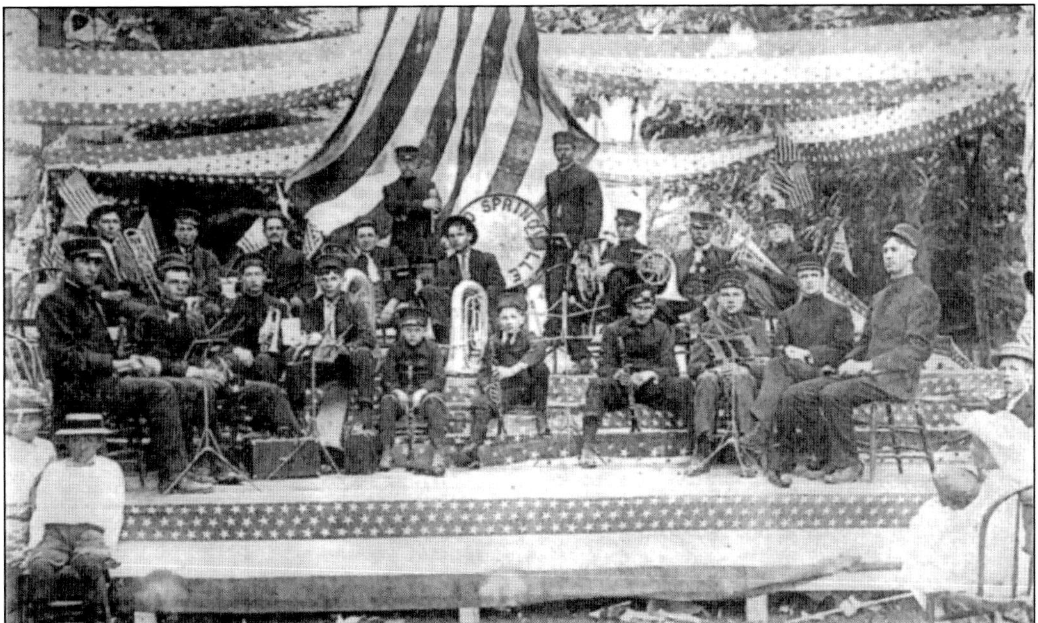

This early Fourth of July image shows the popular Springville Band, which played for many town celebrations. From left to right are (first row) Ralph B. Weight, Joe Allan, Vernon Thorn, Henry Child, Earl Thorn, Wendell Kindred, unidentified, Charles Mitchell, Sam Whittaker, and Claude Weight; (second row) Kenneth Roylance, Tom Kelly, Al Packard, two unidentified, Amasa Haymond, Charlie Allan, and unidentified; (third row) Mr. Inshaw and Will Allan. (Courtesy of the Mapleton Historical Museum.)

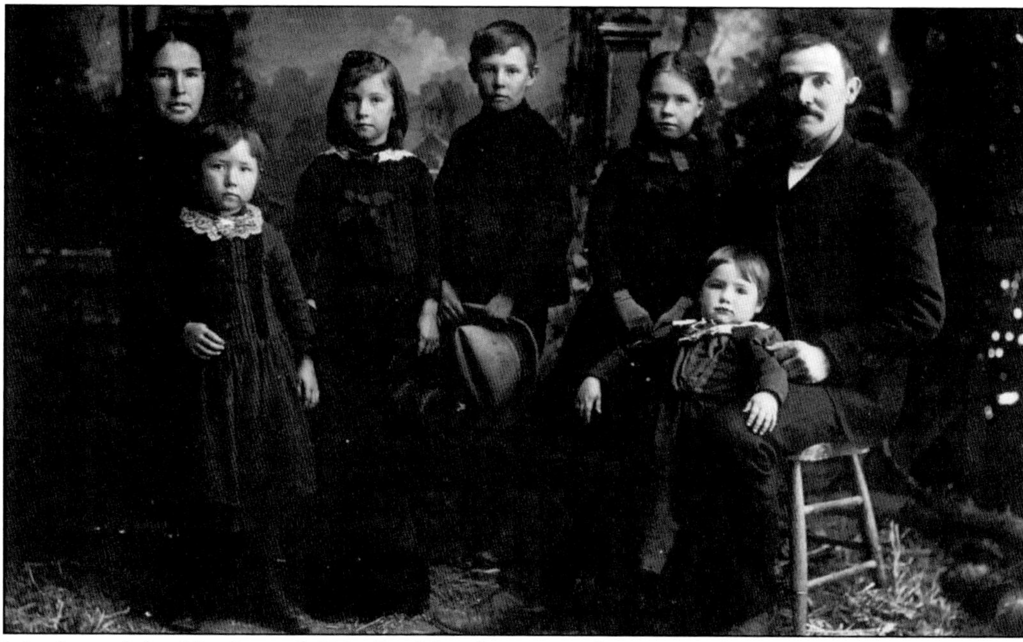

Members of the Charles and Abby Bird family are seen here. From left to right are Jennie, Abby, Hannah, Charlie, Bessie, Charles M., and Emogene. Charles's leg had to be amputated above his knee after an accident. After he recovered, he was fitted for a wooden leg that enabled him to perform his farm work. (Courtesy of Mary Hjorth Fojtek.)

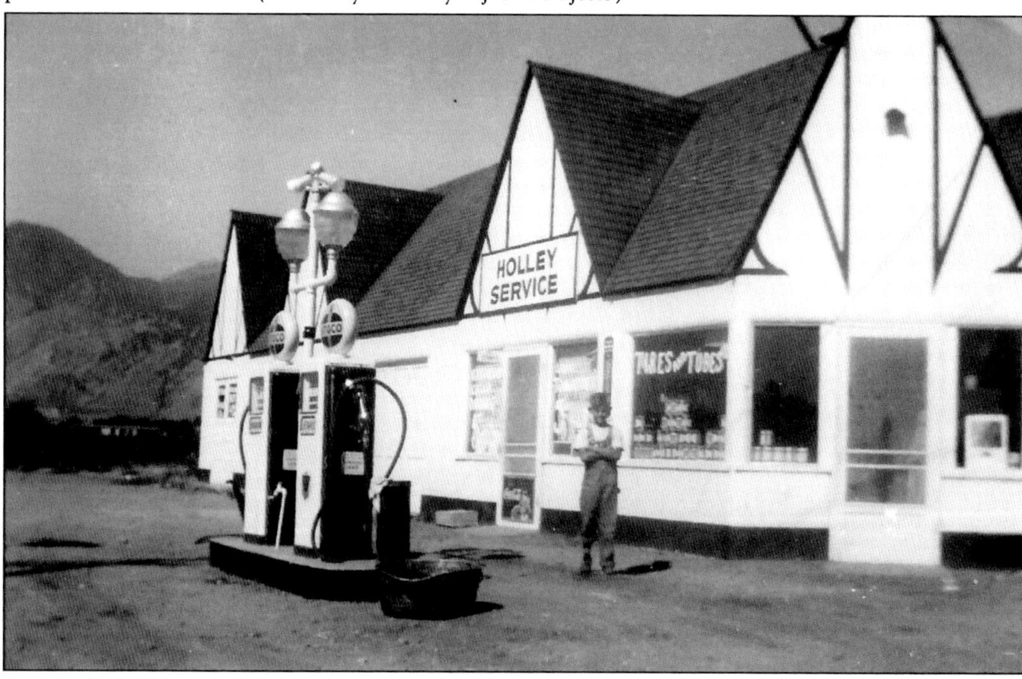

Pictured here is the Holley Service station with Mac Bills standing in front of the store. Holley's combined a small gas station with an all-purpose country store. The Holleys used the credit, trade, exchange, and barter system. Fair prices were easily negotiated in exchange for cash and/or goods. (Courtesy of Kay Bills.)

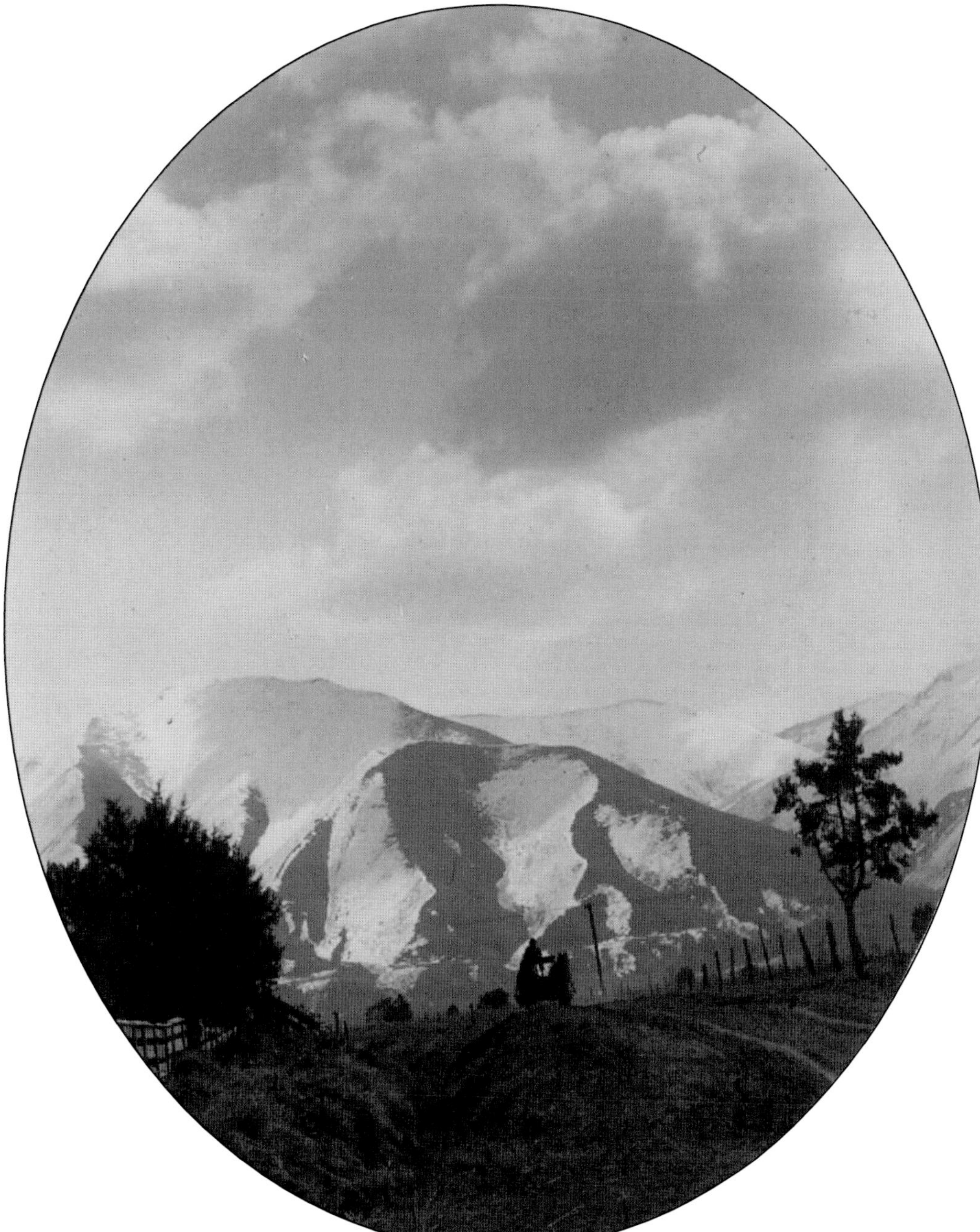

The old hay wagon is pictured here in 1908 traveling up the south side of the road by the Evergreen Cemetery, heading into Mapleton. (Courtesy of Mary Hjorth Fojtek.)

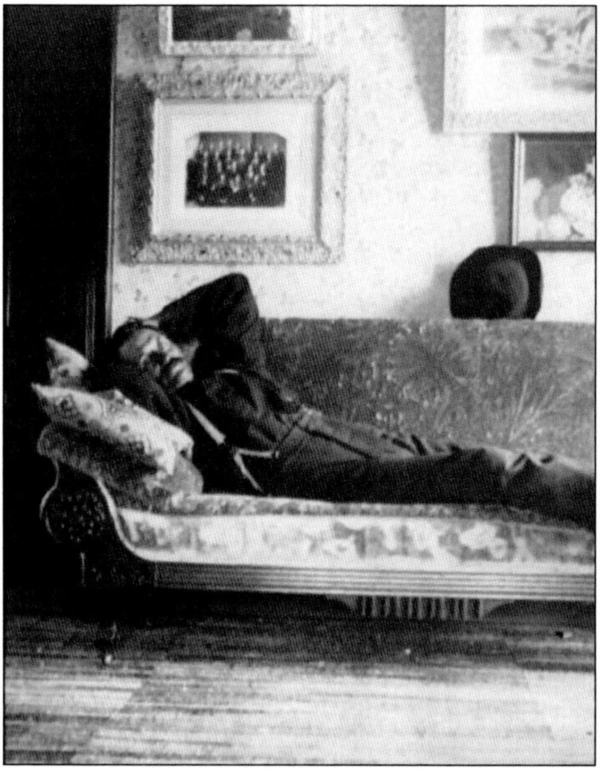

Richard Lovell Mendenhall Sr. rests around 1891 in the family parlor after a hard day's work. Mendenhall homesteaded a section of land in Northwest Mapleton, where he and his wife lived in a small lean-to-type home until 1891, when a two-story brick home was built. (Courtesy of Mary Hjorth Fojtek.)

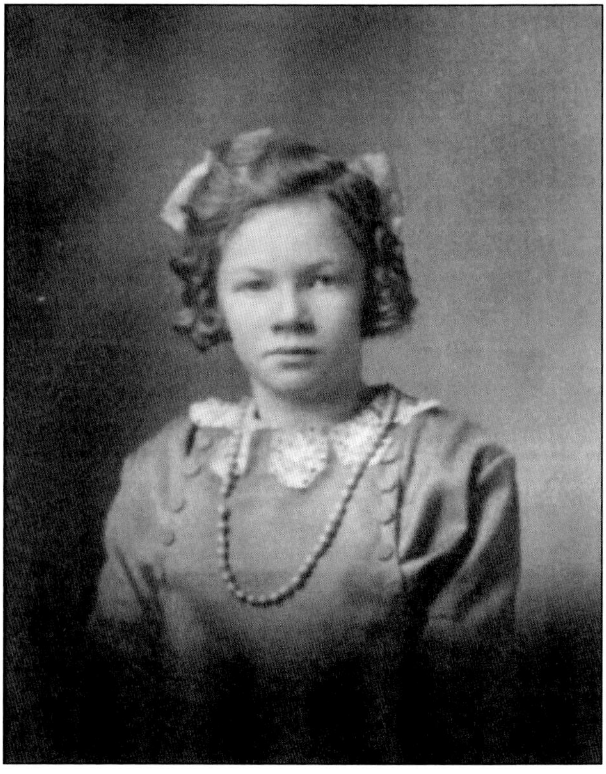

Louise Mendenhall Harmer was the daughter of Richard Lovell Mendenhall Jr. and Hannah Mendenhall. (Courtesy of Mary Hjorth Fojtek.)

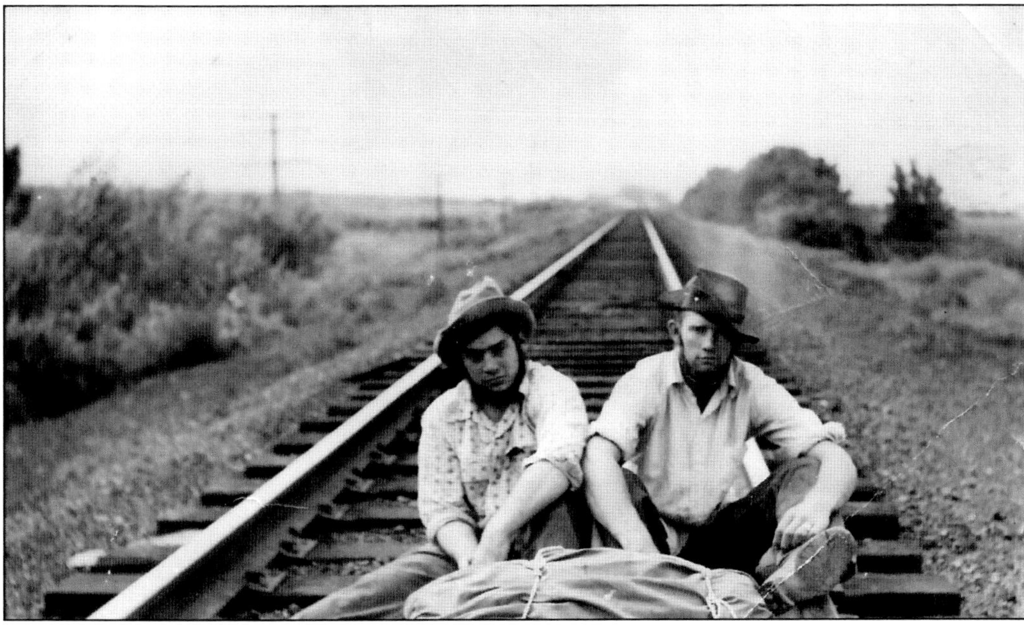

Leon Nebeker (left) and Kay Bills pose for a photograph in August 1949 on the railroad tracks. (Courtesy of Kay Bills.)

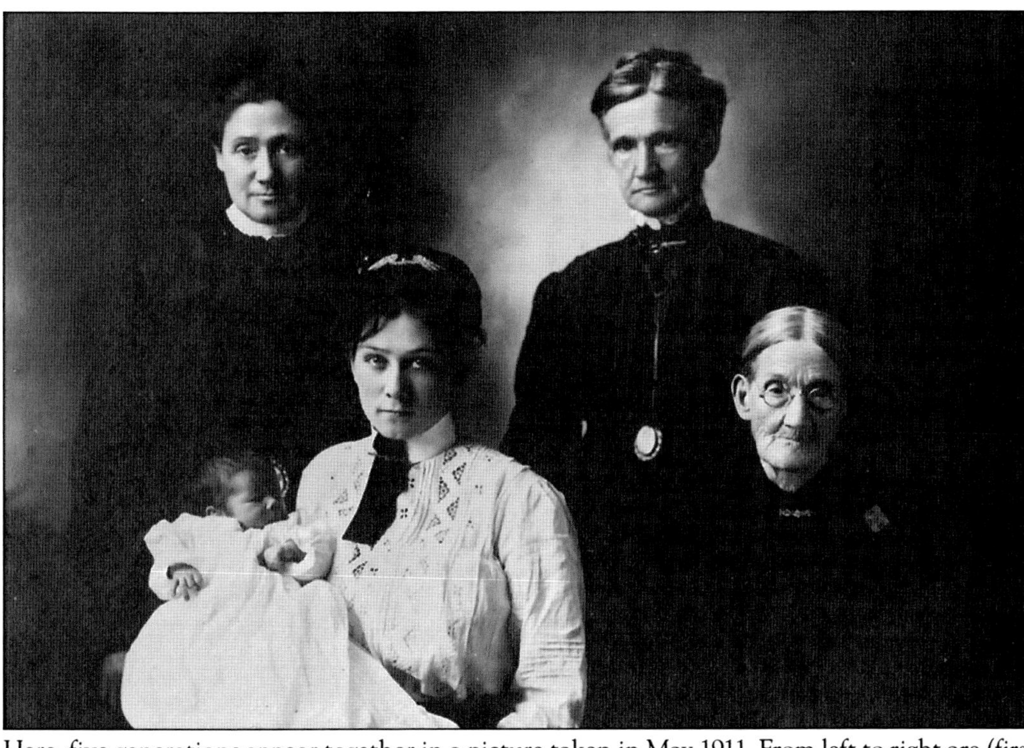

Here, five generations appear together in a picture taken in May 1911. From left to right are (first row) Margaret Larsen (holding Clyde Larsen) and S. Clyde; (second row) Lydia Hunt and M. Sanford. (Courtesy of the Mapleton Historical Museum.)

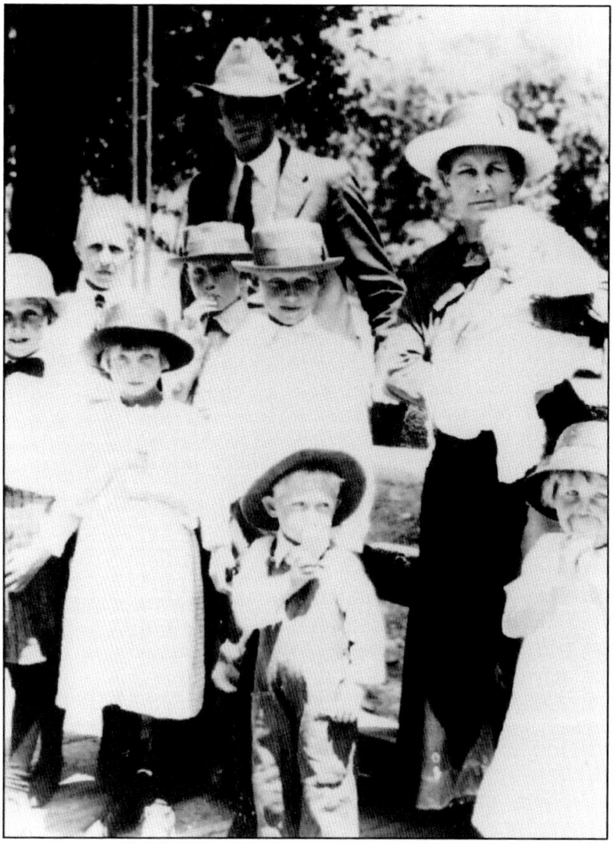

Members of the Anthon Nielson family pause for a photograph. Anthon purchased the Oak Springs Ranch and operated it for a number of years. He also served as the town board president for two terms and in many other capacities around town. (Courtesy of the Mapleton Historical Museum.)

Reed Hales is pictured driving this horse and buggy. (Courtesy of the Mapleton Historical Museum.)

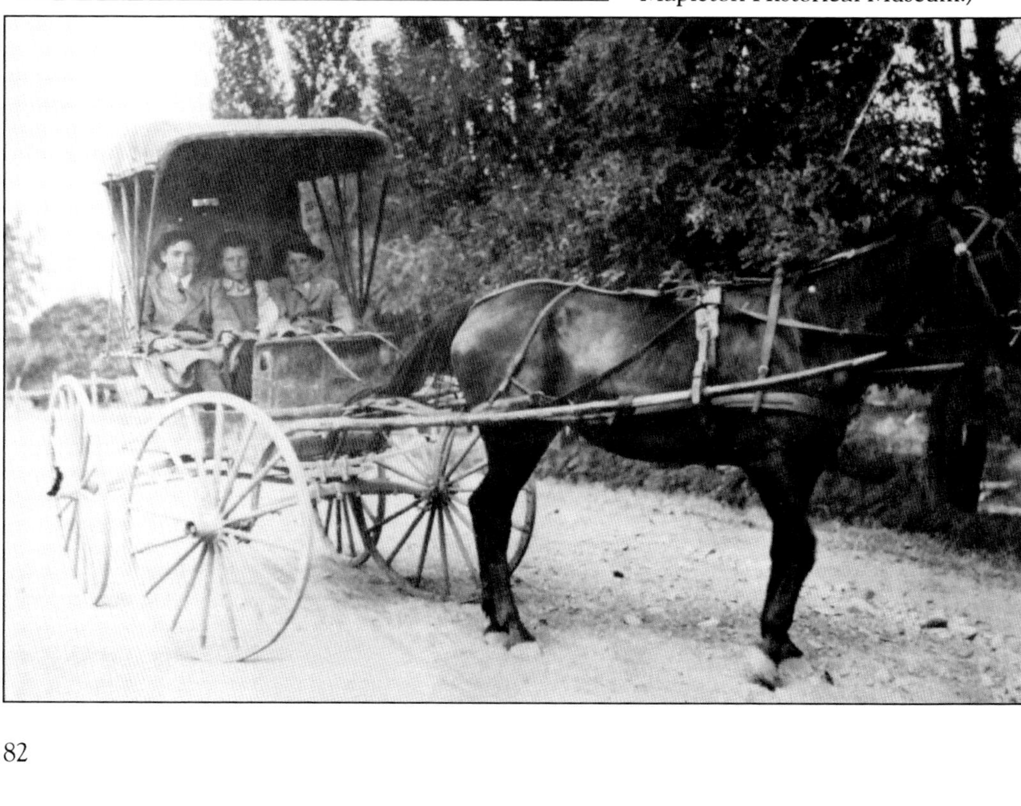

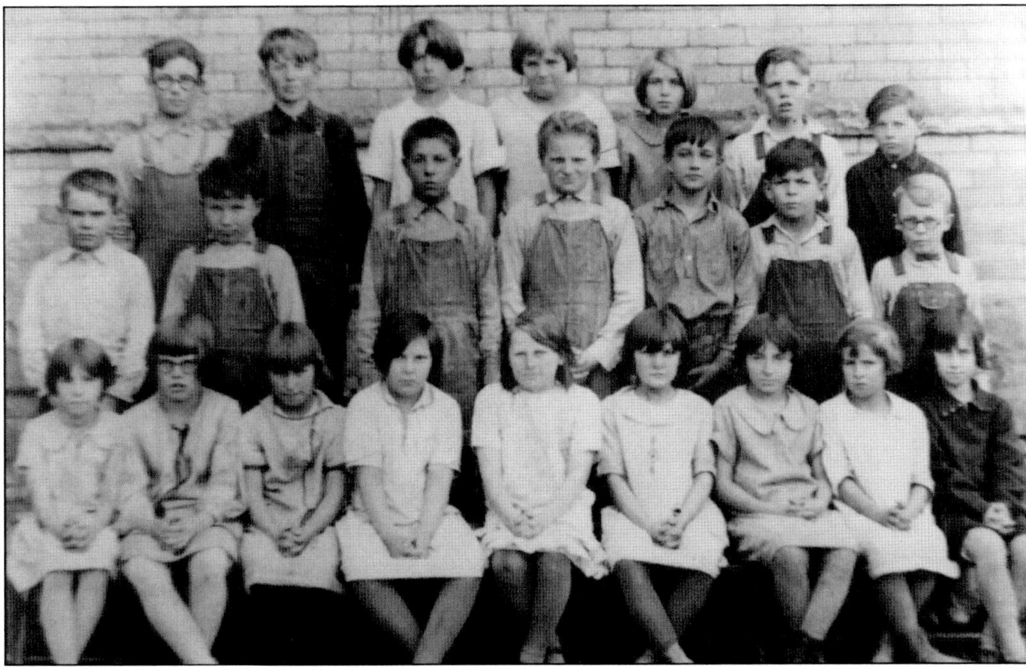

Mapleton School fifth-and-sixth-grade students are pictured in 1928. Students identified are Ray Law, Harold Diamond, Ruth Wiscombe, Lucille Harmer, Ione Nielson, Rex Whiting, Ralph Johnson, Larie Perry, Ella Snow, Faye Whiting, Verla Whiting, Evelyn Ellet, Ted Lee, Cluff Hopla, Carl Curtis, ? Gividen, Lawrence Jordan, Lawrence Whitney, Russell Holley, Erma Holley Thora Whiting, Irene Jensen, and Grace Holley. (Courtesy of the Mapleton Historical Museum.)

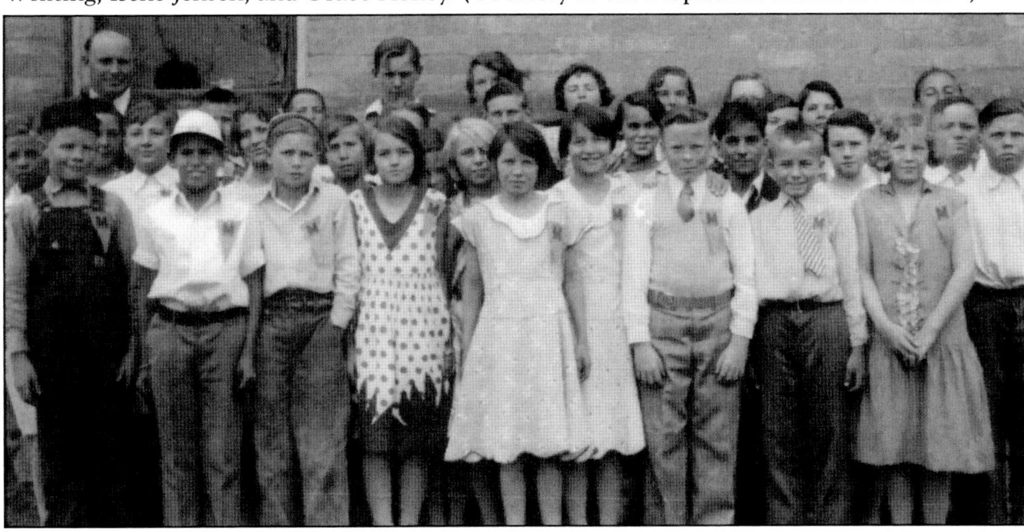

Mapleton School fourth-and-fifth-grade students are pictured in 1932. Teacher Rulon Nelson's students included Ted Dibble, Edna Wiscombe, Cleo Whiting, Beulah Whiting, Irene Bird, Wilma Binks, Hannah Bee Mendenhall, Merrill Allan, Melba Mendenhall, Gertrude Ann Welch, Blaine Harmer, Velma Curtis, Floy Whiting, Joyce Lee Kelsey Johnson, Jane Lee, Johnny Bleggi, Catherine Ann Mendenhall, Thirl Tew, Juan Whiting, Evan Allan, Bernice Binks, Genevieve Bird, Virginia Bird, Mack Holley, Cecil Johnson, Rhea Gividen, and Bevan Lindsey. (Courtesy of the Mapleton Historical Museum.)

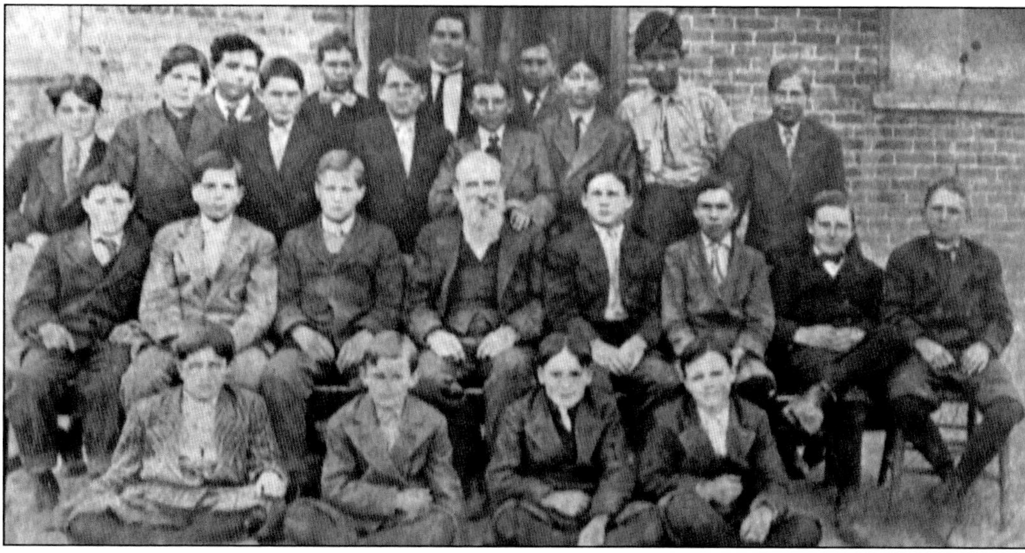

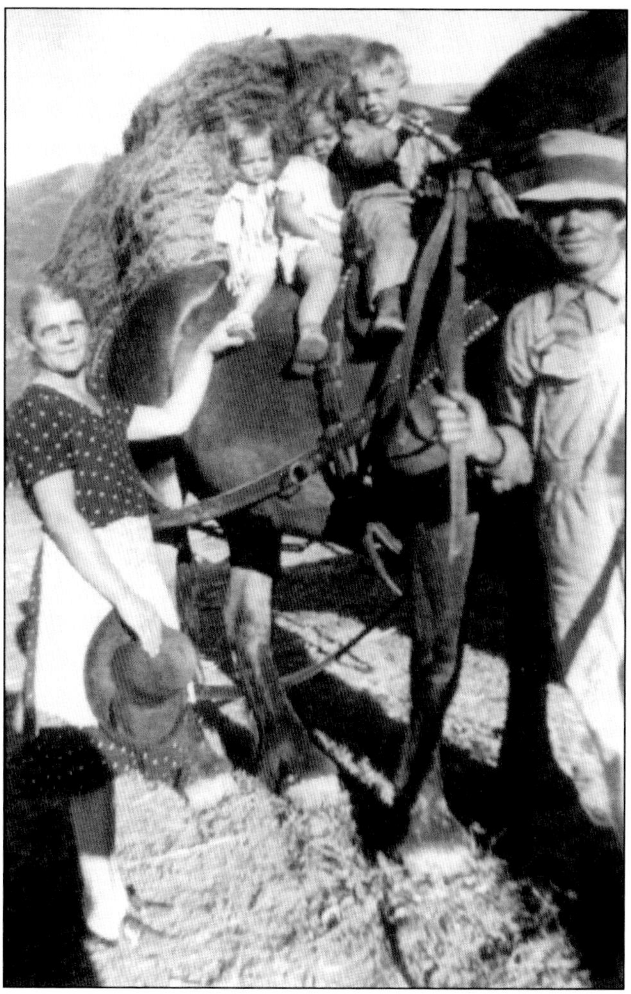

The class of 1909 LDS deacons from Mapleton are, from left to right, (first row) Bryan Tew, James Perry, Lee Warren, and Reese Anderson; (second row) William Holley, Kenneth Fullmer, Ernest Whiting, John Tuckett (teacher), Dave Manwaring, Merrill Bird, Arrus Warren, and Willis Harmer; (third row) Norris Binks, Ernest Snow, Doyal Hill, Paul Holley, William Lee, Glen Holley, Horace Fullmer, William Nielson, Lavell Bird, Joseph Binks, Raymond Dibble, and Roy Jensen. Deacons are between the ages of 12 and 14 and serve in a variety of ways; one weekly duty is to pass the sacrament to the congregation each Sunday. (Courtesy of the Mapleton Historical Museum.)

Charles and Hilda Everett are seen with their children (from left to right) Neal, Blake, and Jesse. Hilda was a true farmer at heart; she took care of the chickens, turkeys, and geese. She also milked the cows when it was necessary. For many years, she supplied the Hungerford Academy in Springville with butter. (Courtesy of the Mapleton Historical Museum.)

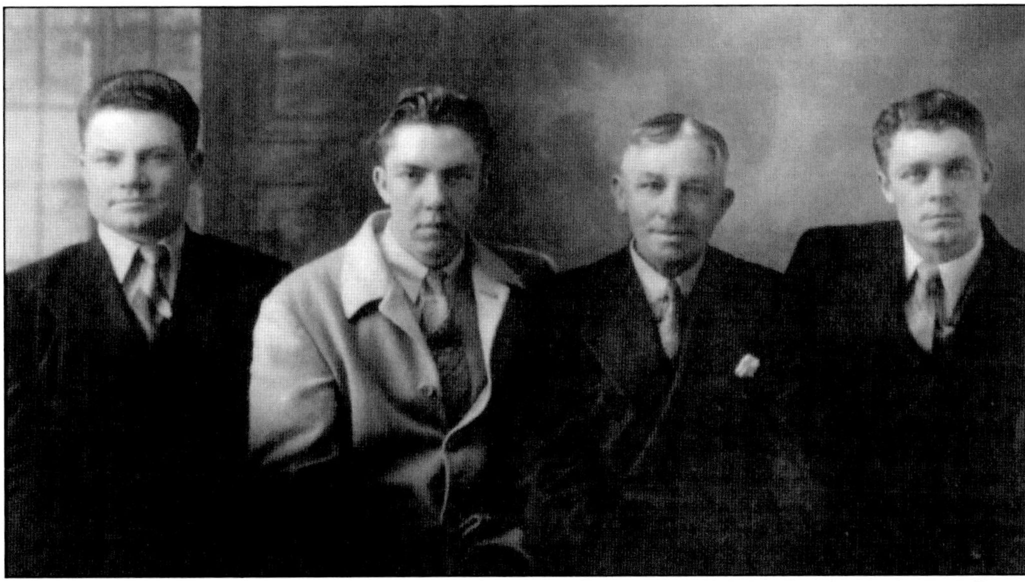

Charles Everett is pictured second from right with his sons, from left to right, Jesse, Neal, and Blake. Charles sold hay to the Provo Fire Department for their horses before motorized vehicles were used. (Courtesy of the Mapleton Historical Museum.)

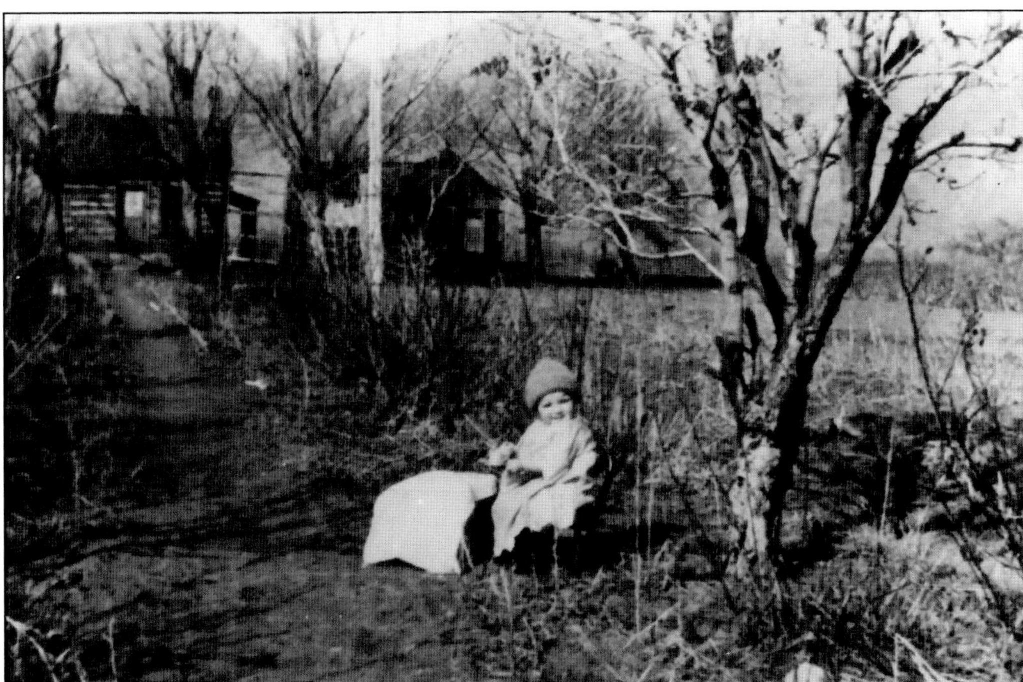

Pictured is Lela Mary Kendall on the original site of the historic log cabin, built around 1885 in Mapleton. During the early years of settlement, much of the recreation and entertainment for bench families focused on the church or the home. Family parties and church outings broke the monotony of daily farm labor. (Courtesy of the Mapleton Historical Museum.)

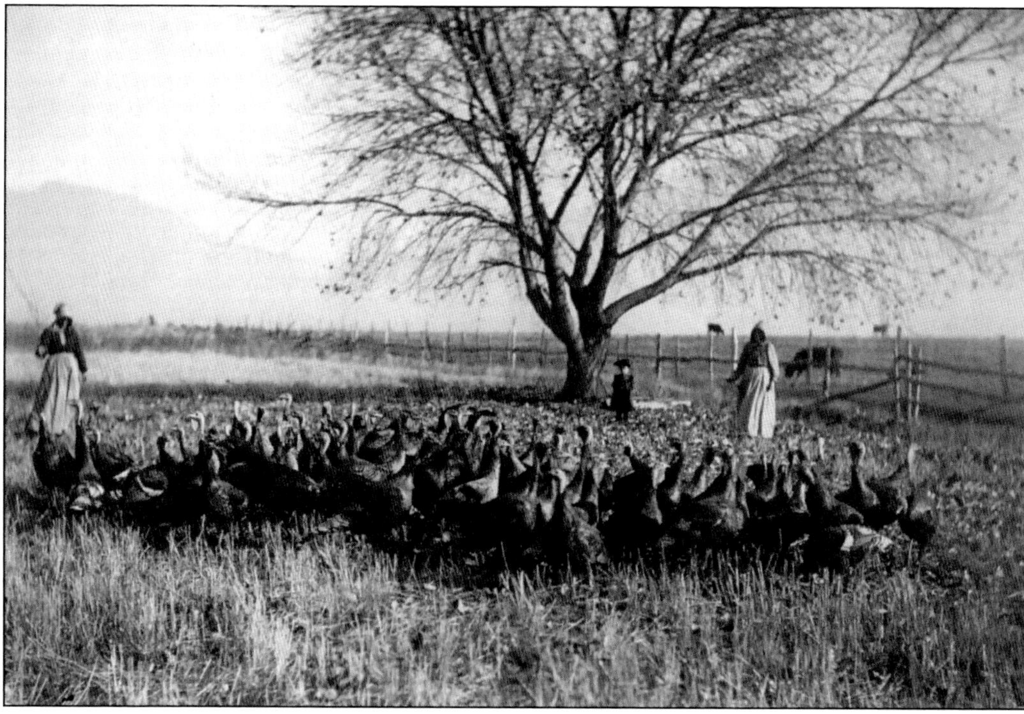

Barbara Coffman (left) along with her mother (right) and a child stand with their flock of turkeys. (Courtesy of the Mapleton Historical Museum.)

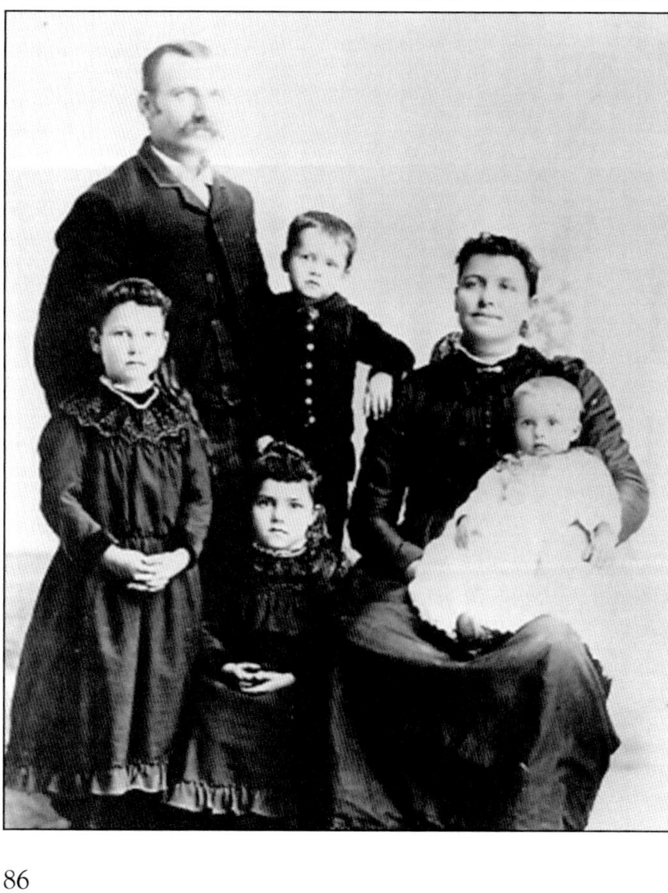

From left to right are (first row) Alice Rebecca Larsen, Florence Victoria Larsen, and Mary Caroline Andersen Larsen holding Clara Elizabeth Larsen; (second row) James Peter Larsen and Wilford Larsen. Tragedy struck the family when the two older children, Hannah and James, died of spinal meningitis. Mary grieved for over a year over the loss. She ceased after receiving a sign that she should grieve no more. They were the parents of 16 children. (Courtesy of the Mapleton Historical Museum.)

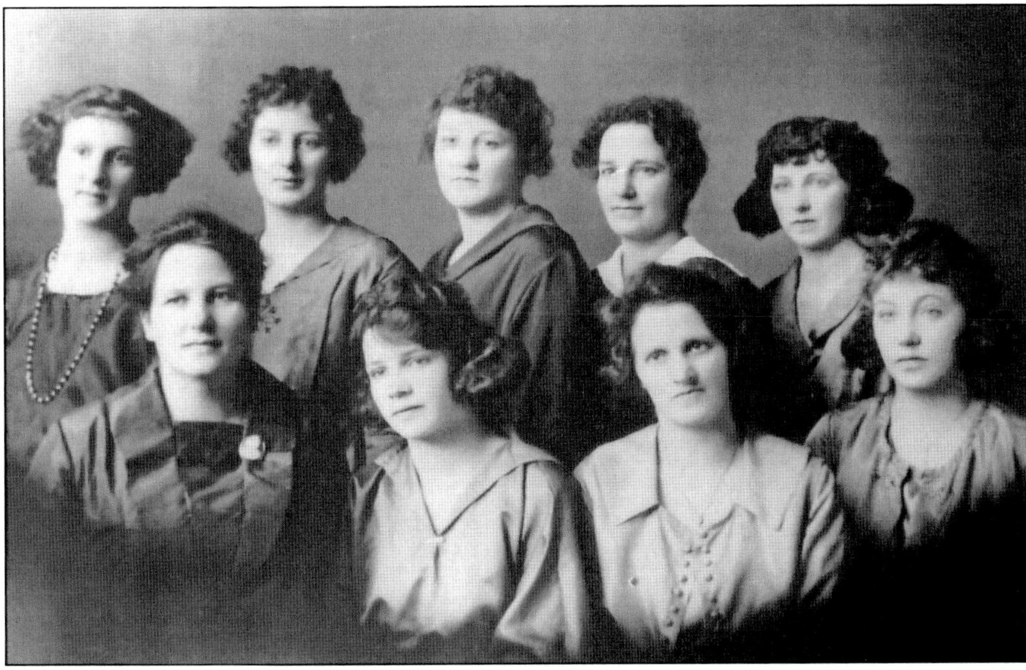

Daughters of James Peter Larsen and Mary Caroline Anderson Larsen are, from left to right, (first row) Alice Rebecca, Ivy, Clara Elizabeth, and Alberta; (second row) Thelma, Alta Christine, Mary Ellen, Florence Victoria, and Ina Jamia. James and Mary taught their children to work as well as play. Their home was one of faith and prayer. (Courtesy of the Mapleton Historical Museum.)

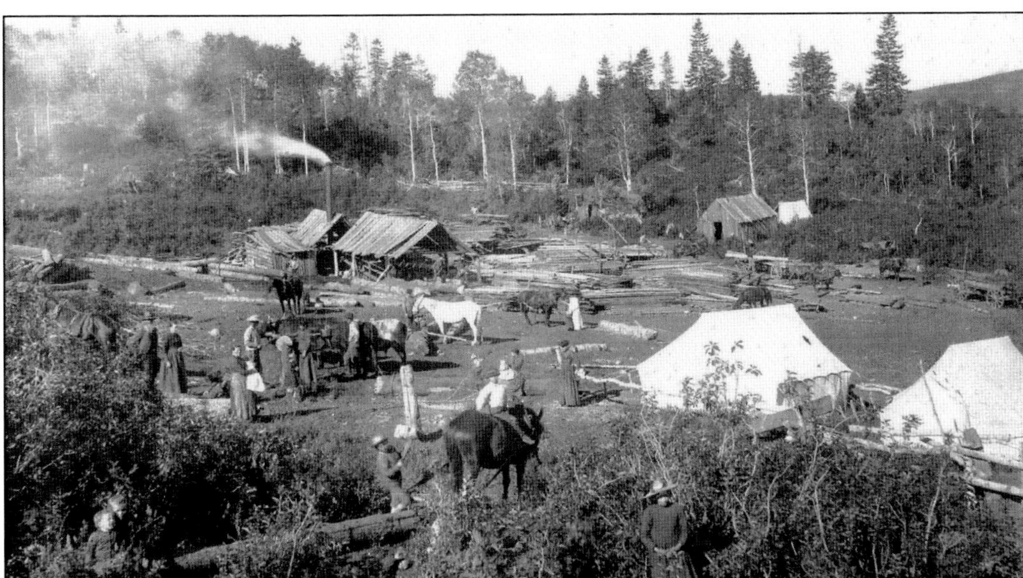

This is a picture of the Whiting Sawmill. It was located above the family ranch, which was homesteaded in 1871. The mill was up the right-hand fork in Hobble Creek Canyon. Near the summit of Hog's Back in the distance are the Bartholomew Mountains. (Courtesy of the Springville-Mapleton Pioneer Museum.)

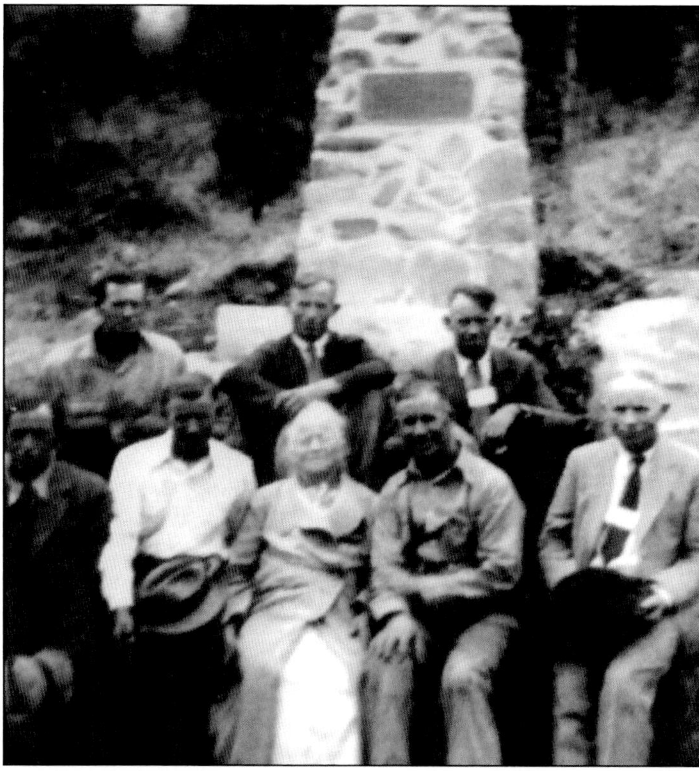

The Whiting monument was erected on the left fork of Hobble Creek Canyon in 1935. Pictured from left to right are (first row) Charles, Bert, Harriet Susannah (mother), Ray, and John Martin; (second row) Victor, Oscar, and Howard. (Courtesy of the Mapleton Historical Museum.)

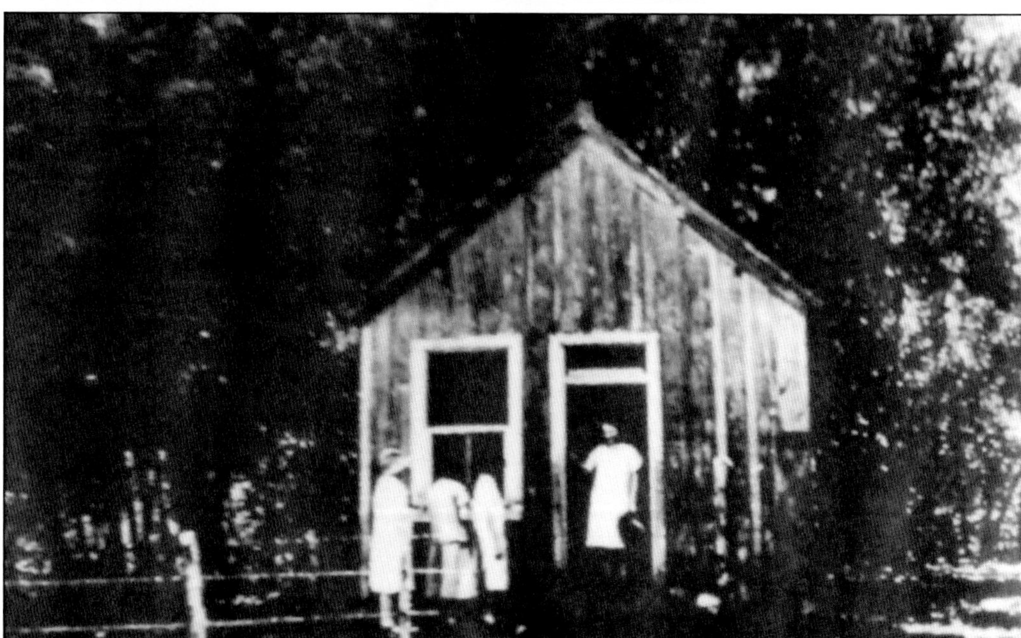

Hobble Creek Schoolhouse, also known as the Oakland School, was in operation from 1892 to 1907; it also functioned as a church. This is where Mary Elizabeth Cox Whiting taught school. Students' tuition was often paid with chickens, butter, eggs, molasses, and dried fruit. (Courtesy of the Springville-Mapleton Pioneer Museum.)

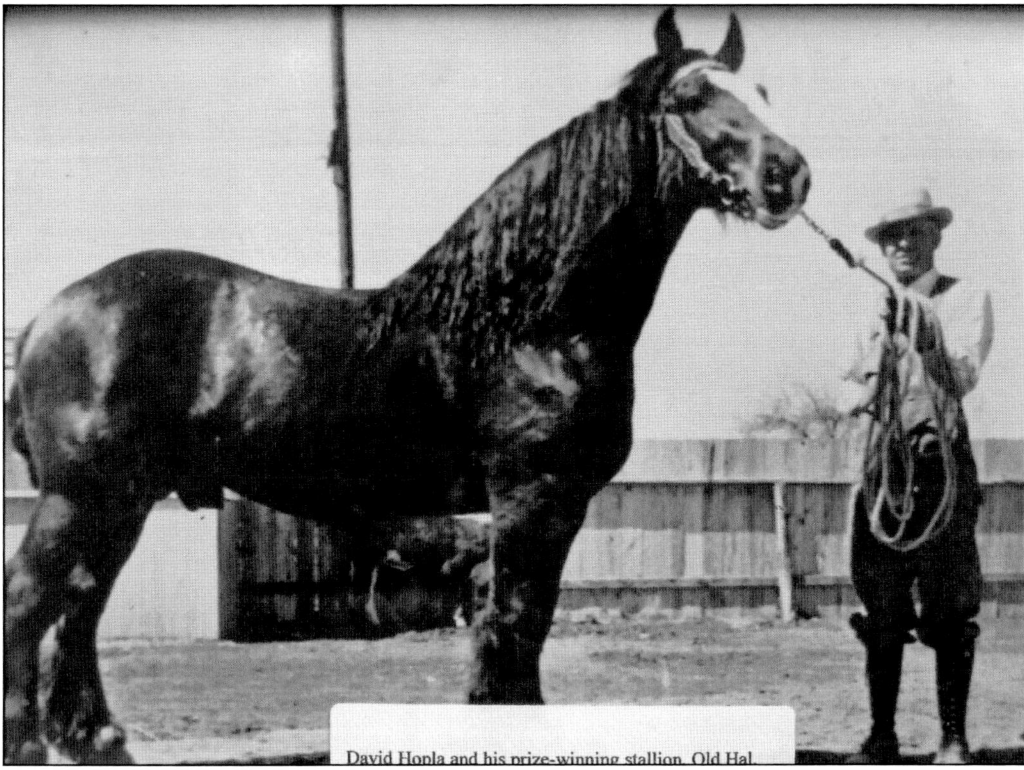

David S. Hopla poses with his prize-winning Shire stallion, "Old Hal." (Courtesy of the Mapleton Historical Museum.)

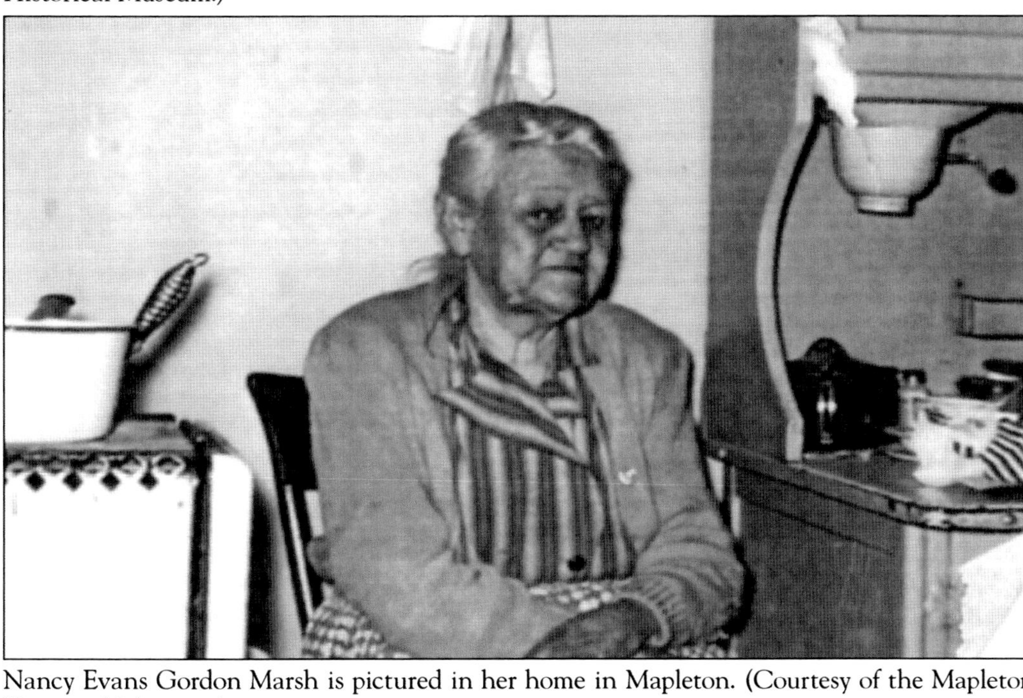

Nancy Evans Gordon Marsh is pictured in her home in Mapleton. (Courtesy of the Mapleton Historical Museum.)

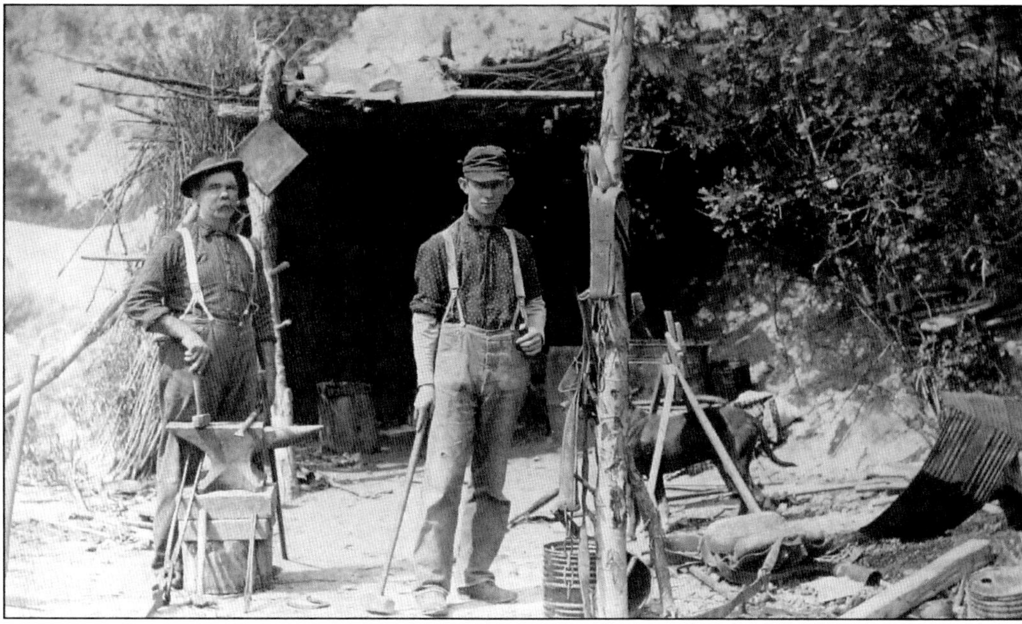

Jack Dyer's blacksmith shop in the Nef Crandall railroad construction camp is pictured around 1896. The two men are Jack Dyer (left) and Joe Crandall. (Courtesy of the Mapleton Historical Museum.)

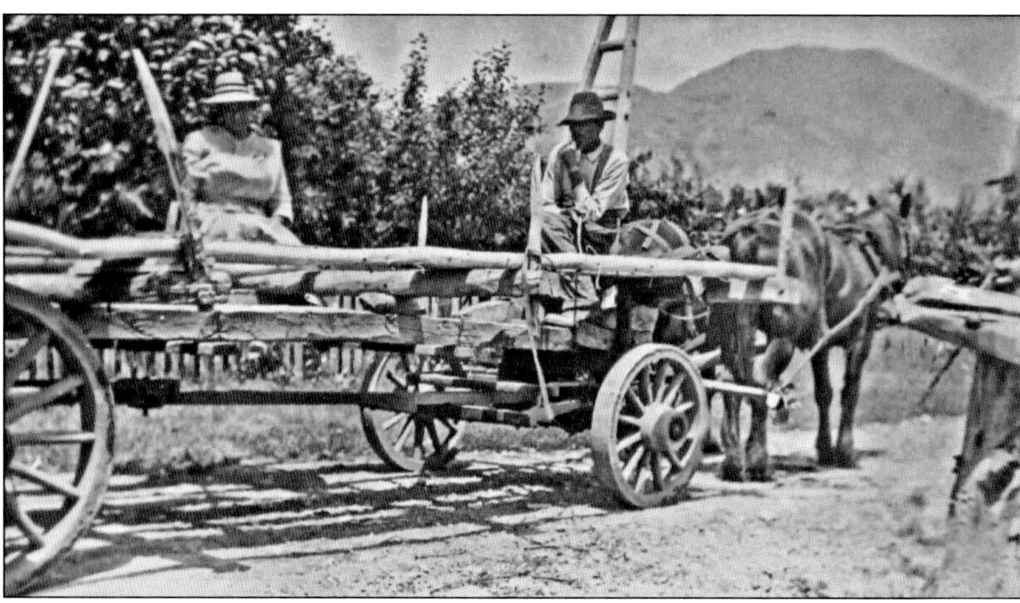

Joseph Knight and his wife are on a hay wagon and are ready to go into town. (Courtesy of the Mapleton Historical Museum.)

Inez Roundy Harmer and her brother Adelbert Roundy pose for a portrait around 1899. Their parents enjoyed taking drives with the buggy and horses. During the winter, the 16 strings of bells would chime merrily in the wind. (Courtesy of the Mapleton Historical Museum.)

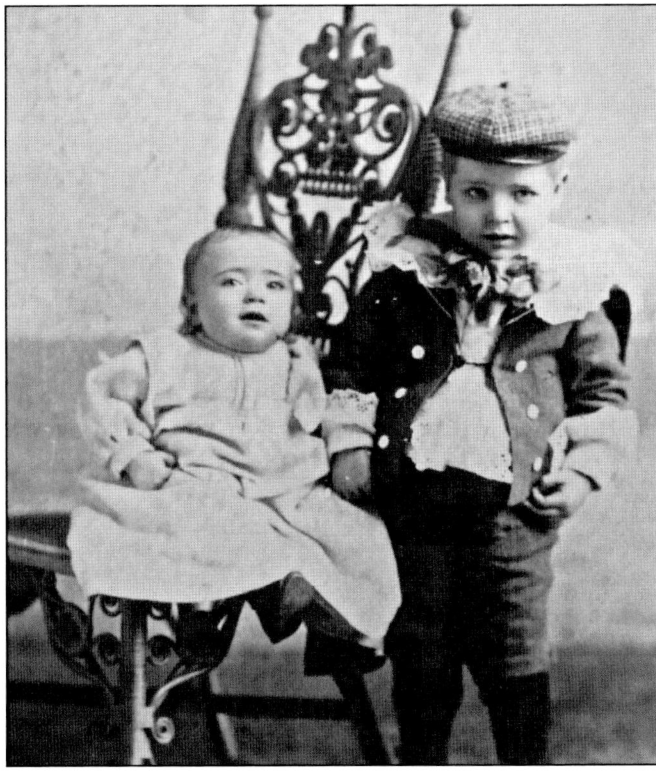

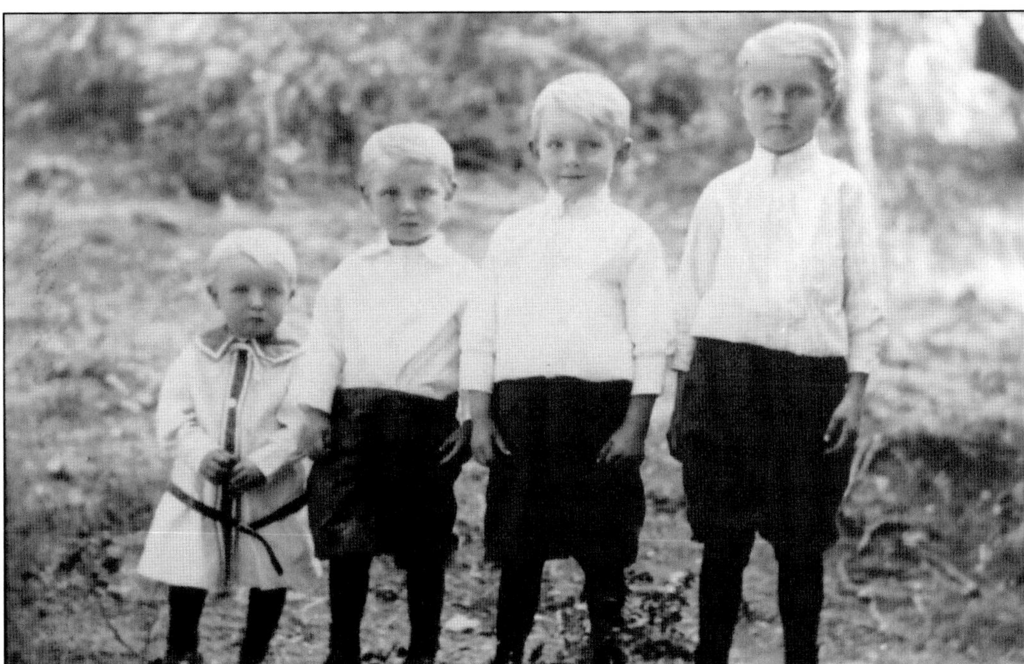

Loren A. and Hattie Nielson's four sons, from left to right, Guy, Ivan, Don, and Glen, are pictured here. Loren served two terms as a member of the town board and then another two terms as president. (Courtesy of the Mapleton Historical Museum.)

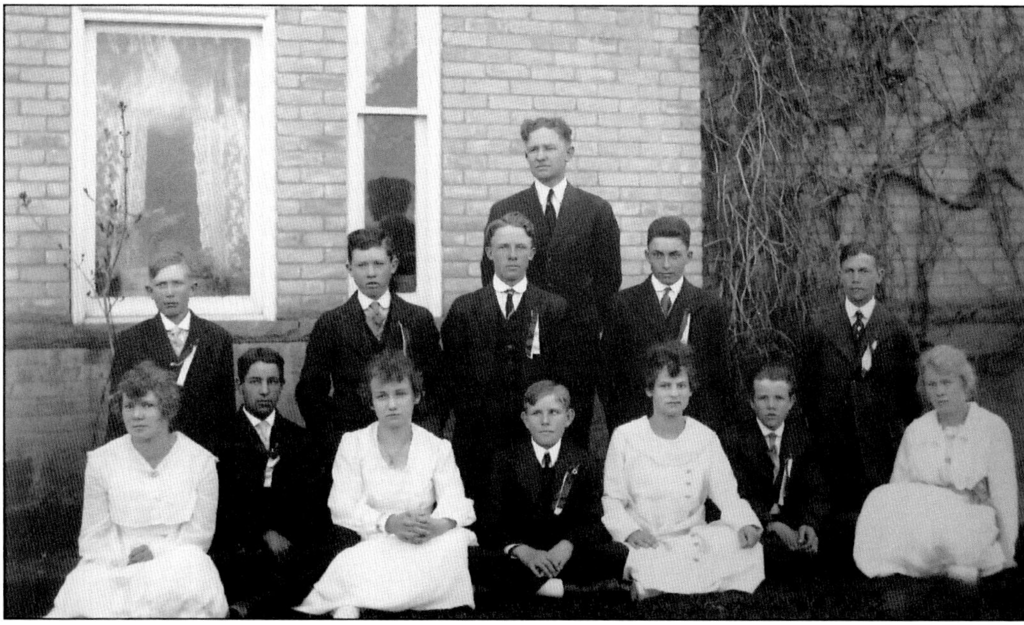

The 1914 Mapleton eighth-grade graduation class is seen here. From left to right are (first row) Elva Harmer, George Synderm, Jessie Wing, Arthur Gallup, Lora Hurst, Leo Llewellyn, and Clara Jensen; (second row) William Snow, Ernest Banks, Arus Bird, Reed Hales, and Kenneth Allan. The school's principal, Jay Dewey, stands proudly in the back. (Courtesy of the Mapleton Historical Museum.)

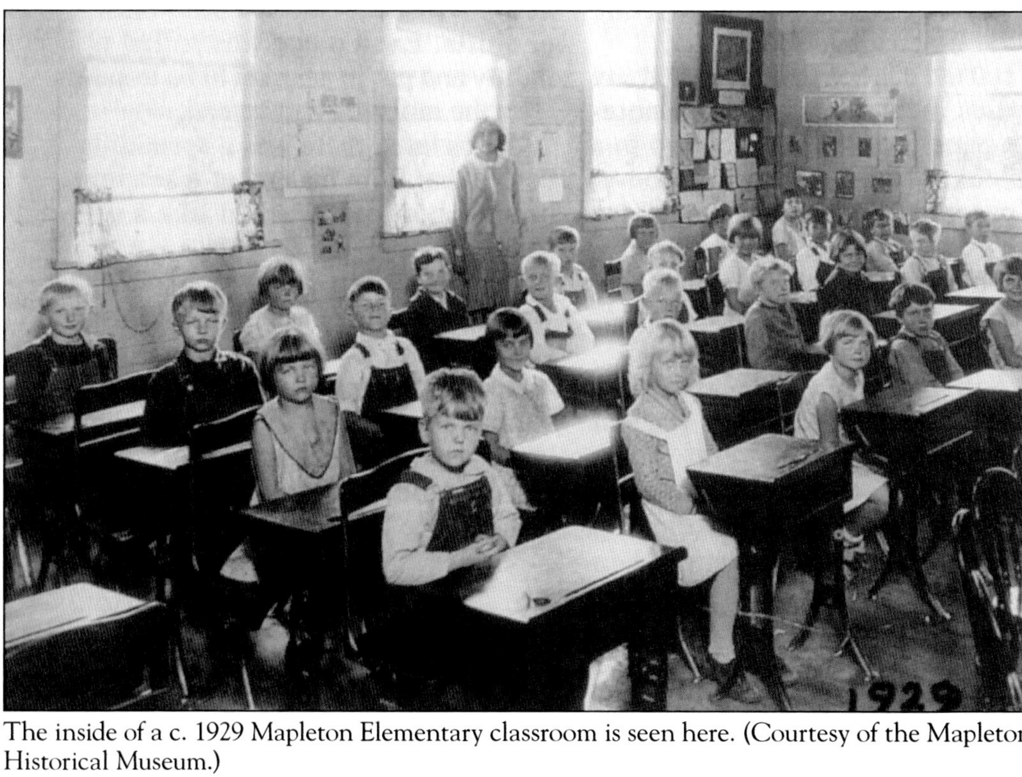

The inside of a c. 1929 Mapleton Elementary classroom is seen here. (Courtesy of the Mapleton Historical Museum.)

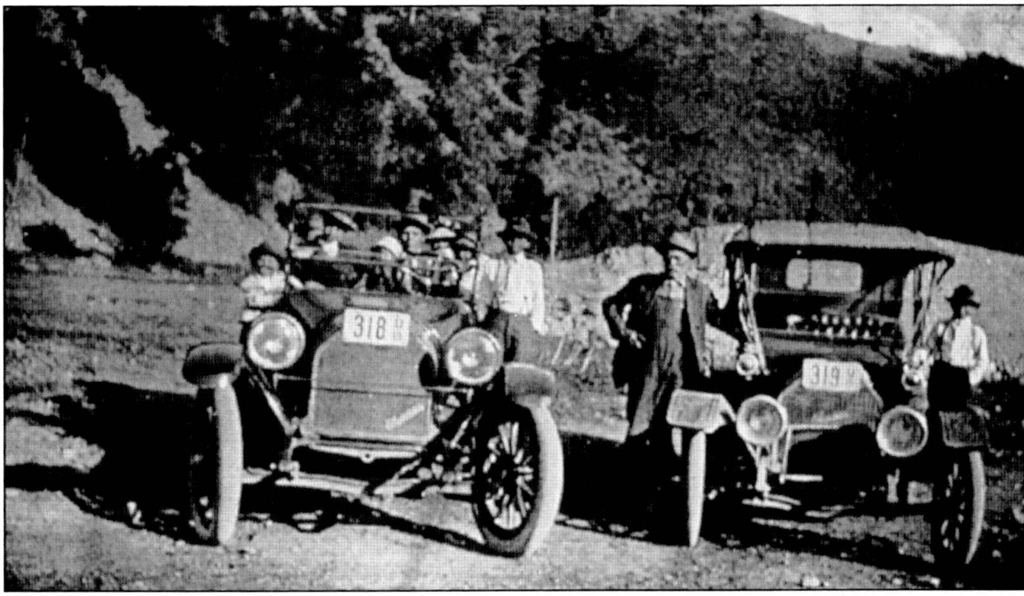

Here, some of the first automobiles in Mapleton are being showcased. Charles Edward Allan is seen on the right in car No. 319. Charles also had the first steam engine–powered threshing machine. (Courtesy of Dean Allan.)

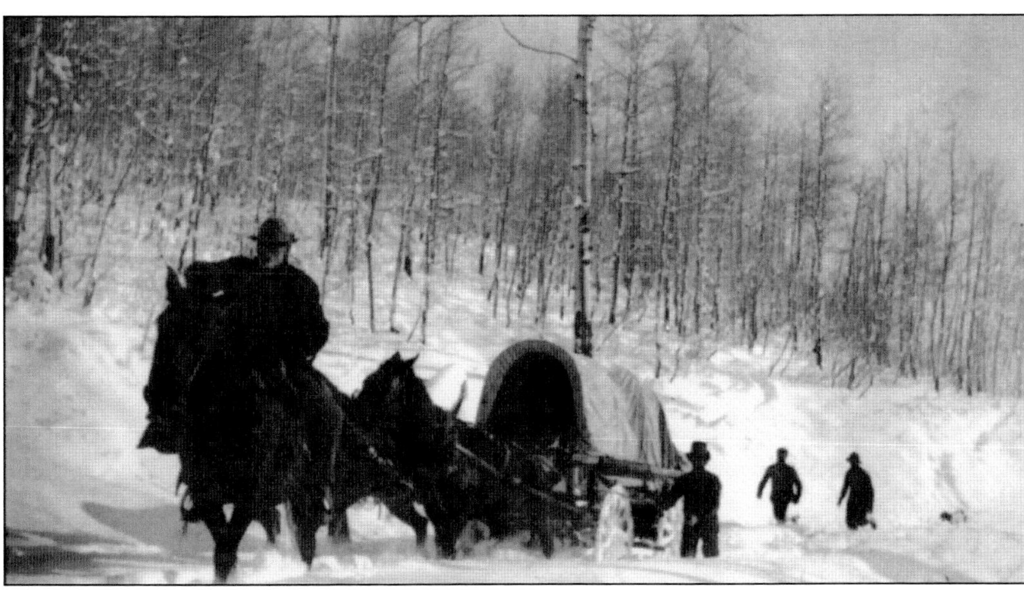

Pictured is a c. 1904 deer hunt in Strawberry with Charles Edward Allan at the head. Charles was an avid outdoorsman and used his skills to hunt for food to sustain his family. (Courtesy of the Samuel Loraine Allan family.)

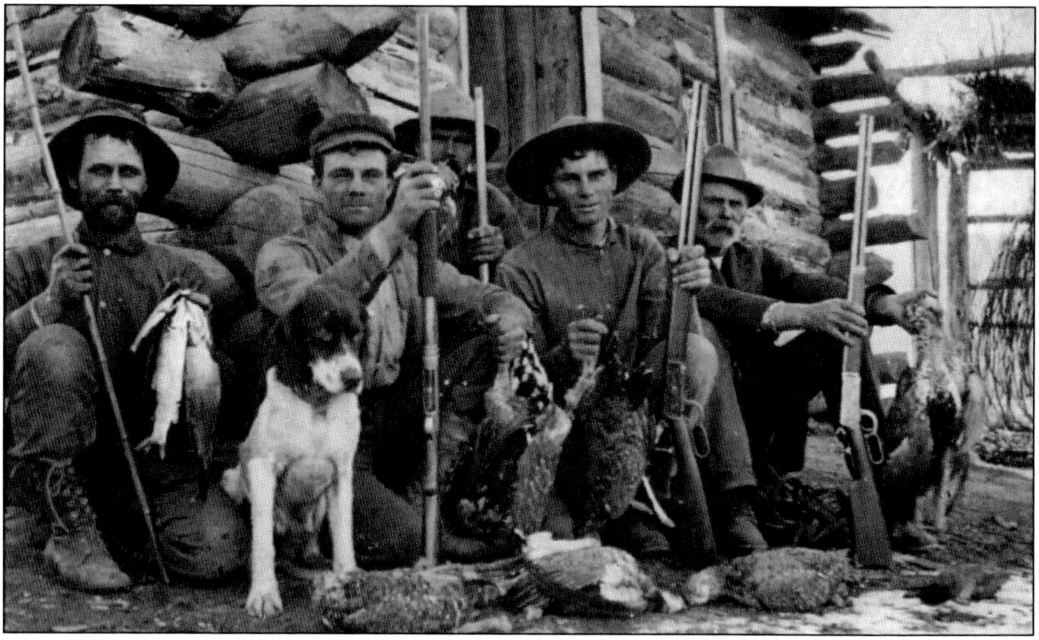

This 1904 photograph depicts the fishing and hunting success of the Allan family; from left to right are William (Dean Allan's grandfather), Joe, Charles, Henry, and Charles Edward. (Courtesy of the Samuel Loraine and Dean Allan families.)

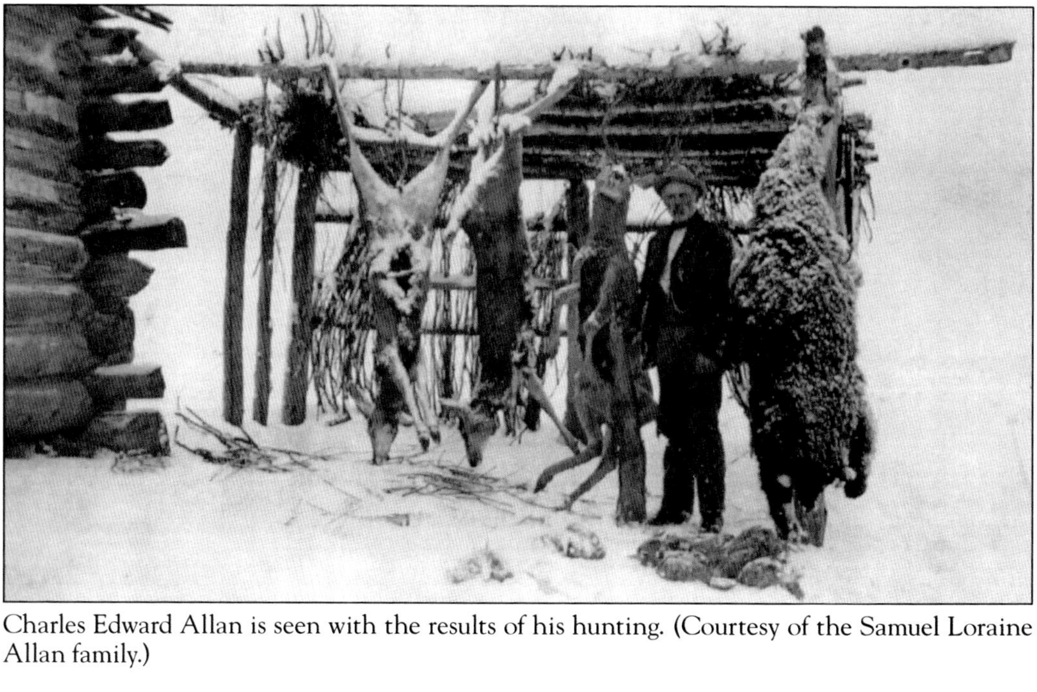

Charles Edward Allan is seen with the results of his hunting. (Courtesy of the Samuel Loraine Allan family.)

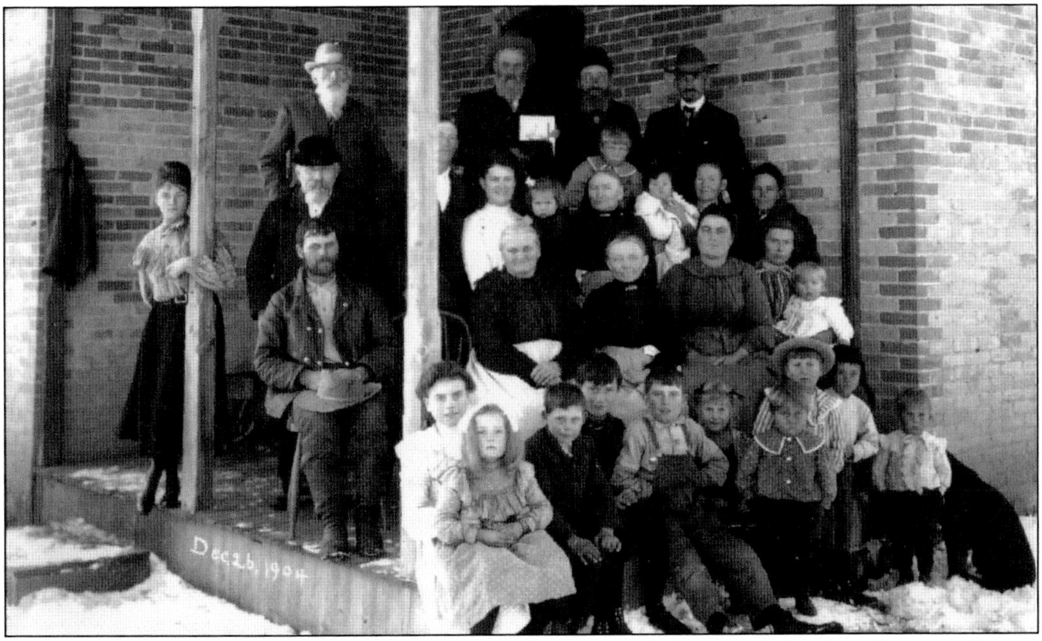

Taken on December 26, 1904, this photograph shows the old home of Charles Edward Allan at 435 West 1600 South. From left to right are (first row) Hannah Allan holding Hazel Twede Baird, Joseph Hafen, Alma Hafen, James Allan, Doris Twede Jensen Tanner, and four unidentified; (second row) William Benjamin Allan, Elizabeth Watkins Allan, Hannah Jensen Boel, Ann Rebecca Allan Twede, and Elizabeth "Lizzy" Jensen Twede (holding ? Twede); (third row) Delia Hafen (arm around pole), Hans Peter Jensen, Herman Twede, Zetta Hafen Larsen (holding Rachael Hafen), Maria Jensen, William Warner Allan, LaVell T. Allan, Edith Viola Twede Allan, and Tora Twede Hafen; (fourth row) Christian Fredrick Nielsen Twede, Charles Edward Allan, Christian Petersen Boel, and John Hafen. (Courtesy of Dean Allan and Collin Allan.)

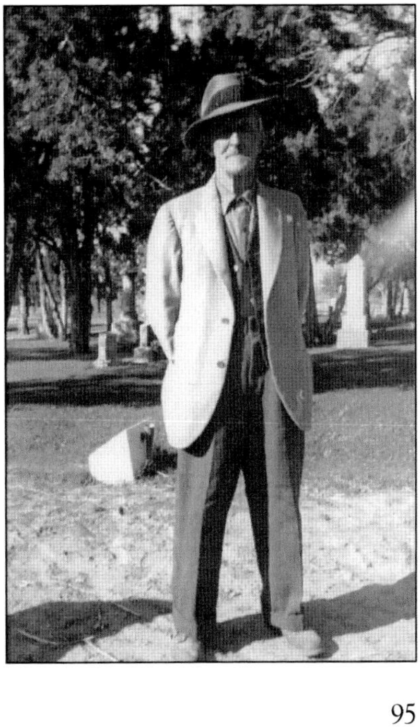

Grant Psimer, son-in-law of the Simplers, is pictured at the Evergreen Cemetery. (Courtesy of Mary Hjorth Fojtek.)

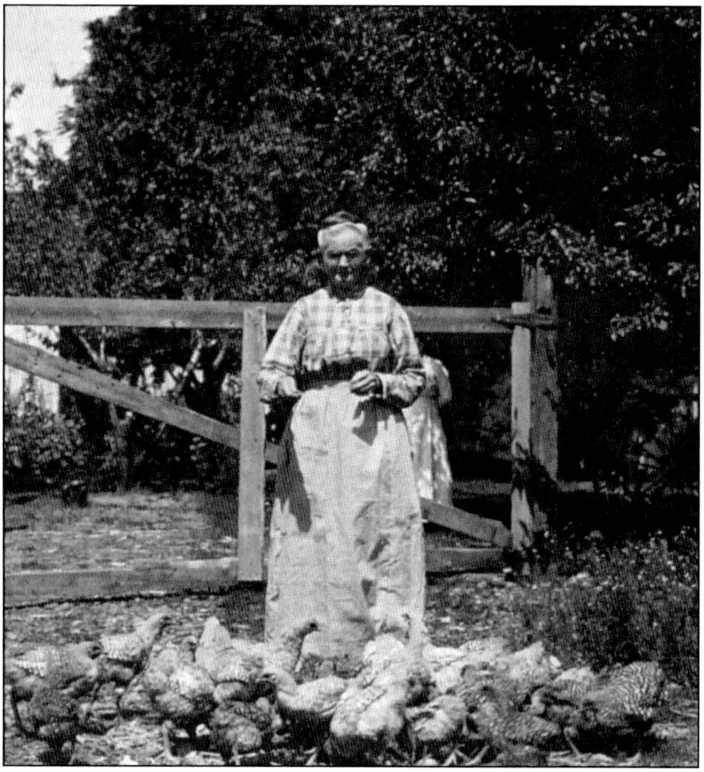

Sarah Simpler is seen here with the chickens. (Courtesy of Mary Hjorth Fojtek.)

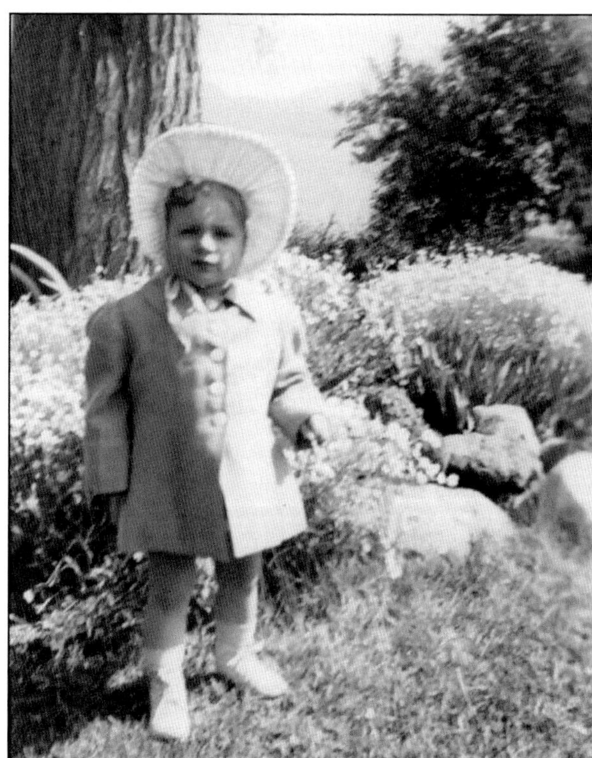

LeAnn Clement Neuenschwander stands outside in her Easter best. (Courtesy of Mary Hjorth Fojtek.)

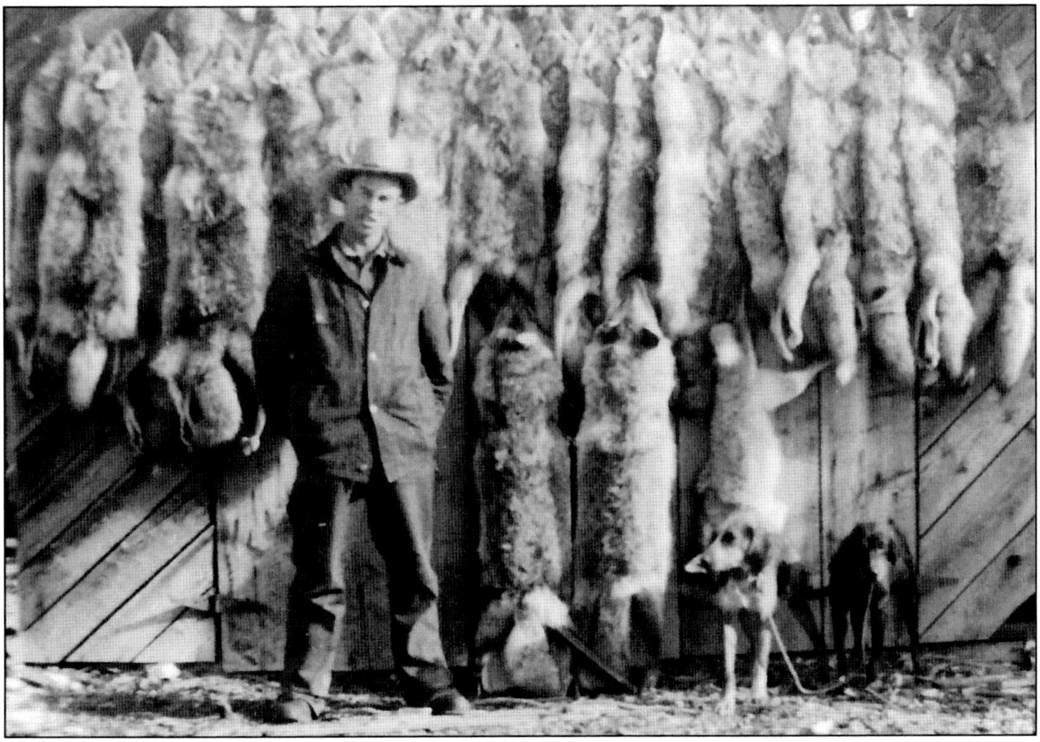

Brown Cazair and his hunting dogs stand with their animal skins and pelts hung out to dry. Mountain wildlife was plentiful, and the cold winters assured thick pelts. (Courtesy of the Mapleton Historical Museum.)

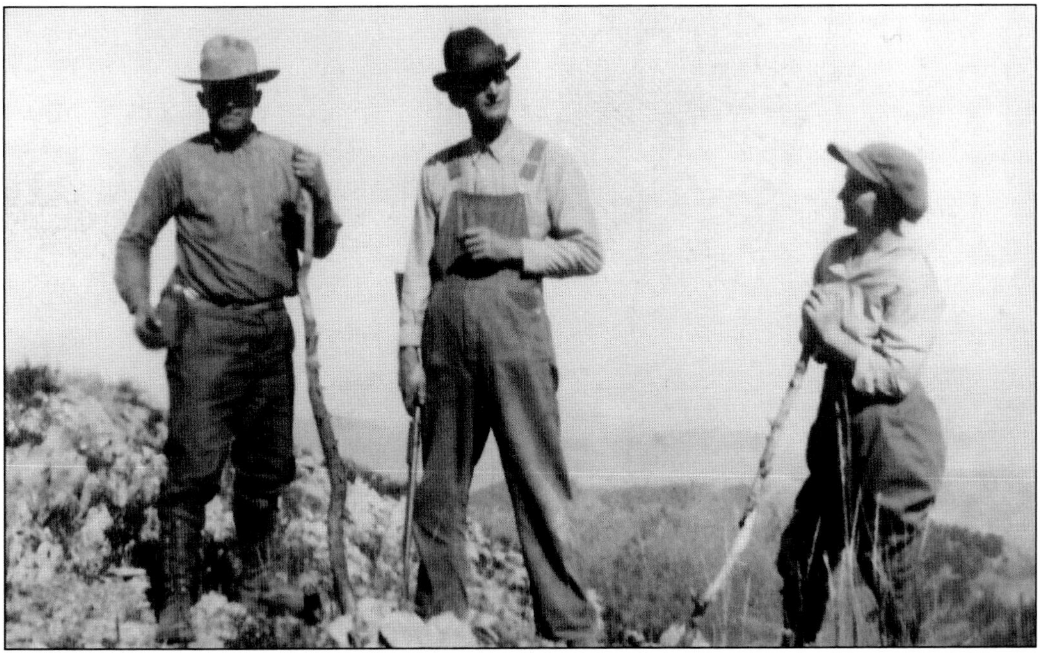

From left to right are hikers Edward Clyde, Amoyt Charington, and Hilda Charington on the summit of Maple Mountain on October 1, 1922. (Courtesy of the Mapleton Historical Museum.)

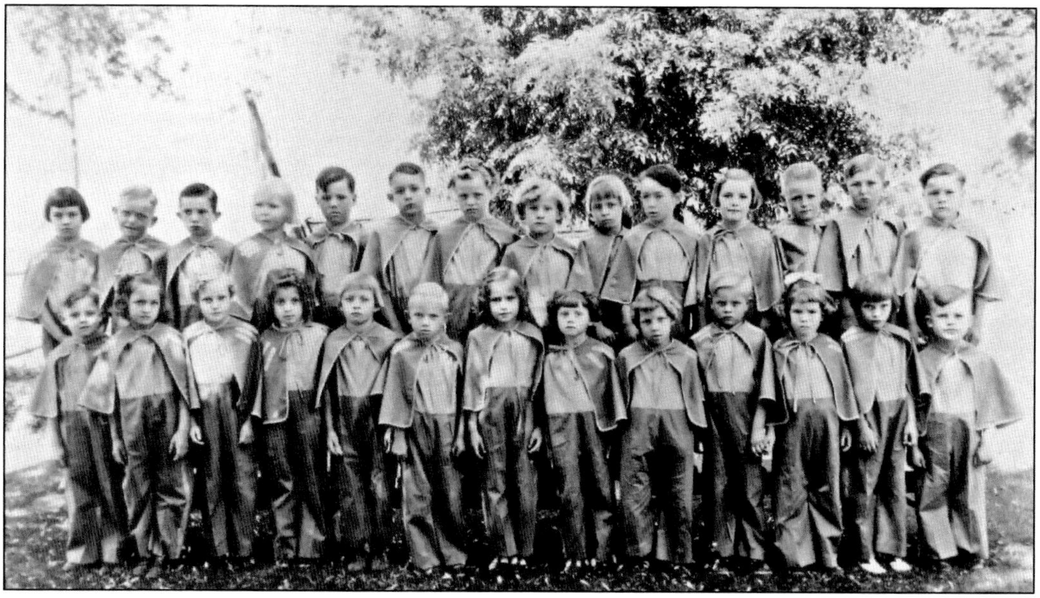

Mapleton Elementary students are shown at an event. Those identified are Diana Bird, Marilyn Whiting, Blaine Hales, Ned Whiting, Michael Whiting, Gayle Whiting, and Marilyn Johnson. (Courtesy of the Mapleton Historical Museum.)

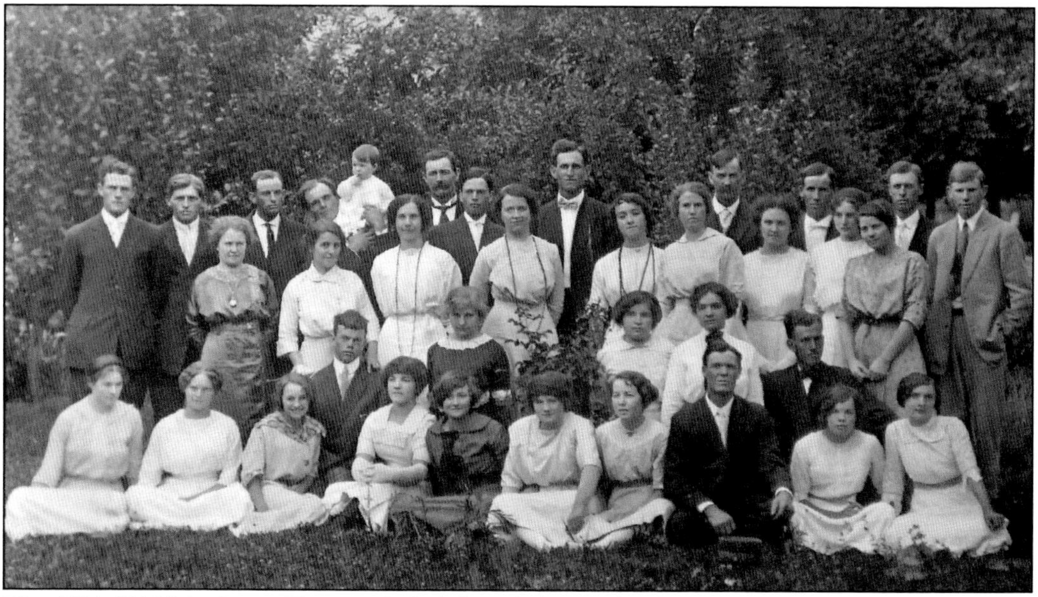

The 1911–1912 Mapleton Choir included, from left to right, (first row) Jennie Houtz Tew, Olive Fullmer Palfreyman, Elizabeth Jolley Dallin, Edna Whiting Mills, Delphia Jolley, Ardell Perry Warner, Alta Law Anderson, Lee Manwaring, Hilda Broomley, and Josephine Roundy; (second row) Mina Bird Larsen, Cordelia Brooks Allan, Mendenhall Berry, Reba Tew Allred, Zinna Law, Hilda Peterson, Lillie Hurst Tew, Sinna Houtz Whiting, Eva Marshbanks Bird, and Victor Whiting; (third row) William T. Tew Jr., Gibson Palfreyman, Chris Larsen, Joseph Allan with baby Verna, Afton Waters, Aaron B. Mendenhall, Lester Peterson, Samuel Fullmer, Ray Whiting, and Austin Houtz. Choirs were a wonderful pastime for Sunday afternoons after church services. (Courtesy of the Mapleton Historical Museum.)

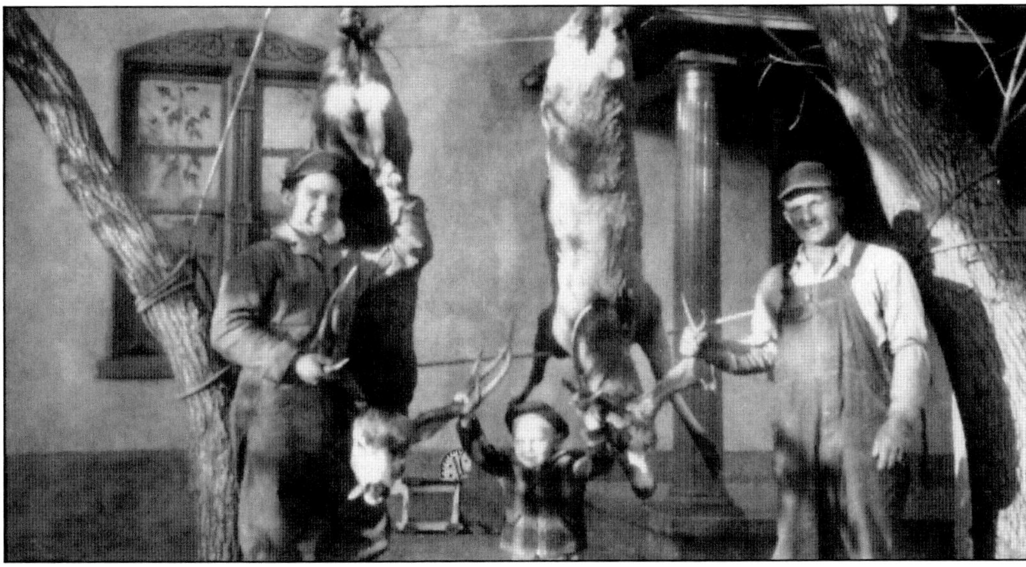

Farrus Larsen (left) and Blaine Larsen (right) are showing off their hunting success with the help of Blaine's young son. (Courtesy of the Mapleton Historical Museum.)

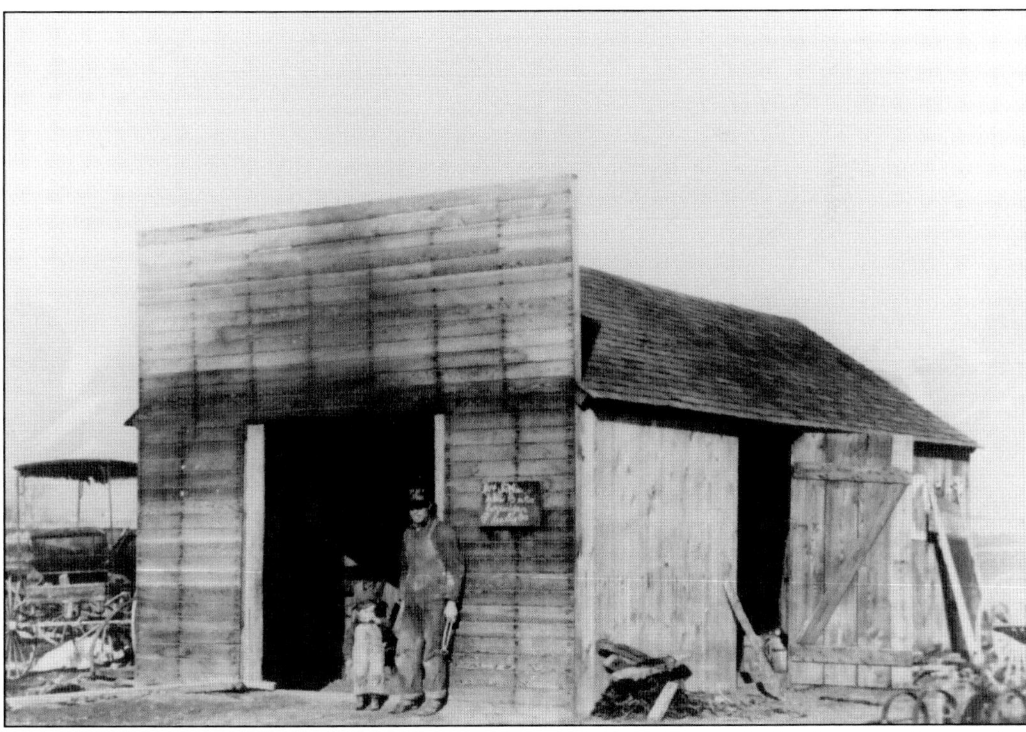

Charlie Whiting is seen with his blacksmith shop and his son Leonard; the photograph was taken in 1914. Charles and Olive, his wife, raised 10 children, and Leonard was the oldest. (Courtesy of the Mapleton Historical Museum.)

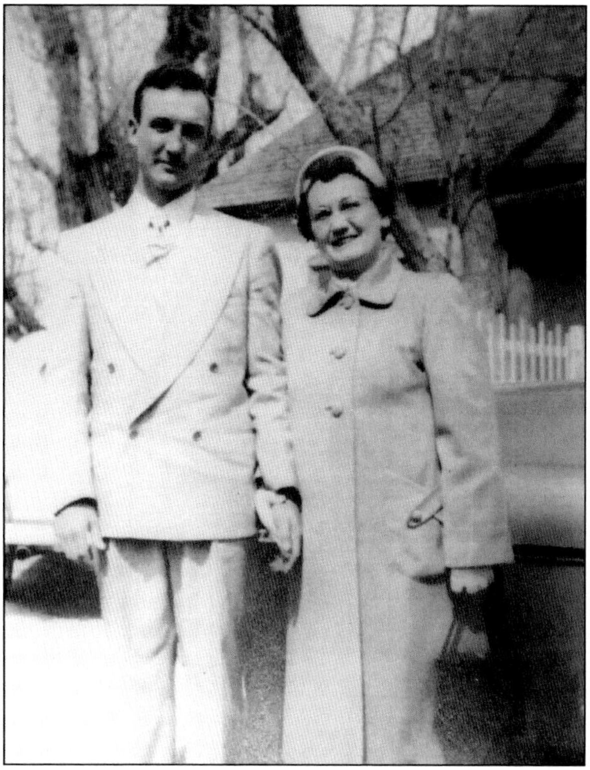

Ferrus Larsen is seen lovingly holding the hand of his mother, Jessie Wing Larsen. For years, 800 West in Mapleton was known as "Larsen Lane" because of all the Larsen families that lived on the street. (Courtesy of the Mapleton Historical Museum.)

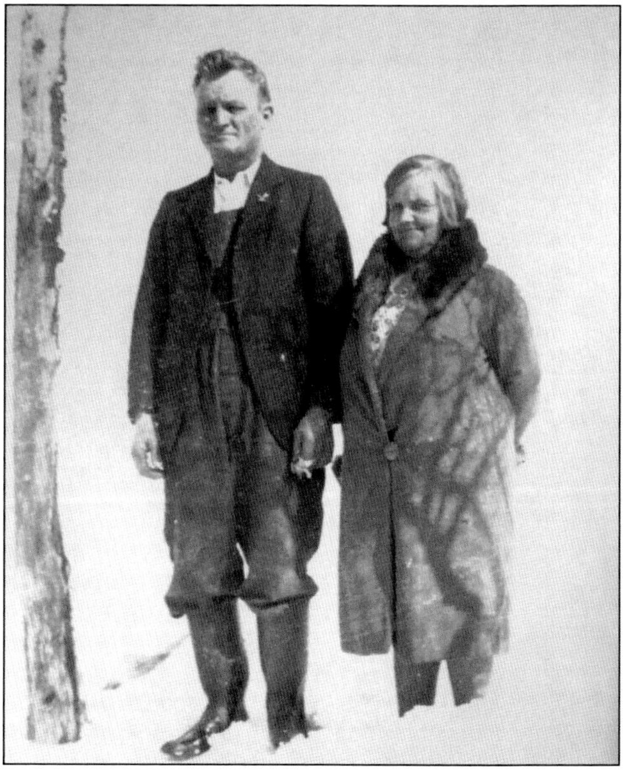

George and Marie Stone are pictured standing in several inches of snow. (Courtesy of the Mapleton Historical Museum.)

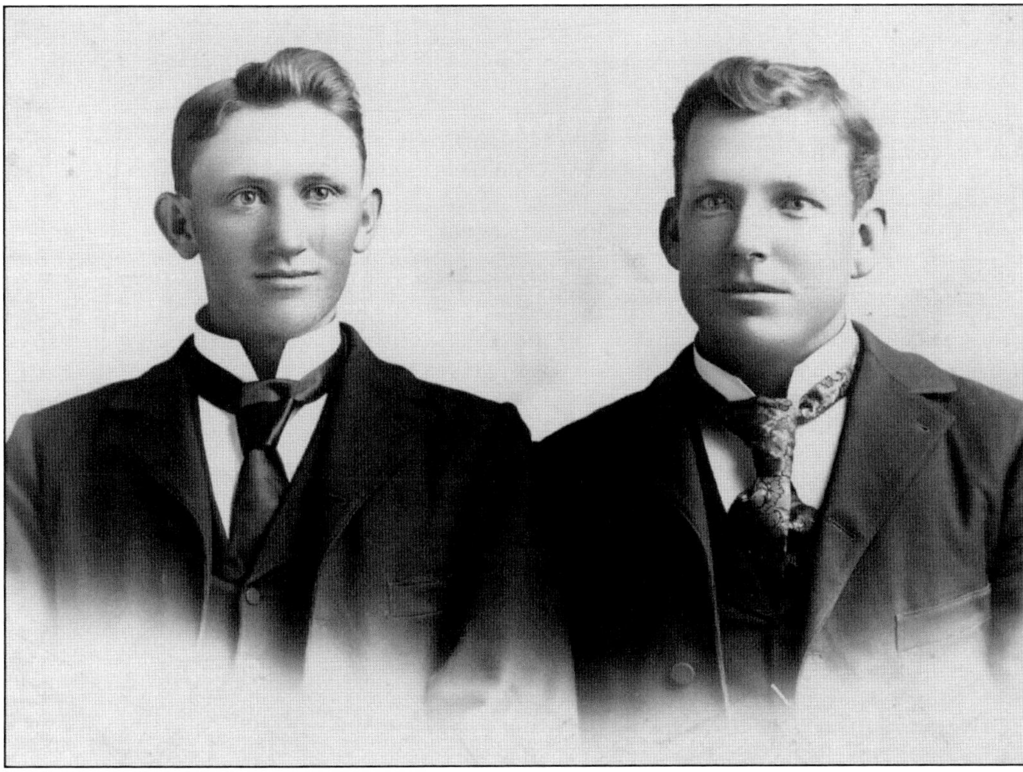

Richard Lovell Mendenhall (left) is pictured in this George Edward Anderson photograph with H. Lee Boyer. (Courtesy of Mary Hjorth Fojtek.)

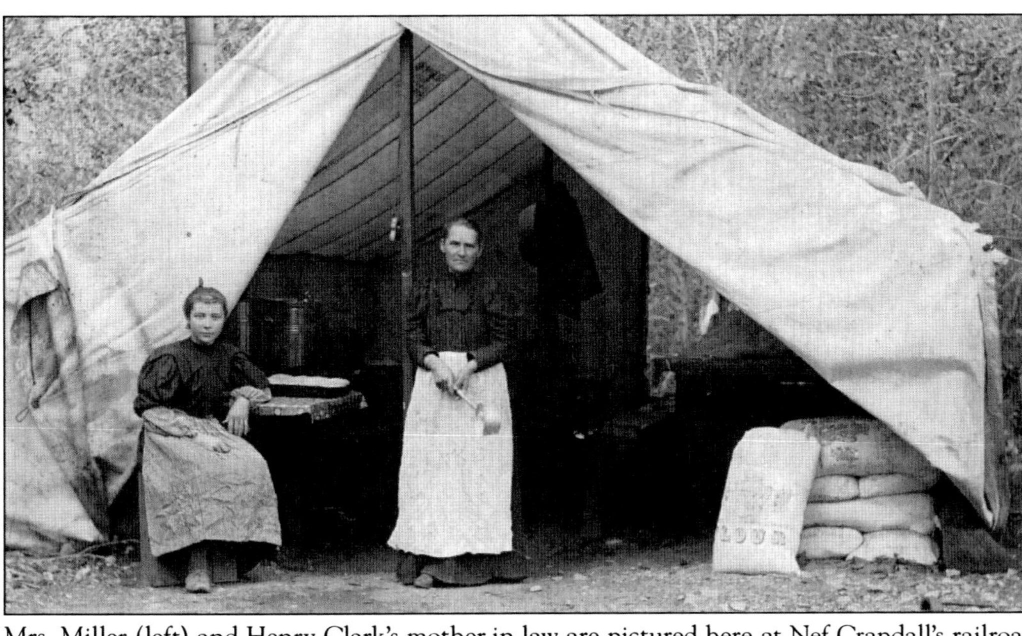

Mrs. Miller (left) and Henry Clark's mother-in-law are pictured here at Nef Crandall's railroad construction camp in Sevier Canyon. (Courtesy of the Mapleton Historical Museum.)

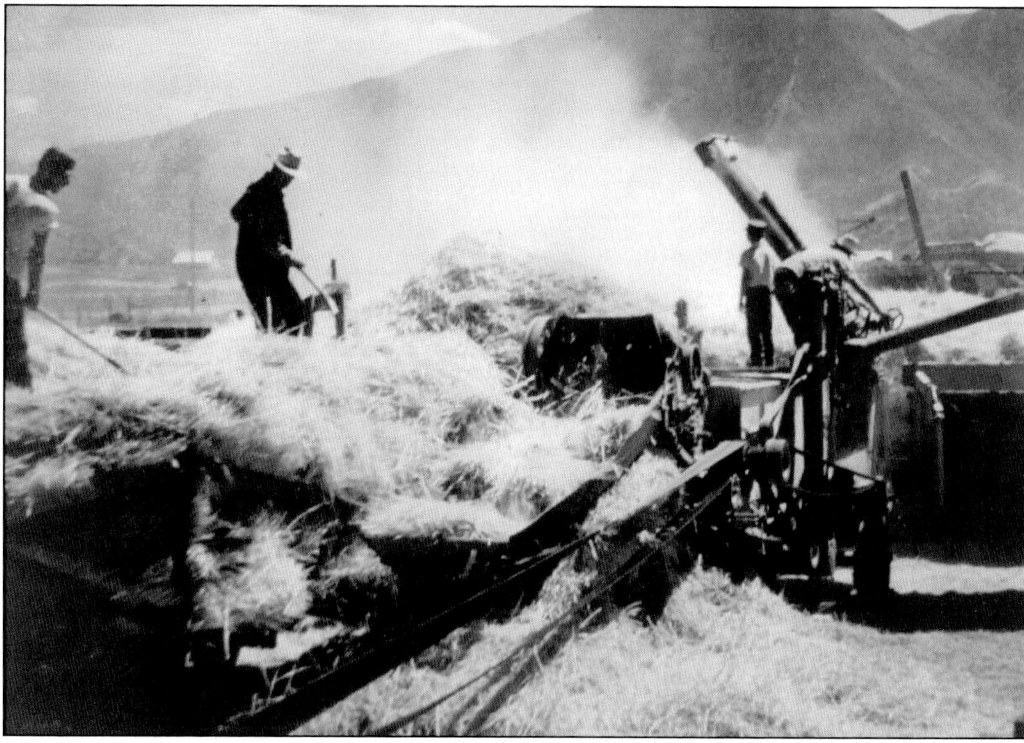

Threshing machines, like the one seen here, were used to remove the grain, separate the grain from the cob or husk, clean the grain, and gather it. (Courtesy of the Mapleton Historical Museum.)

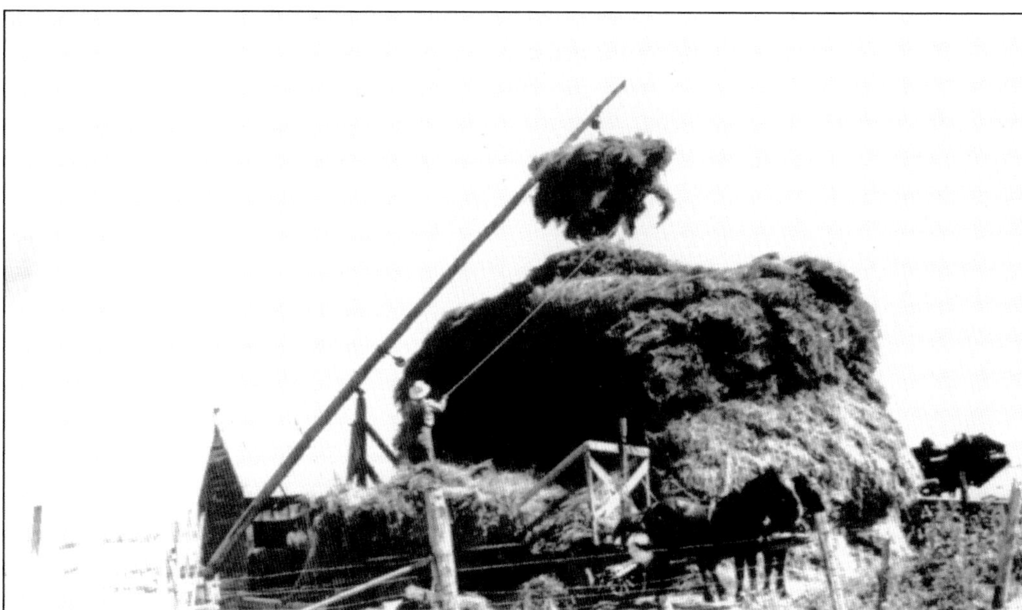

The hay was lifted to the top of the stack by a derrick, a weight and pulley arrangement using a crane. The derrick is in the center with horse teams and rakes "pushing" hay to the loading area. (Courtesy of the Mapleton Historical Museum.)

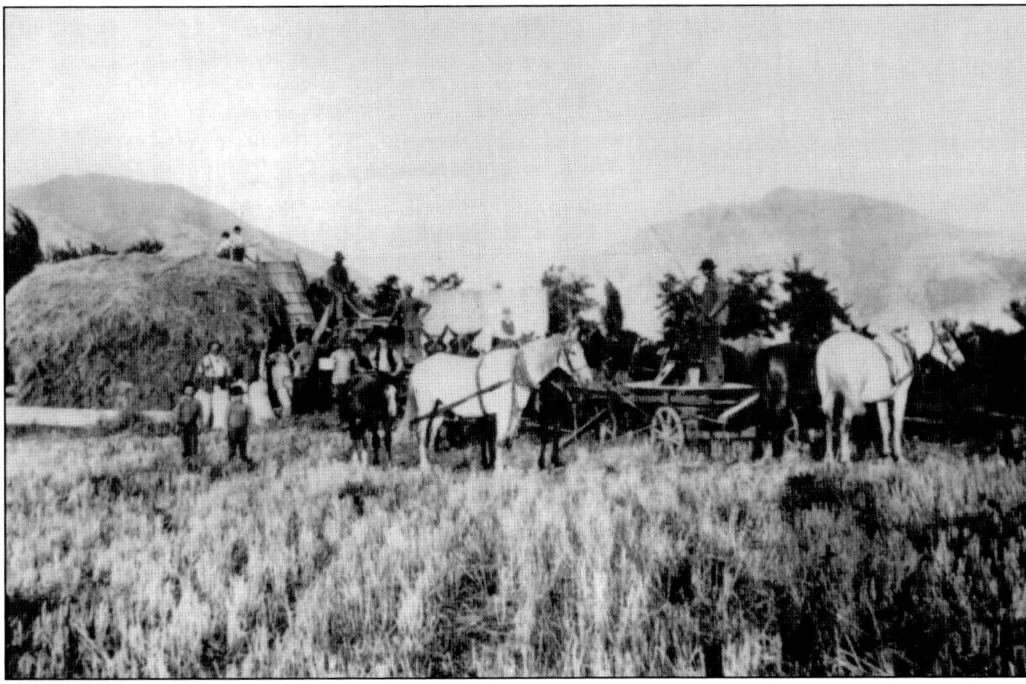

Here, a group of neighbors is seen joining together in an effort to put up the hay using a horse-powered thresher. (Courtesy of the Mapleton Historical Museum.)

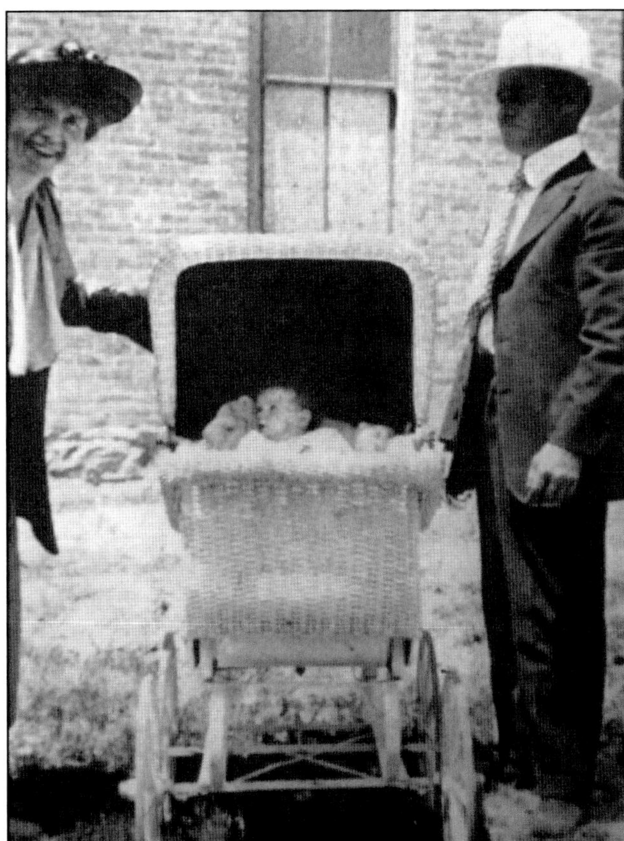

Edwin Snow Jr. and his mother, Frances Perry Snow, are pictured along with a carriage and Edwin Jr.'s infant child. Edwin Jr. (right) played the trombone in the Mapleton band. The band performed at many town meetings and celebrations. (Courtesy of the Mapleton Historical Museum.)

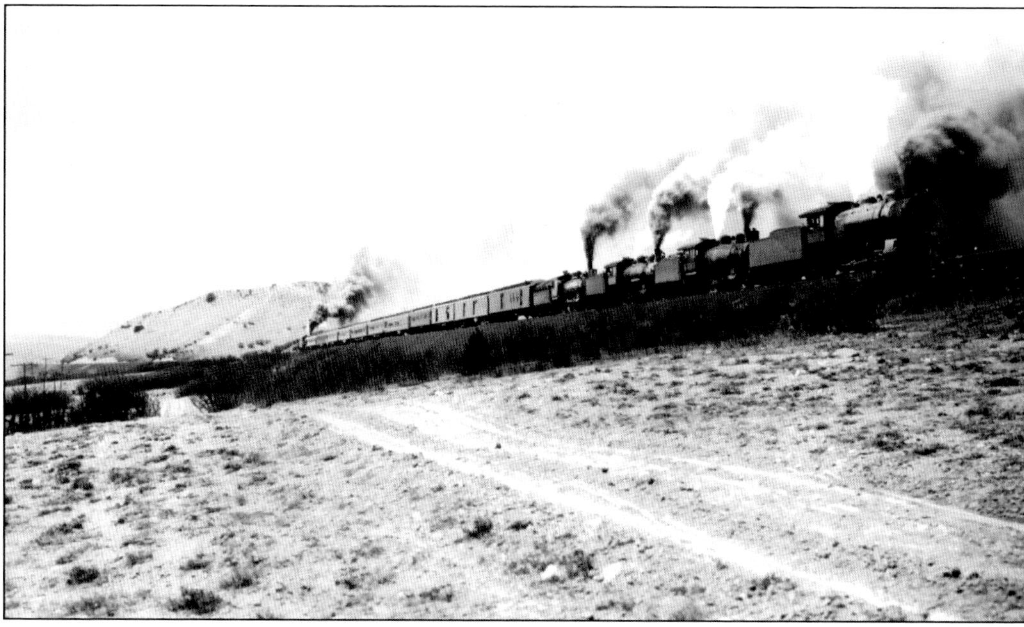

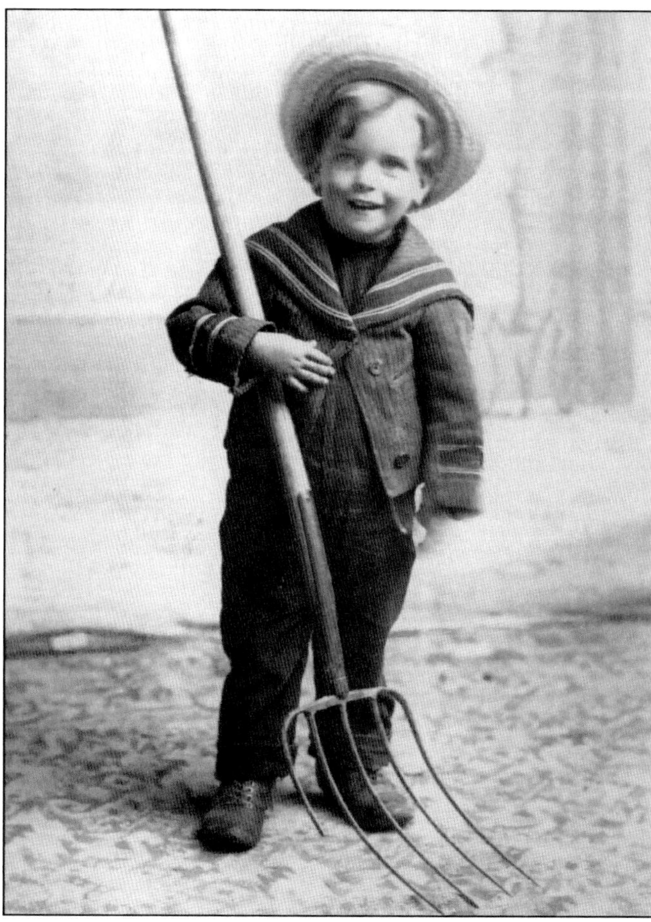

A train is puffing its way through Mapleton as it heads up to Spanish Fork Canyon on April 26, 1911. (Courtesy of the Mapleton Historical Museum.)

Barney Mendenhall is seen here. Barney's father, John, raised sugar beets, livestock, hay, and grains, and had a sizable fruit orchard. (Courtesy of the Mapleton Historical Museum.)

George Wing guides his prized horses in a pulling contest. This type of entertainment was a favorite during the summer holiday celebrations. (Courtesy of the Mapleton Historical Museum.)

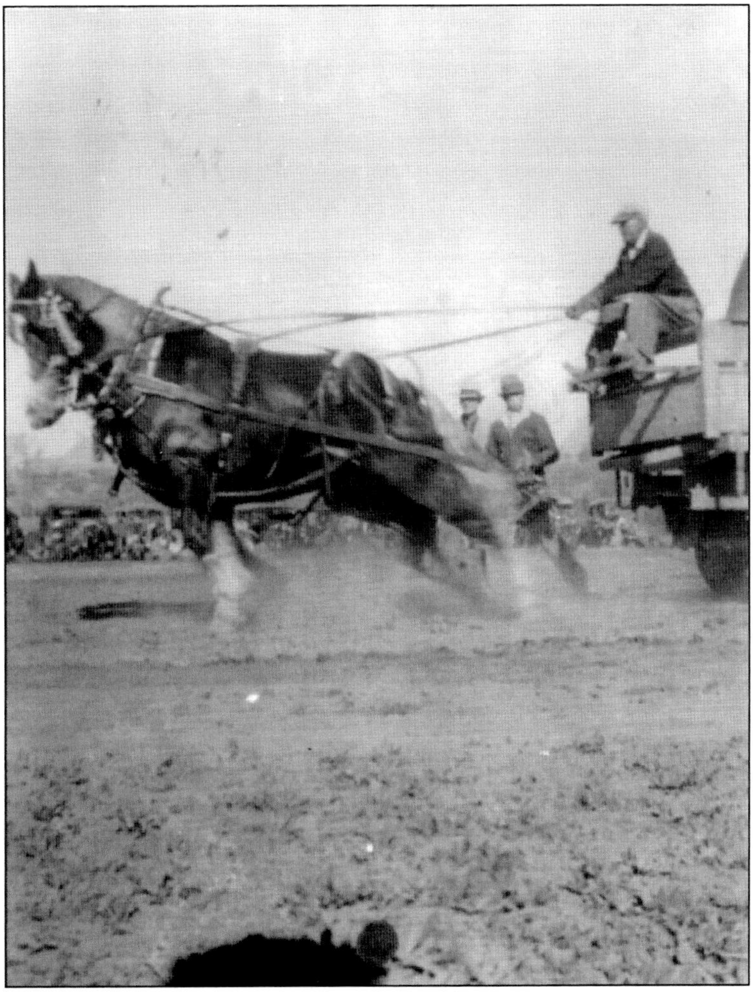

Brothers Elmer (left) and Joe Wiscombe are busy planting grain. (Courtesy of the Mapleton Historical Museum.)

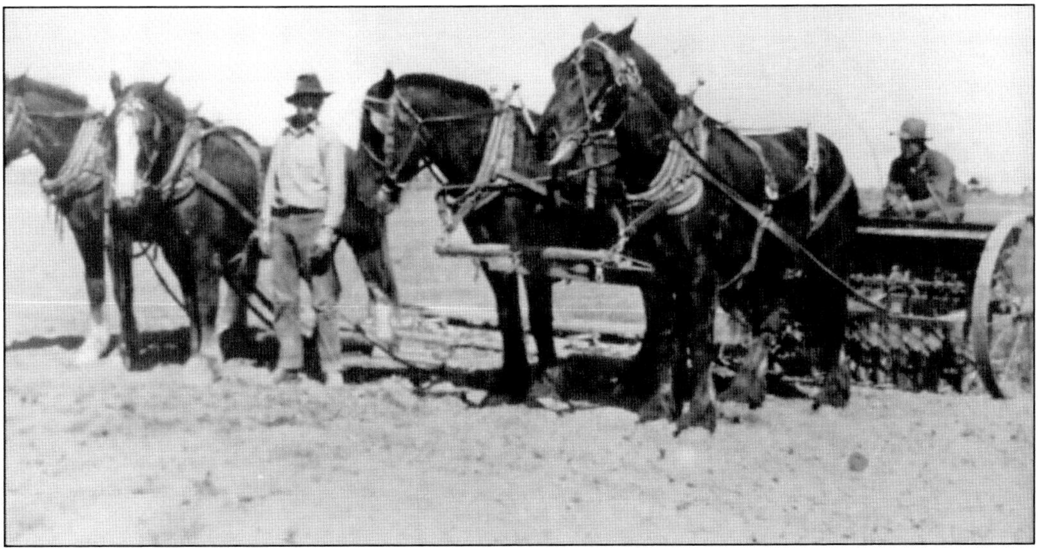

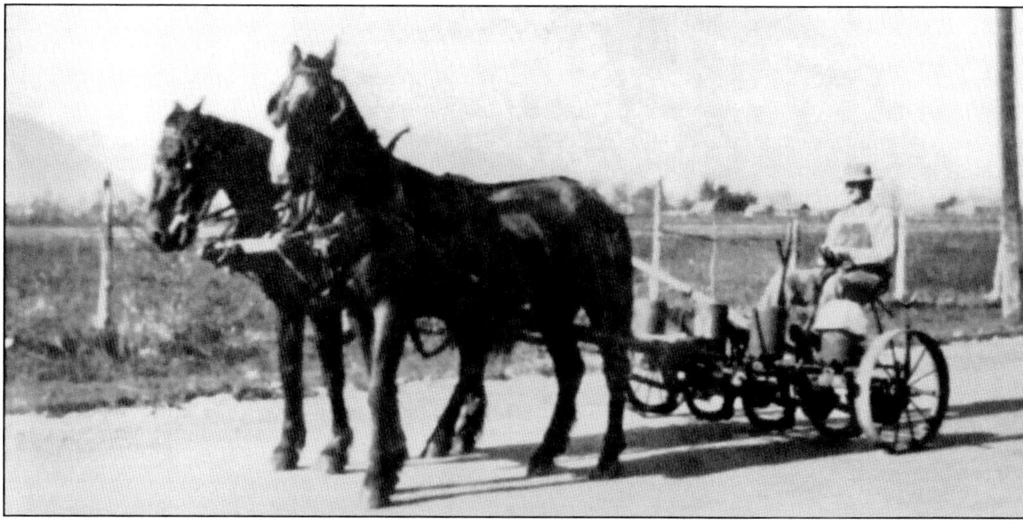

James Wiscombe sits atop his sugar beet drill planter being pulled by two horses. Utah was one of the first states to successfully manufacture refined sugar from sugar beets. The leftover pulp was fed to the livestock. (Courtesy of the Mapleton Historical Museum.)

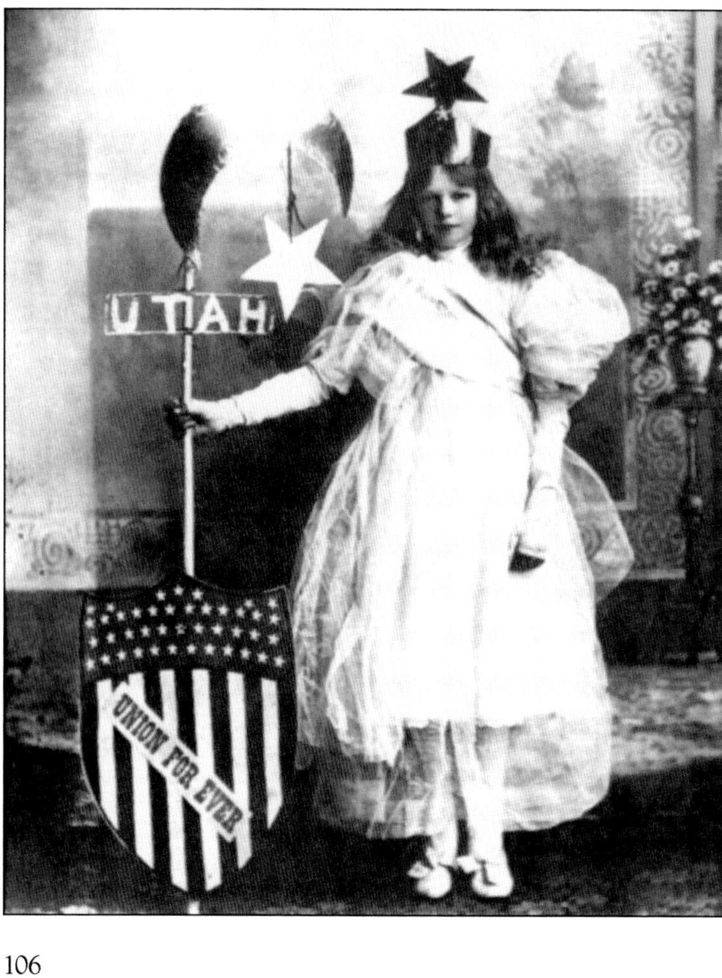

Pictured is the 1896 Statehood Day queen Matilda "Tillie" Houtz, 12 years old. A total of 24 young ladies on white horses, along with 24 young men dressed in white, paraded with her. The Goddess of Liberty, Tillie was chained to a pole on the float so she could pose gracefully as she rode along the dirt roads. George Edward Anderson took this photograph, and Rell G. Francis preserved it. (Courtesy of the Mapleton Historical Museum.)

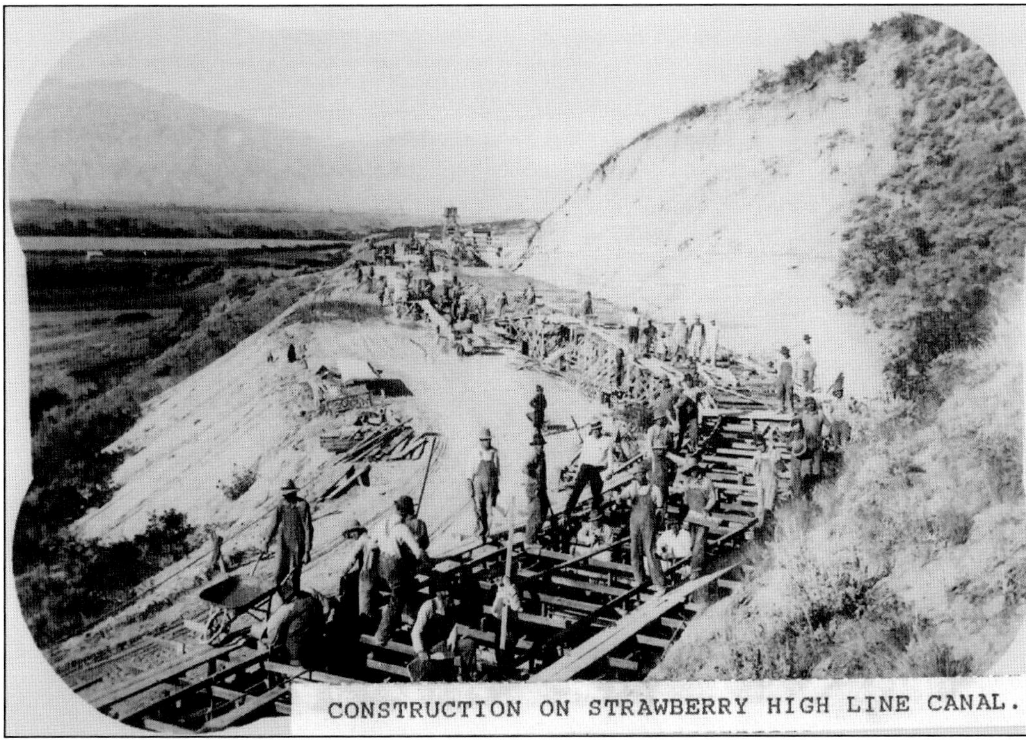

In 1912, construction crews were busy building the Strawberry High Line Canal. (Both courtesy of the Mapleton Historical Museum.)

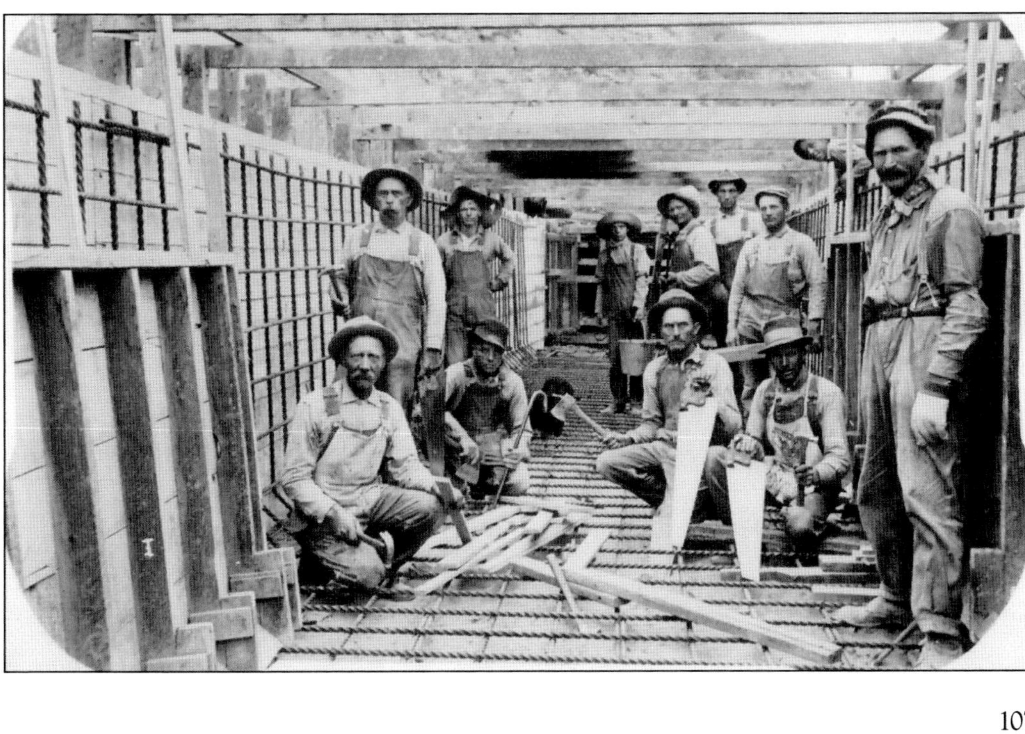

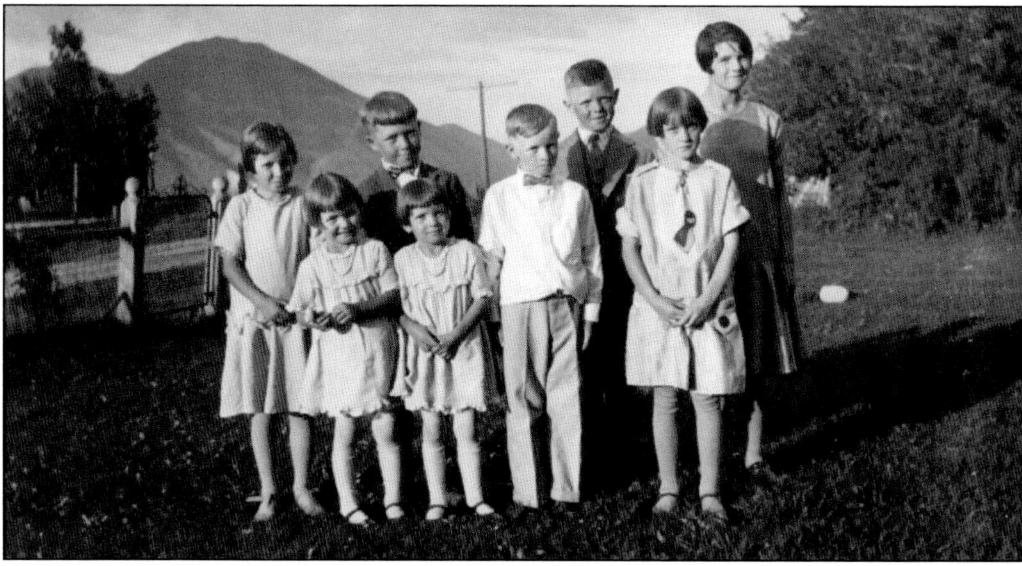

Pictured here from left to right are (first row) Virginia and Genevieve Bird and Earl and Erma Mendenhall; (second row) Ruth and LeRoy Hill and Leo and Leah Manwaring; they are all sets of twins and first cousins and are pictured in the following images as babies. This photograph was taken at the home of Abby Ann and Charles Monroe Mendenhall on a Sunday as the twins visited with their grandparents and each other. (Courtesy of Mary Hjorth Fojtek.)

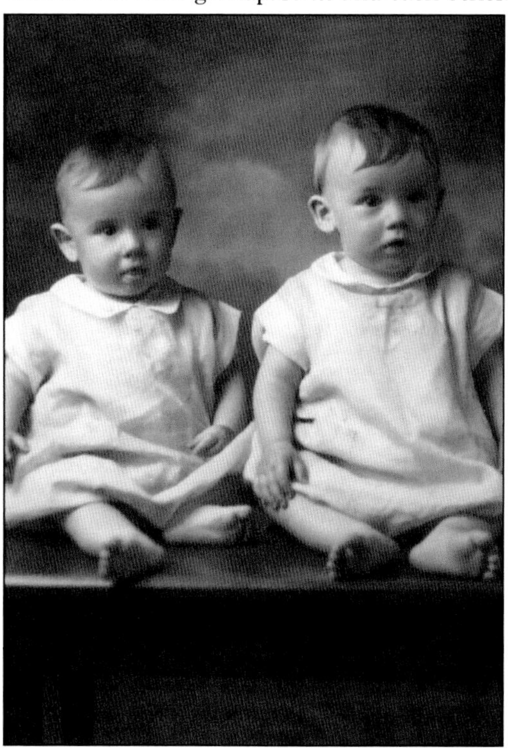

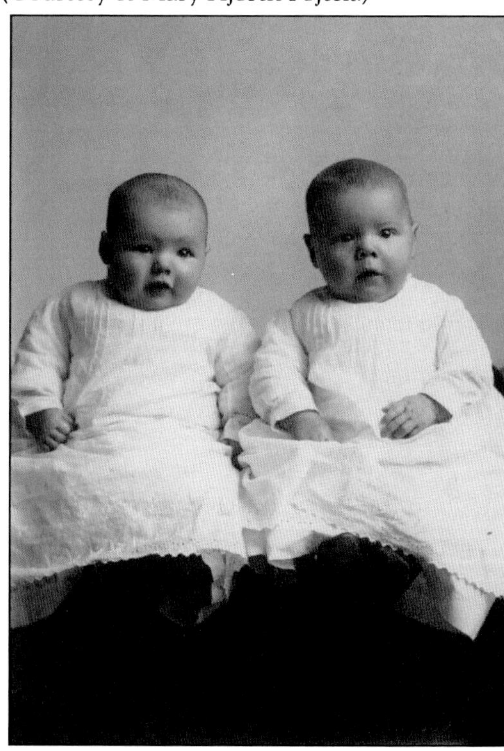

At left, Richard (left) and Ralph Bird, sons of Merrill Bird born July 5, 1929, have their first portrait taken. At right are Leo (left) and Leah Manwaring, children of Emogene Bird Manwaring born July 15, 1914. (Both courtesy of Mary Hjorth Fojtek.)

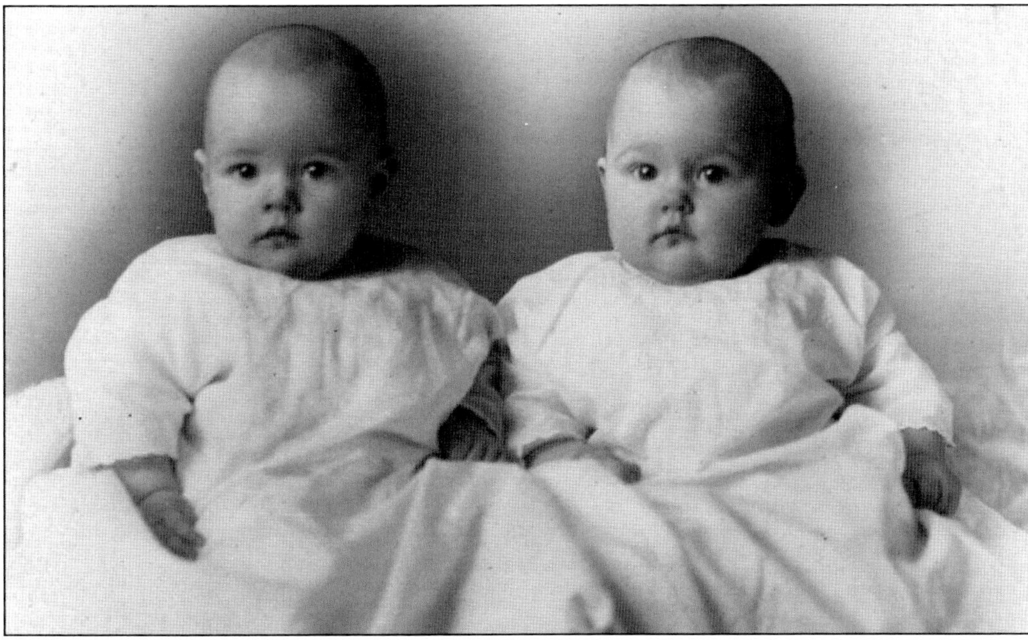

Pictured above in 1918 are infant twins Earl (left) and Erma Mendenhall, children of Richard Lovell Mendenhall born August 29, 1917. Both are adorned in traditional white christening gowns. Below at left, Genevieve (left) and Virginia Bird, daughters of Freeman Bird born January 31, 1921, hold hands wearing similar delicate white dresses. Below at right, LeRoy (left) and Ruth Hill, children of Jennie Bird Hill born May 22, 1917, pose for their first portrait. (All courtesy of Mary Hjorth Fojtek.)

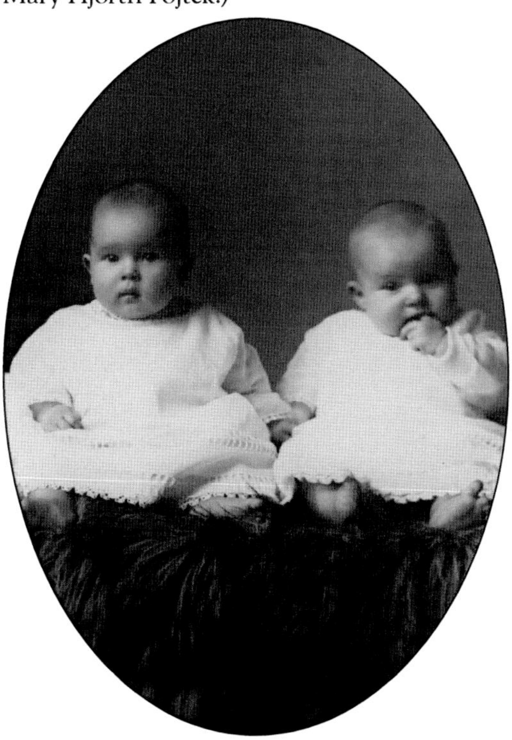

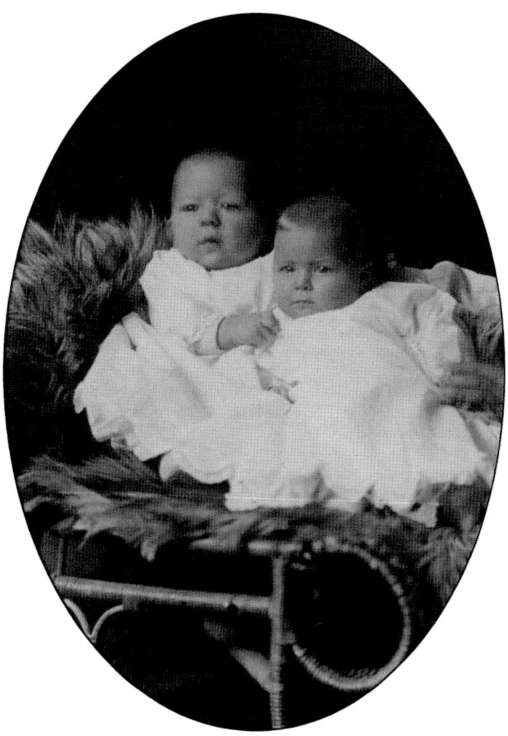

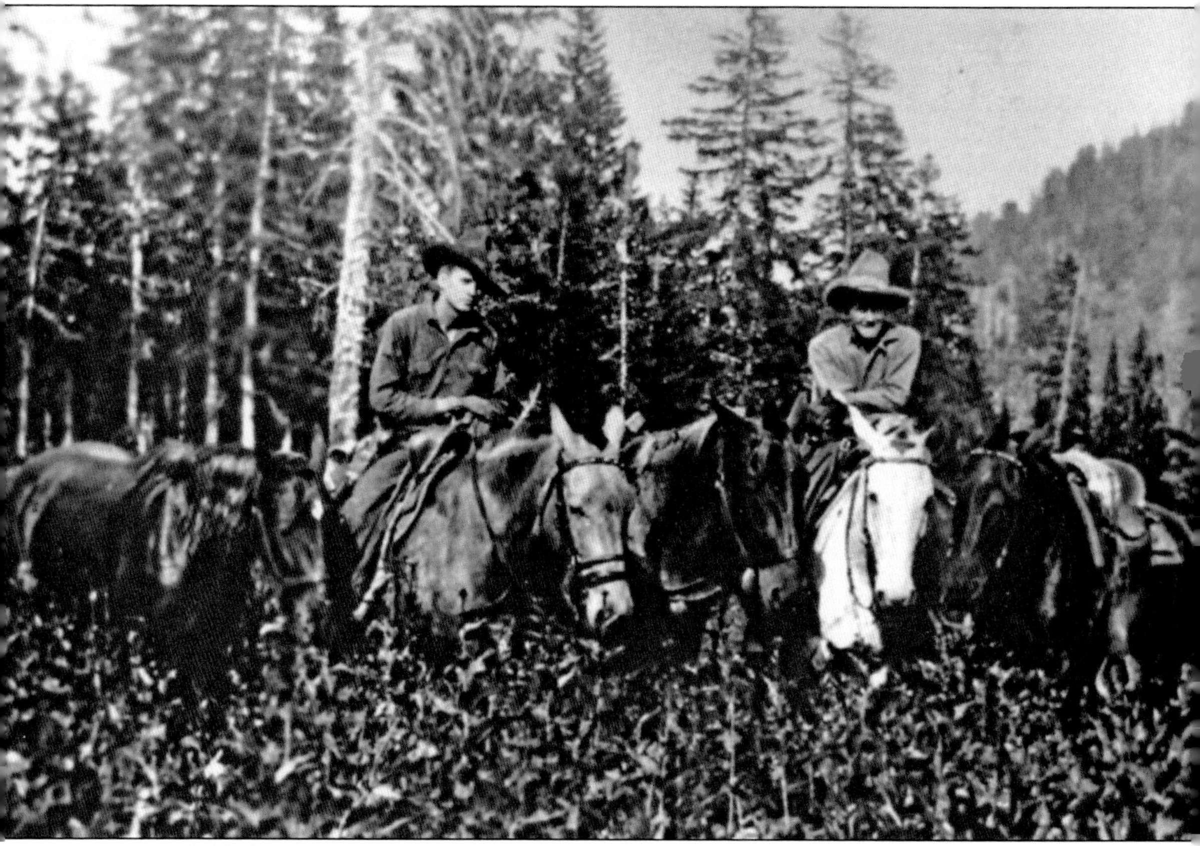

Myron Childs (left) and Wendell Mendenhall are pictured herding sheep on Maple Mountain. (Courtesy of the Mapleton Historical Museum.)

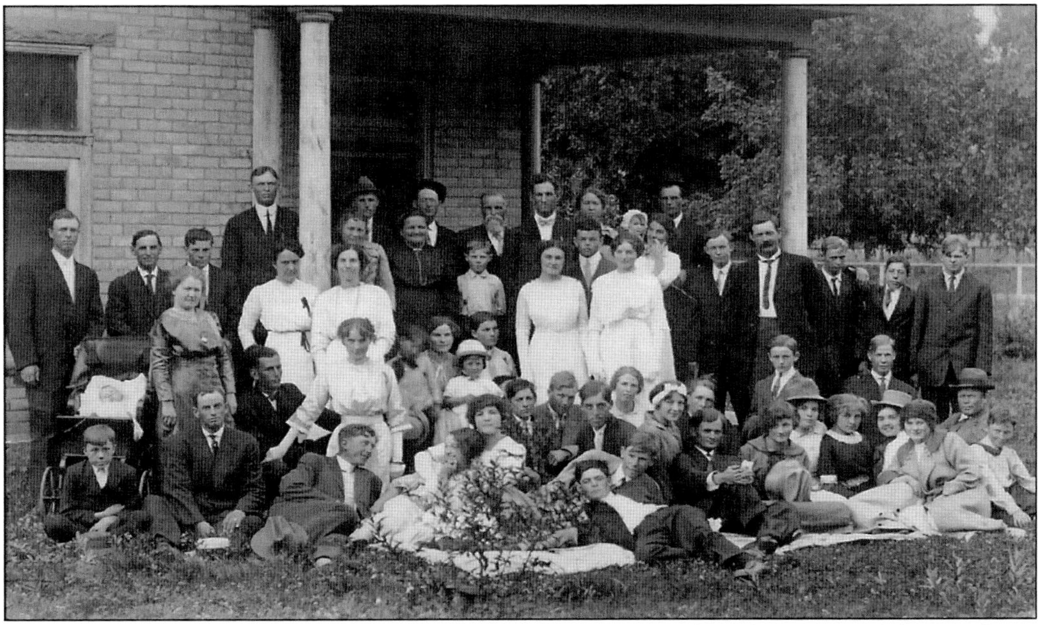

Members of the choir assembled outside for this casual group shot. (Courtesy of the Mapleton Historical Museum.)

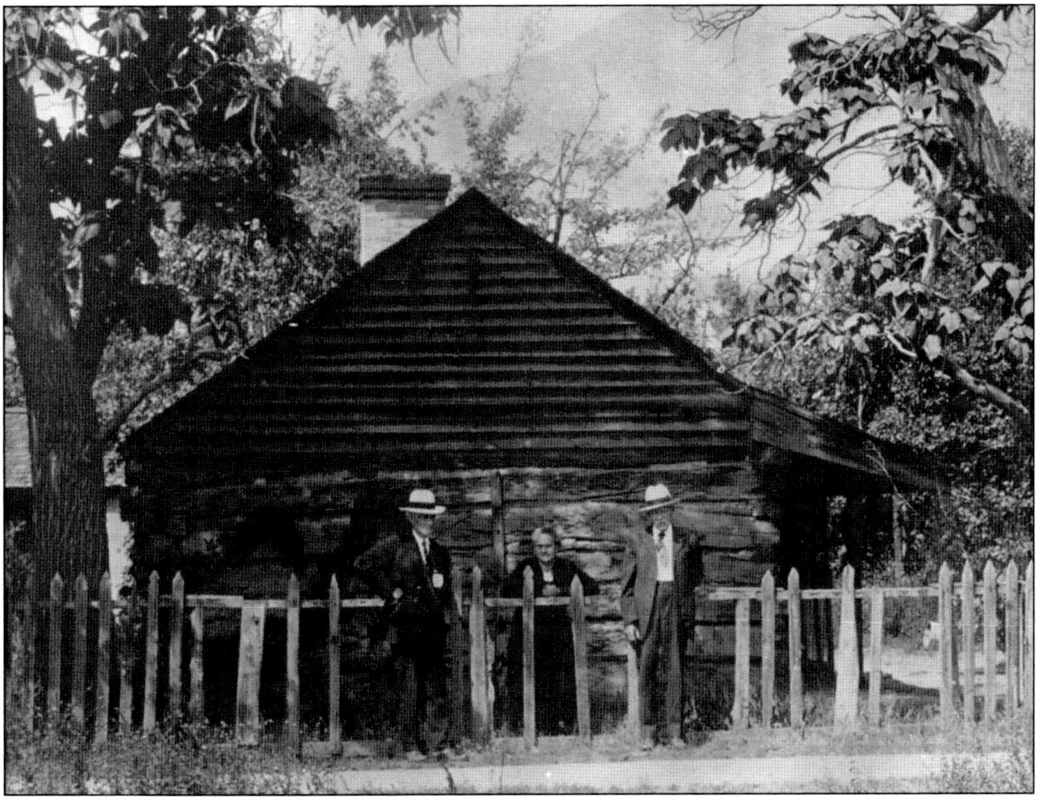

Willis K. Johnson (left) is standing in front of his cabin and wearing a hat, while friends Hannah B. and Thomas L. Mendenhall lean on the fence. (Courtesy of the Mapleton Historical Museum.)

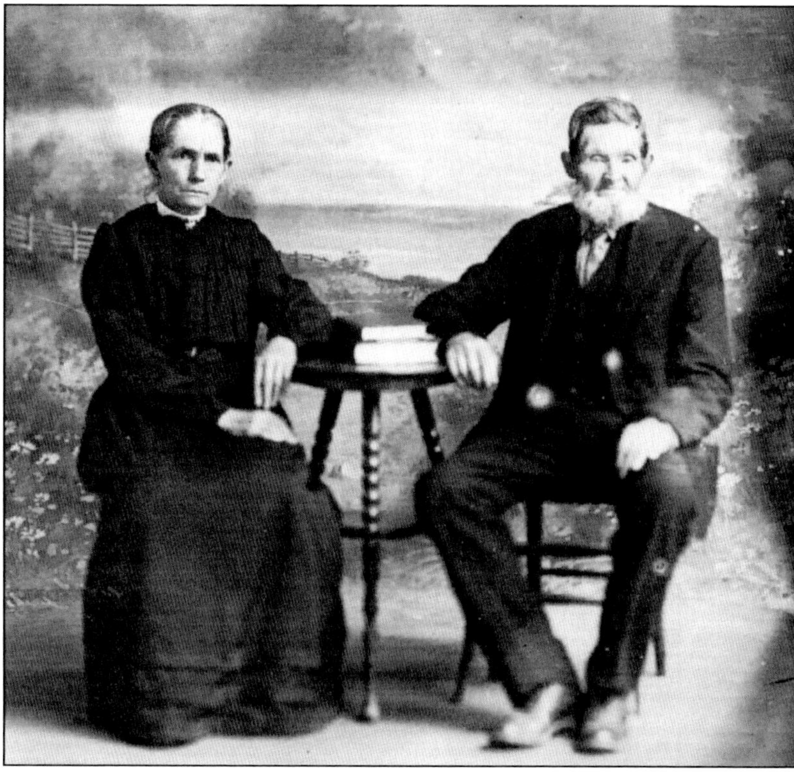

Sarah Jane and Uriah E. Curtis are pictured here. (Courtesy of the Mapleton Historical Museum.)

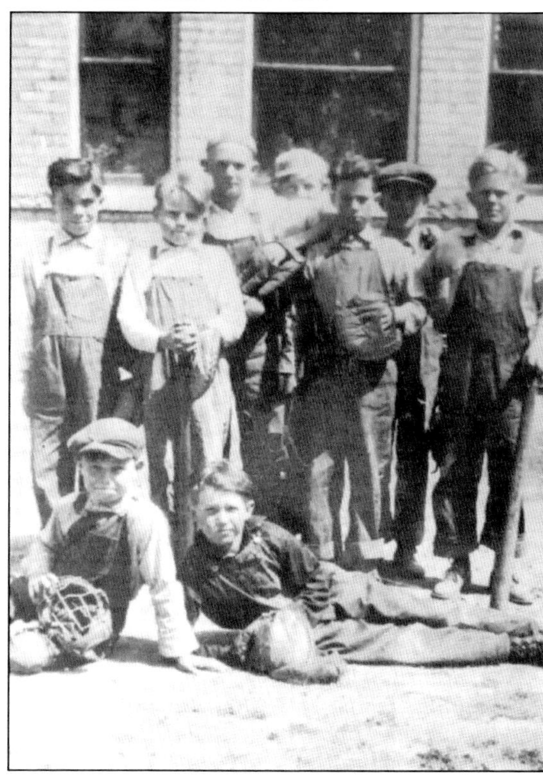

Mapleton's baseball team is pictured here in 1925. From left to right are (first row, sitting) Maurice Bird and Donald Johnson; (second row, standing) Jack Whiting, Don Fuller, Arthur Mendenhall, and Ralph Wing; (third row) Howard Larsen, Guy Nielson, and Robert Johnson. (Courtesy of the Mapleton Historical Museum.)

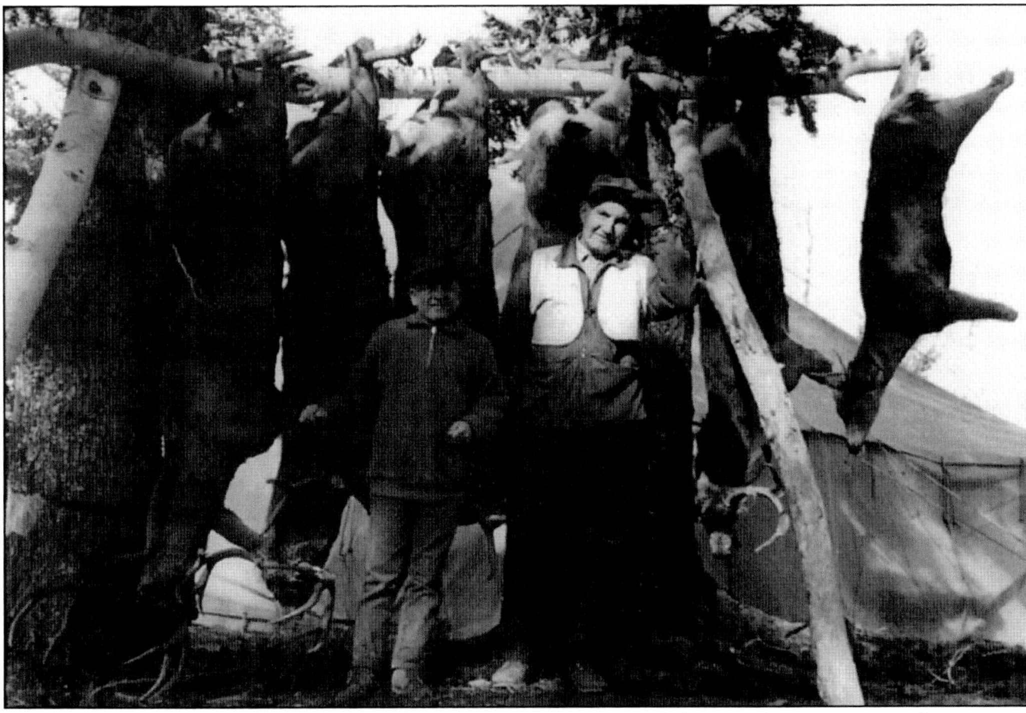

These hunters are proudly posing with their kills. (Courtesy of the Mapleton Historical Museum.)

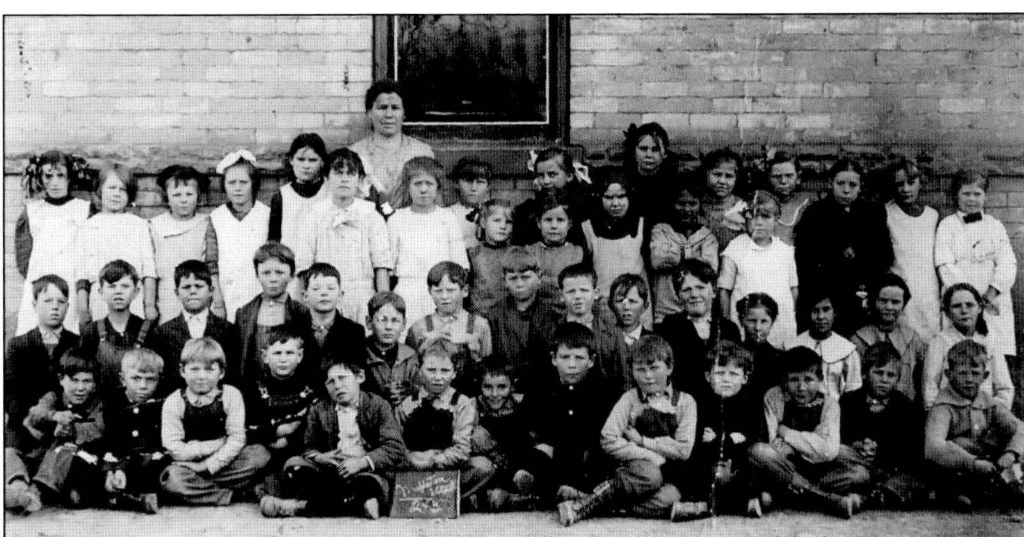

Second-and-third-grade students and their teacher take a break to pose in a joint class photograph outside the school entrance. (Courtesy of the Mapleton Historical Museum.)

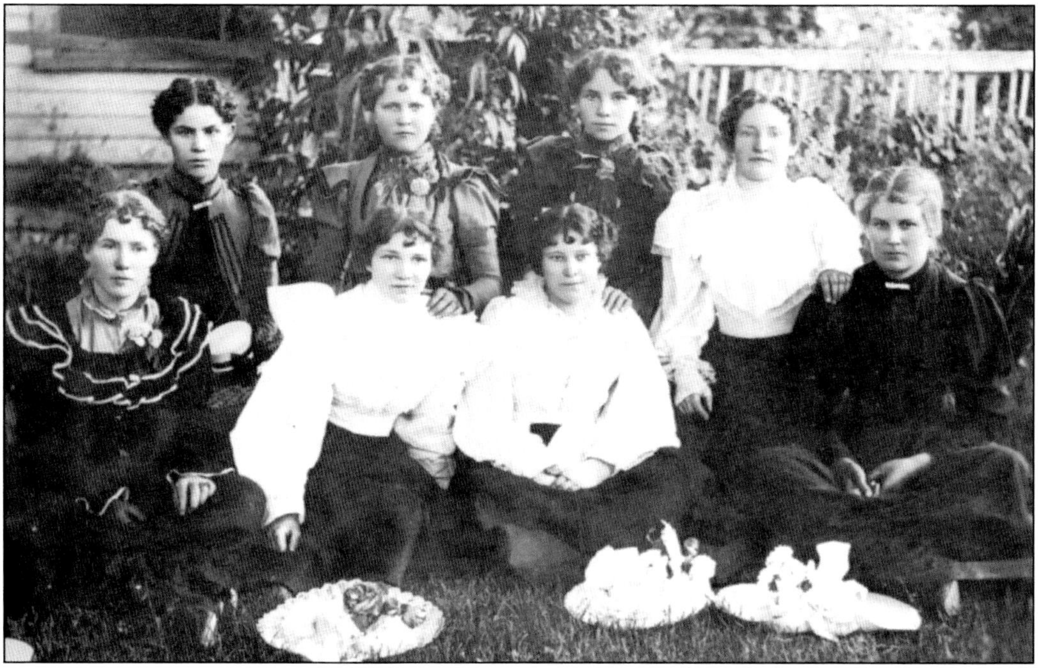

The strawberry "pickers" pictured here are, from left to right, (first row) Mary Jensen, Myrtle Bird, Stella Hatch, and Hannah Holam; (second row) Hattie Whiting, Belle Whiting, Ethel Whiting, and Francis Probart. (Courtesy of the Mapleton Historical Museum.)

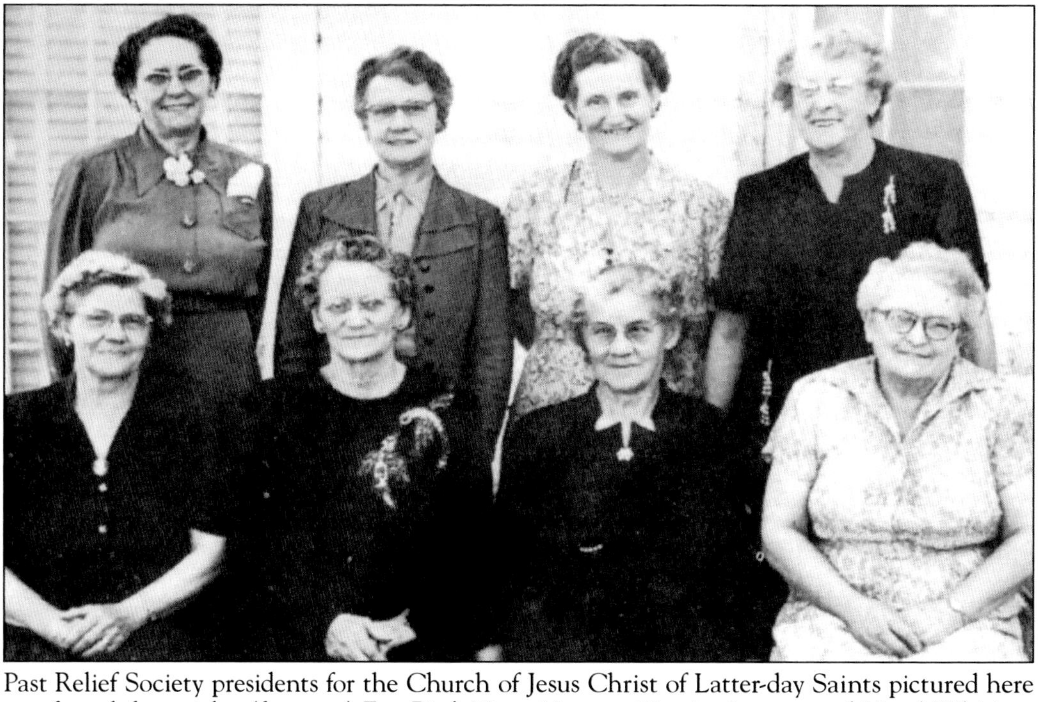

Past Relief Society presidents for the Church of Jesus Christ of Latter-day Saints pictured here are, from left to right, (first row) Eva Bird, Nena Harmer, Harriet Jensen, and Hazel Whiting; (second row) Martha Whiting, Amanda Binks, Gladys Parry, and Sadie Whiting. (Courtesy of the Mapleton Historical Museum.)

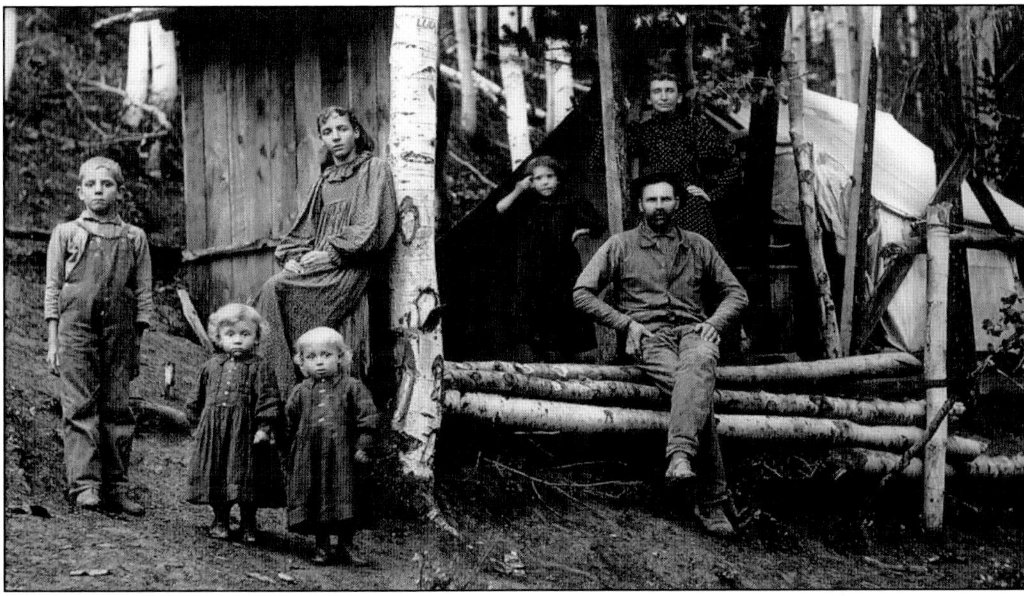

The John Sylvester and Evalyn "Eva" Maude Matson Perry family is pictured camping out while John worked for the railroad near Alpine, Utah, around 1896–1897; from left to right are George Stephen, twins Jesse and Jasper, Edith Estella Perry Snow and Maple Perry Hutchings, John Sylvester, and Evalyn Maud Matson. Maple Perry Hutchings was mother of Miss America Colleen Hutchings and NBA player Mel Hutchings. George Edward Anderson took this photograph, and Rell G. Francis preserved it. (Courtesy of M. Lee Taylor.)

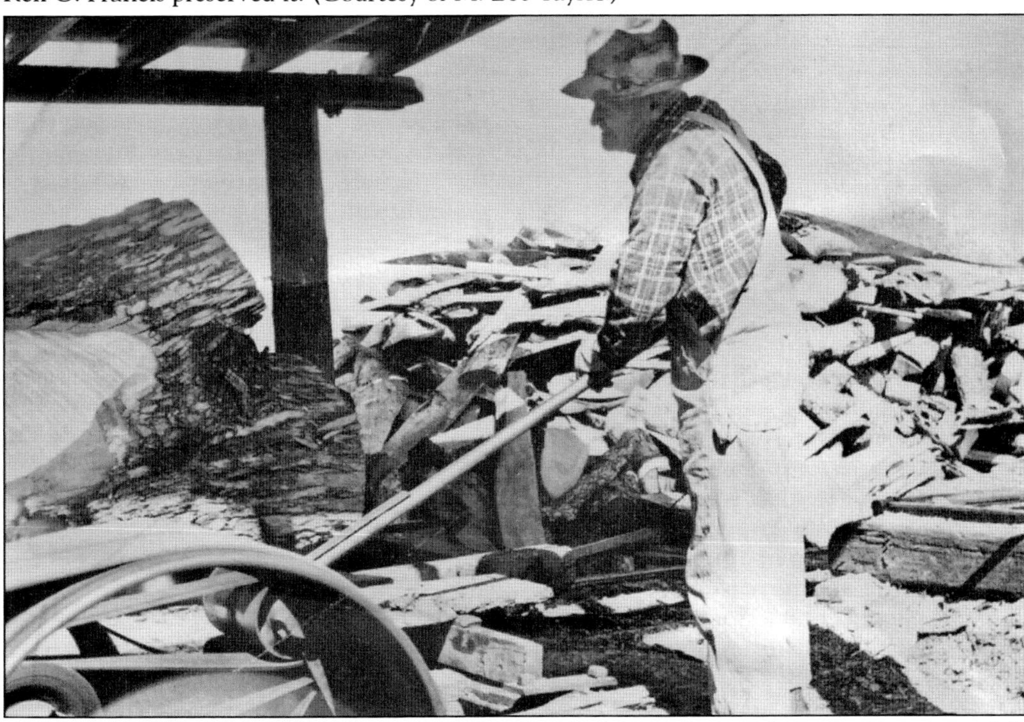

Clint Young is working at the sawmill cutting railroad ties. He was the only man west of the Mississippi River cutting them around 1975. (Courtesy of the Mapleton Historical Museum.)

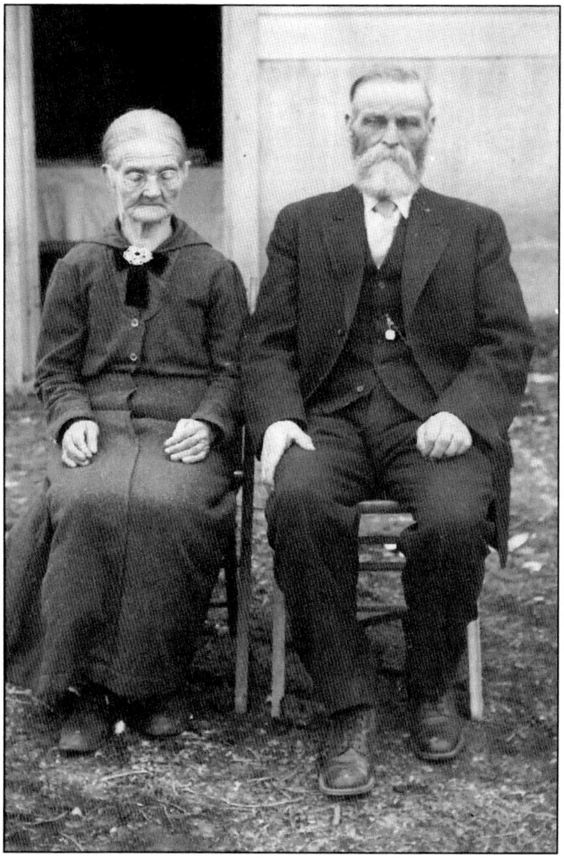

Levi Kendall and his wife, Eliza, built the log cabin that is on display at the Mapleton City Park. He was a veteran of the Echo Canyon and Indian Wars. They were some of the first settlers to live in Mapleton in the 1880s. They arrived in Salt Lake Valley on July 24, 1847, with the first company of pioneers. Brigham Young, the second prophet in this last dispensation for the Church of Jesus Christ of Latter-day Saints, legally adopted Levi. (Courtesy of the Mapleton Historical Museum.)

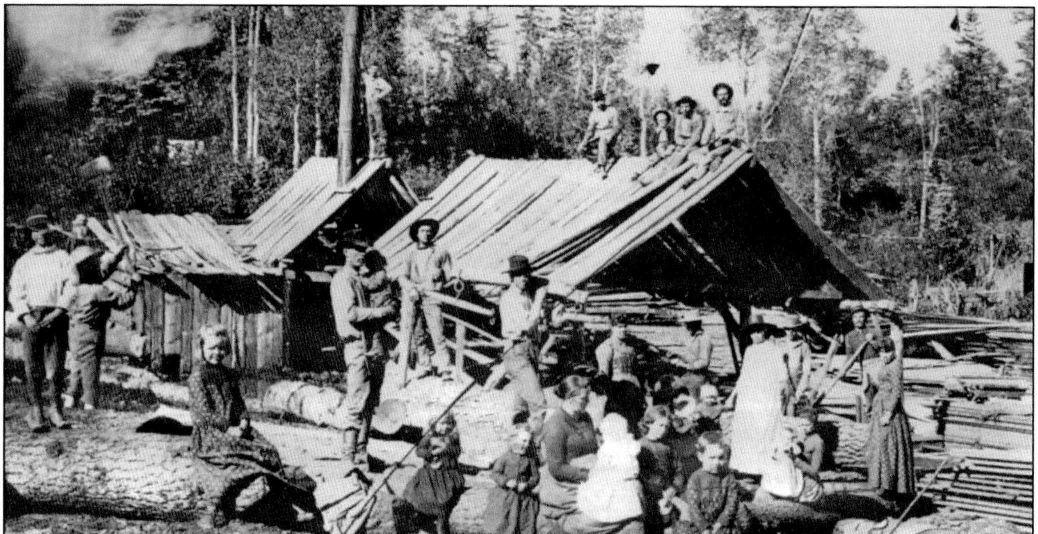

Workers at the Whiting sawmill, as well as family members, are pictured here. This close-up photograph shows the actual operation of the mill and the steam-powered saw. George Edward Anderson took this photograph, and Rell G. Francis preserved it. (Courtesy of the Mapleton Historical Museum.)

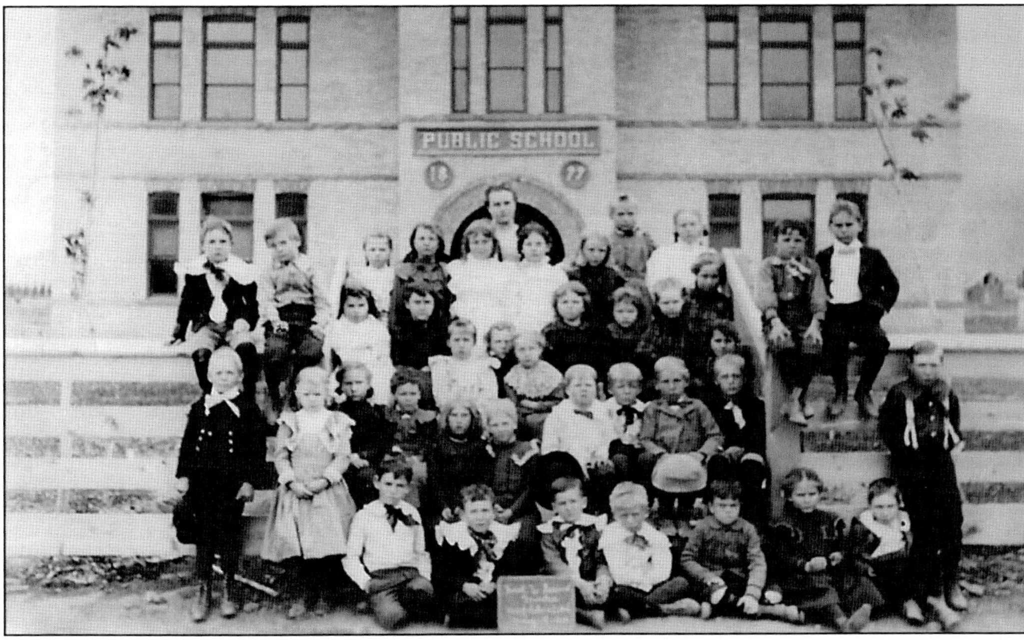

This c. 1900 photograph shows Central School Elementary students. Pictured are, from left to right, (front row) Howard Johnson, Dave Hopla, Elmo Whiting, Morris Johnson, Bird Tew, Phenny Gallup, Douglas Hatfield, and Clarence Hatfield; (second row) Paul Sourwine, Prudence Sourwine, Priscilla Gallup, Alice Jackson, Hilda Peterson, Ora Hatfield, Frank Jensen, Reid Fullmer, Oscar Whiting, Cyrus Matson, and Clara Larson (behind Matson); (third row) Elsie Waterman, Nell Lee, Phenie Fullmer, Ora Roylance, Vera Fullmer, Ora Rockwell, Ellen Larsen, Olive Fullmer, and Eva Fullmer; (fourth row) Freeman Bird, Hollis Bromley, Vera Roylance, Kate Hopla, Mary Larsen, Deseret "Retta" Mendenhall, Hatsie Holley, Vera Matson, Molly Cone, Reed Fullmer, Randall Whiting, and teacher Anna Whitney. George Edward Anderson took this photograph, and Rell G. Francis preserved it. (Courtesy of the Mapleton Historical Museum.)

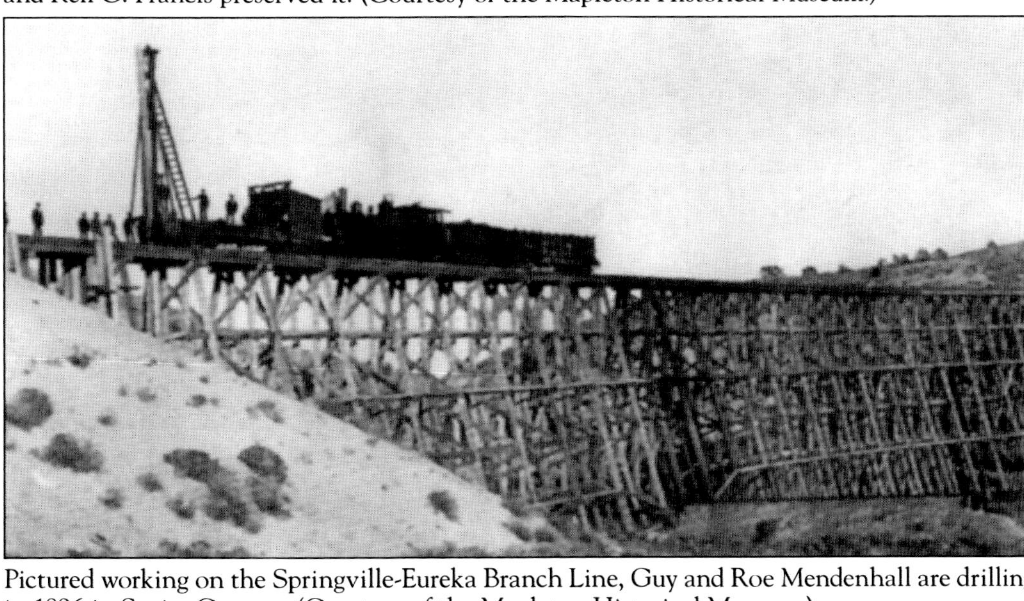

Pictured working on the Springville-Eureka Branch Line, Guy and Roe Mendenhall are drilling in 1896 in Sevier Canyon. (Courtesy of the Mapleton Historical Museum.)

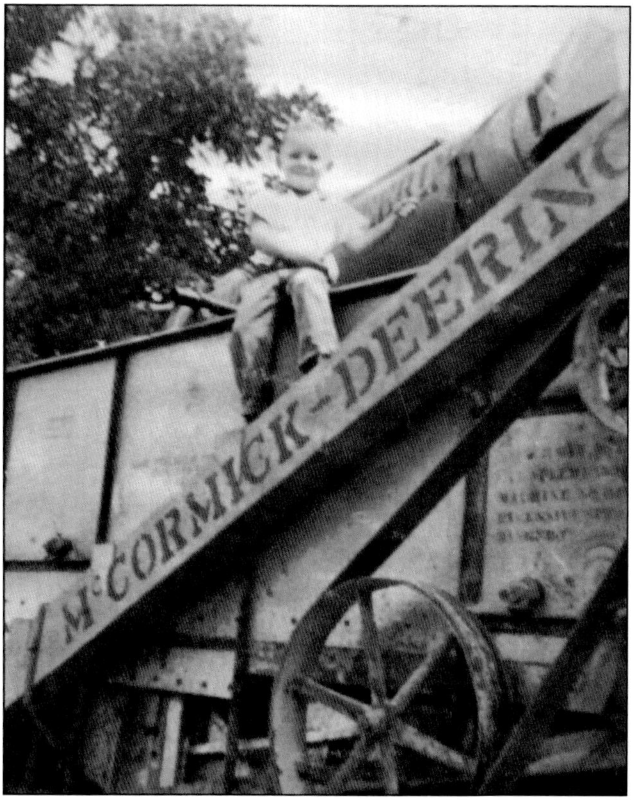

Young Russell Harmer is seen sitting atop a McCormick-Deering thresher. (Courtesy of the Mapleton Historical Museum.)

A railroad steam shovel is pictured around 1914. The Utah Railway built a track adjacent to the Denver & Rio Grande between Provo and Thistle, Utah. The steam shovel is loading flatcars to carry gravel for the new railroad. George Edward Anderson took this photograph, and Rell G. Francis preserved it. (Courtesy of the Mapleton Historical Museum.)

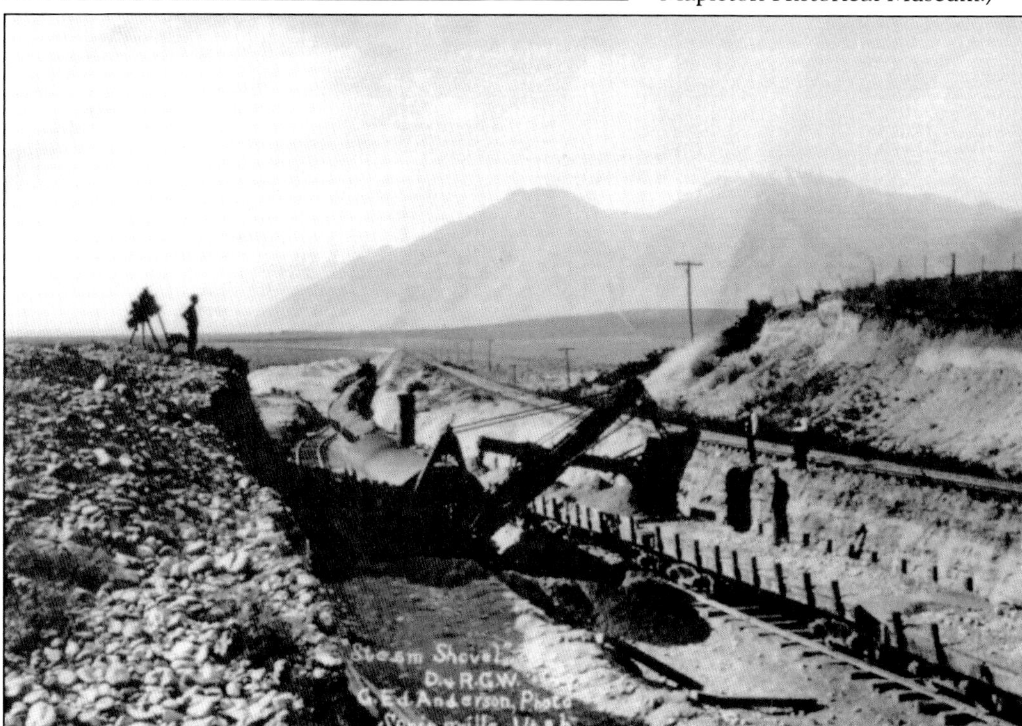

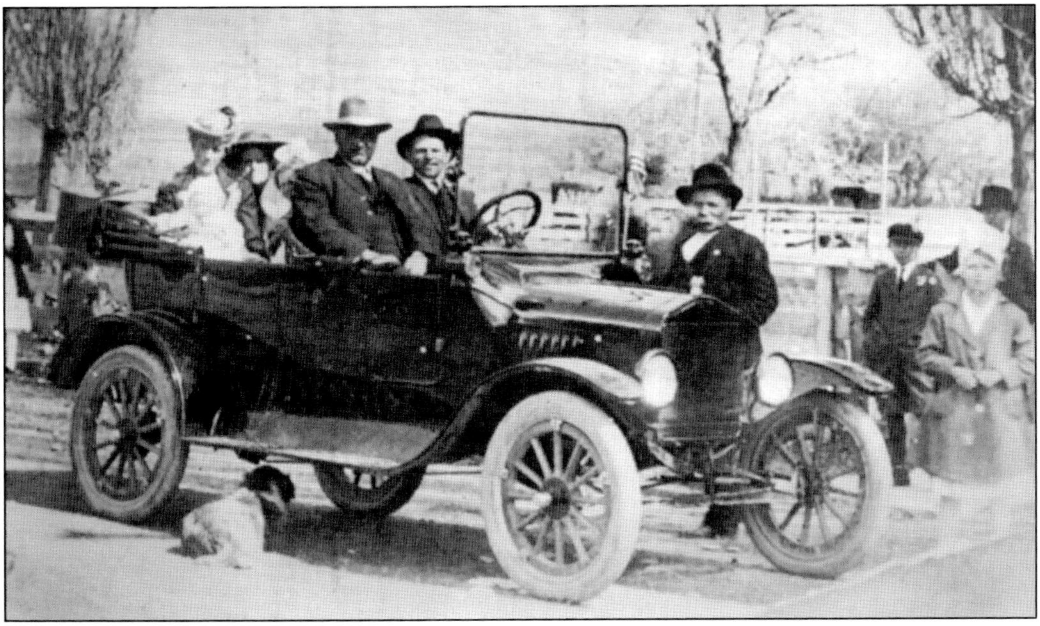

This c. 1915 George Edward Anderson photograph shows, from left to right, Esther Walters holding daughter Ruth Holley, Uda Holley, Martin Walter (front seat), Dallas Holley (driving his Model T), and George B. Matson (near front of car). Those at far right are unidentified. Dallas and his neighbor Martin Walker constructed an icehouse, which provided ice year-round. (Courtesy of the Mapleton Historical Museum.)

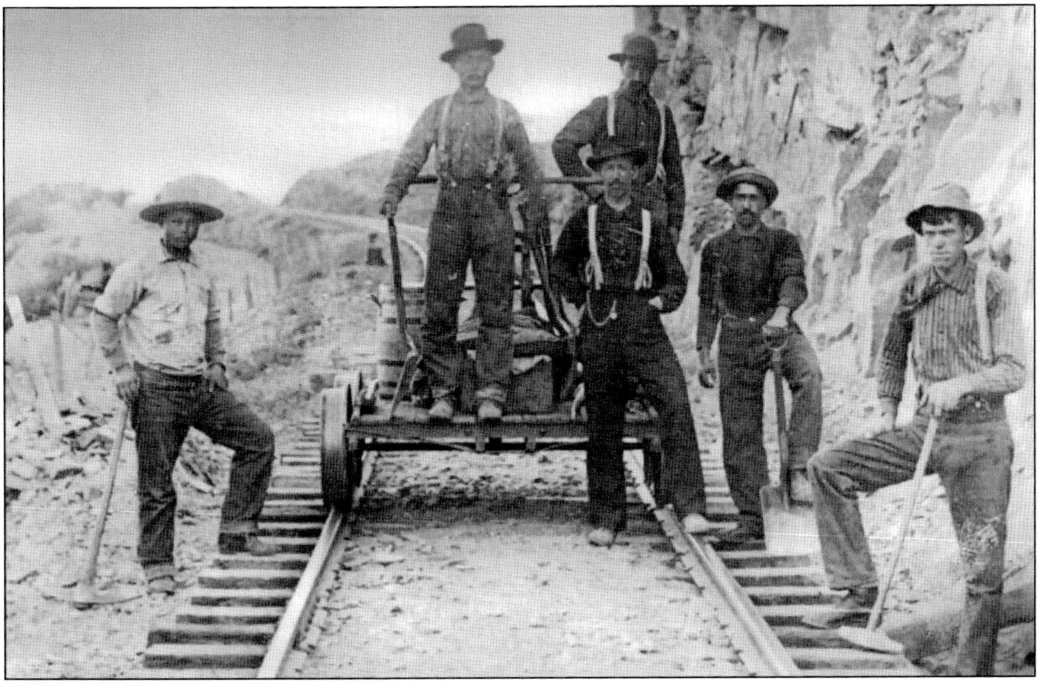

Pictured around 1900 in this George Edward Anderson photograph are members of the railroad section crew working on laying track through Mapleton. (Courtesy of the Springville-Mapleton Pioneer Museum.)

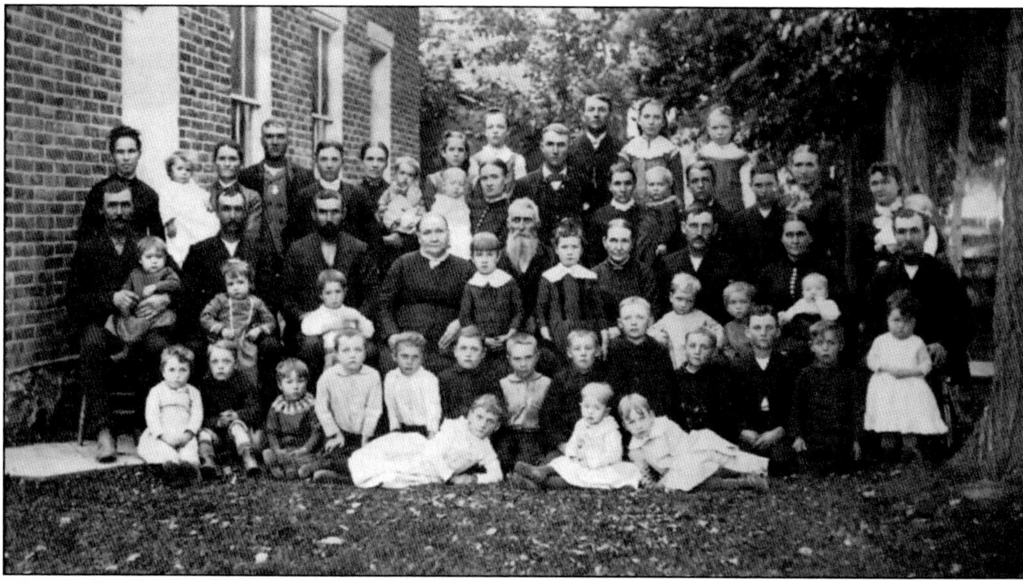

The Richard Bird family is pictured around 1888. Members are, from left to right, (first row) Minerva Johnson, Ada Kindred, and Eliza R; (second row) Haxel, Richard, Jennie, Lester, Reed, Arthur D., Oliver Huntington, Charles Monroe Jr., Vernon Ray, Franklin M. Johnson, James Bayard Johnson, Roswell D., and Mina; (third row) Charles Monroe Sr., Emmogene, Martin William, Bessie, unidentified, Emmeline Crandall, Laura, Richard, Hannah, Laura Crandall, Willis Kelsey Johnson, Harrison Johnson, Chester Johnson, Sarah Mendenhall Johnson, Richard Johnson, and Roswell Darius; (fourth row) Abby Ann Whiting, Elizabeth Mendenhall, Bella, Amasa, Richard L., Dressor, Launa Mariah, Amasa E. Kindred, Arris, Margaret Bird Huntington, Presinda Huntington, Martin William, Willis Kelsey Johnson III, Mary Ann, and Emmeline Steele; (fifth row) Delbert, Francis, Ida, Sarah Emeline, and Winnifred. In 1868, Richard was called on a mission for the Church of Jesus Christ of Latter-day Saints; he went to colonize the "Big Muddy" in Southern Utah. George Edward Anderson took this photograph, and Rell G. Francis preserved it. (Courtesy of the Mapleton Historical Museum.)

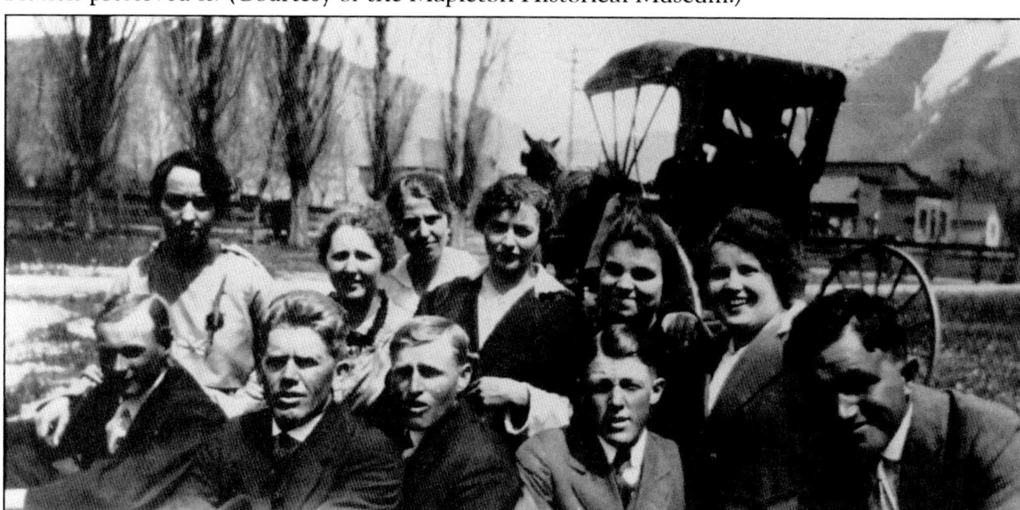

This group was photographed around 1918; the mode of transportation was the buggy. (Courtesy of the Mapleton Historical Museum.)

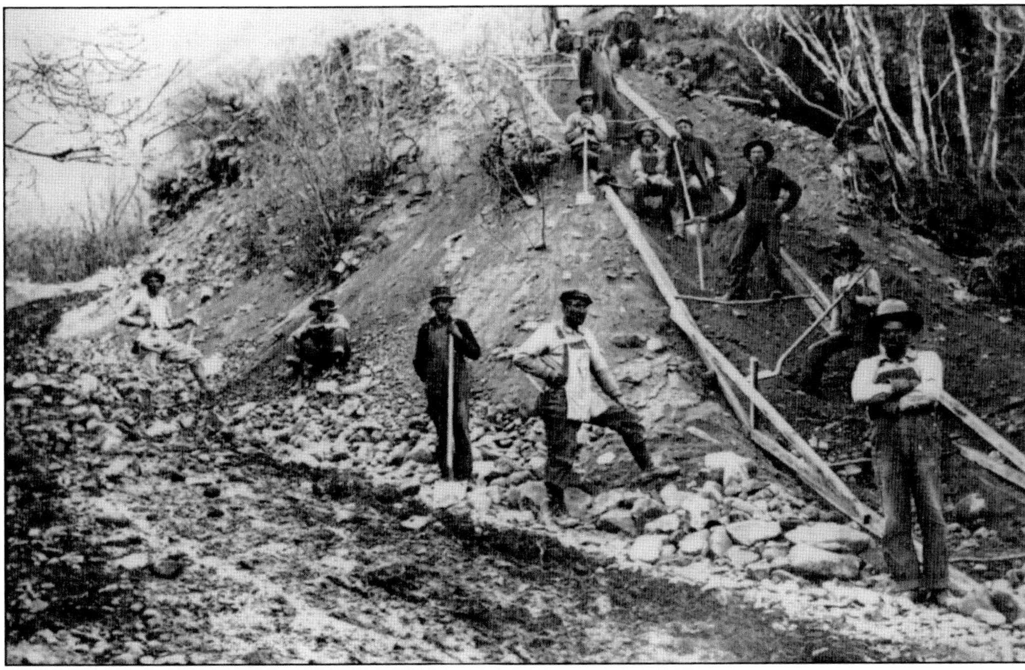

This c. 1915 construction crew was creating a cement ditch for irrigation water in Mapleton Canyon, also known as "Maple Canyon." Dallas Holley is at far right with arms folded. George Edward Anderson took this photograph, and Rell G. Francis preserved it. (Courtesy of the Mapleton Historical Museum.)

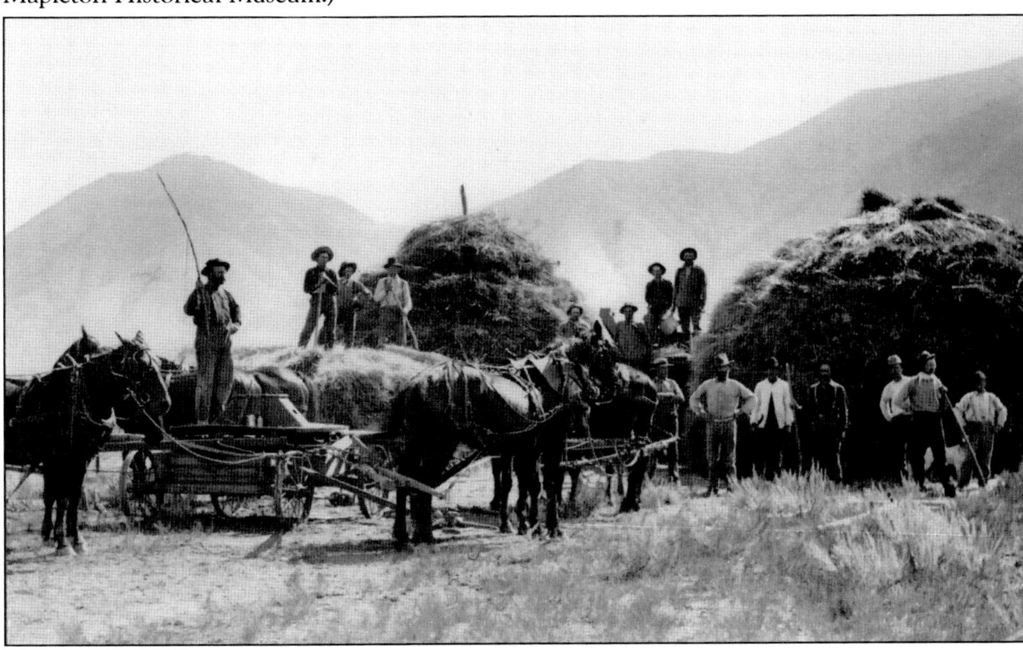

This c. 1898 threshing crew is pictured in southern Mapleton on land owned by Lewis Perry. Amos Benoni Warren is shown with whip in hand; others pictured are the Lewis and Perry brothers and Wells Snow. George Edward Anderson took this photograph, and Rell G. Francis preserved it. (Courtesy of the Mapleton Historical Museum.)

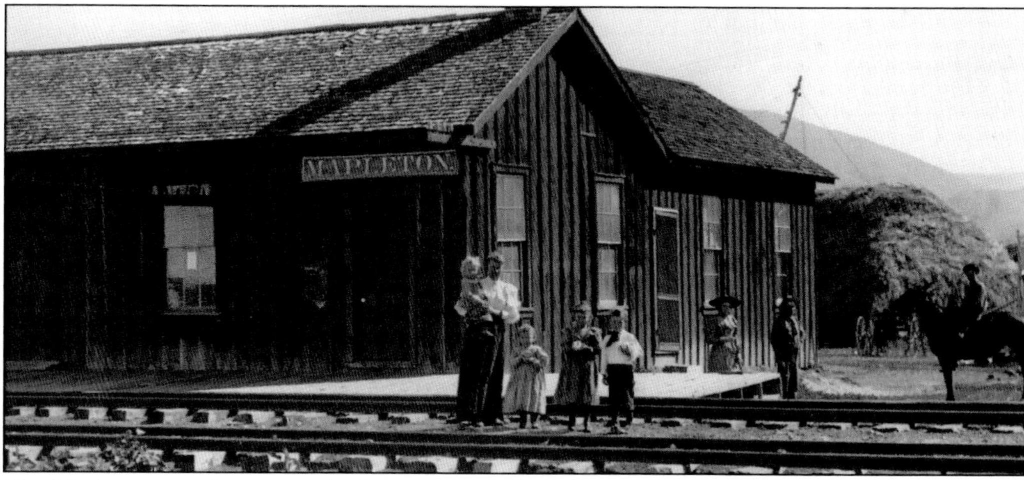

The Mapleton train depot is on the Denver & Rio Grande section in the southwest area. Stationmaster Thomas Waterman is pictured with his wife and children. The depot has now been moved and remodeled as a home at 800 West and 800 South. George Edward Anderson took this photograph, and Rell G. Francis preserved it. (Courtesy of the Mapleton Historical Museum.)

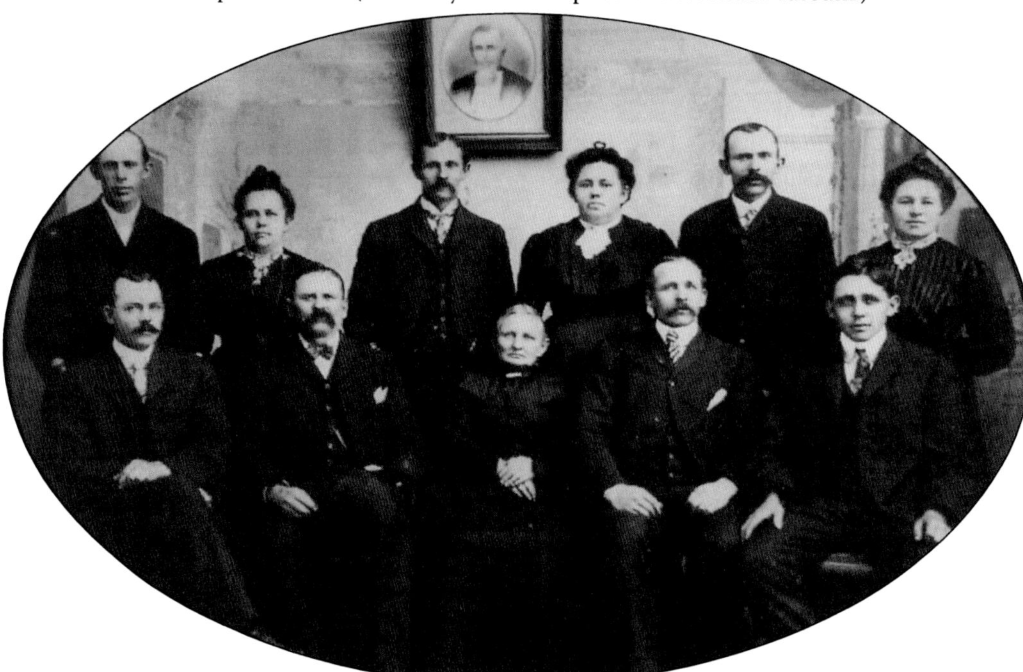

The family of Stephen Chadwick Perry and his third wife, Mary Boggs, is pictured here. Stephen Chadwick Perry's portrait, painted by John Hafen, is on the back wall. Stephen married Mary, the 14-year-old daughter of Francis and Evaline Boggs. Francis served in the original vanguard company of pioneers with Brigham Young. By trade, Stephen made chairs. His children remember playing on the stacks and helping their father cure and weave the rawhide netting that made the seat. Many of his chairs are still in existence today. From left to right are (first row) Mark, George, Mary Boggs, Hyrum B., and Marion; (second row) Parley Pratt, Lucy, Harvey, Luella, Horace Brigham, and Frances. George Edward Anderson took this photograph, and Rell G. Francis preserved it. (Courtesy of M. Lee Taylor.)

These 1916 graduates are, from left to right, (first row) Lerea Roundy, Lula Evans, Glyda Jackman, and Norma Holley; (second row) Willis Bird, George Murray, Roland Hill, teacher Leland Dewey, Liza Halverson, Irene Roundy, Lorna Whiting, and Thelma Lee; (third row), Edward Perry, Tom Carrick, Ammon Johnson, and Barney Mendenhall. (Courtesy of Bagley Studio.)

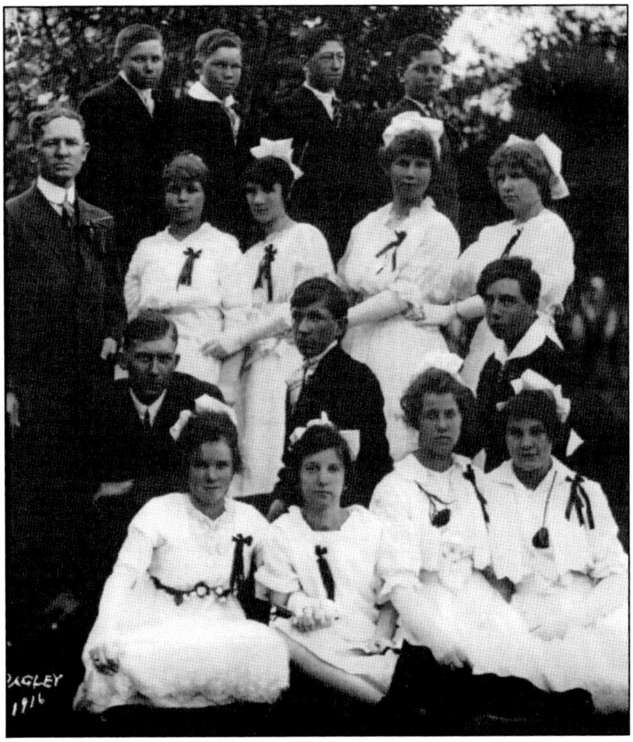

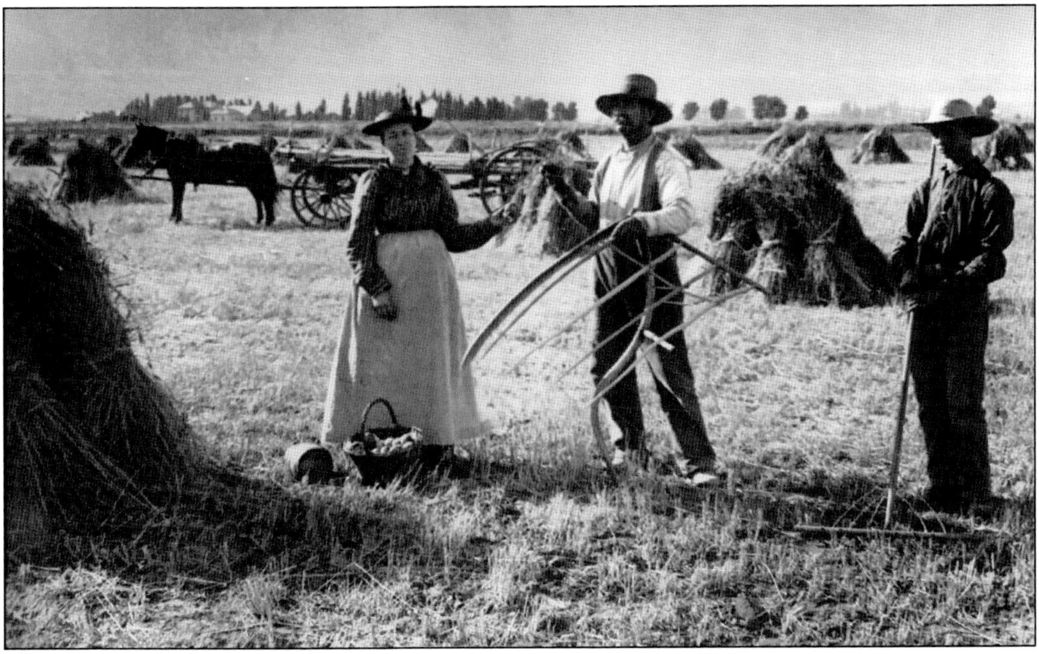

Ether Blanchard Farm is in full threshing operation around 1902. Ether is holding a turkey-wing cradle scythe, his wife, Sylvia G., has brought lunch, and his son Achilles "Chillis" is on the right. Chillis did not attend school during harvest time but instead provided much-needed help around the farm. Ether harvested the 13 acres using wheat stalk cords to tie the grain. George Edward Anderson took this photograph, and Rell G. Francis preserved it. (Courtesy of the Mapleton Historical Museum.)

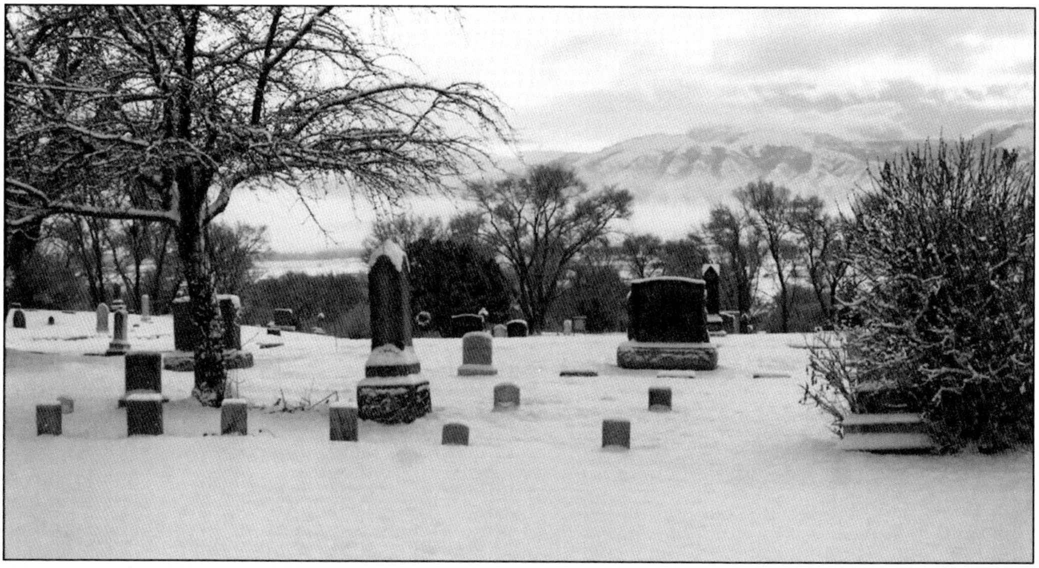

The grounds of Evergreen Cemetery are seen here in a picturesque winter scene. (Courtesy of the Mapleton Historical Museum.)

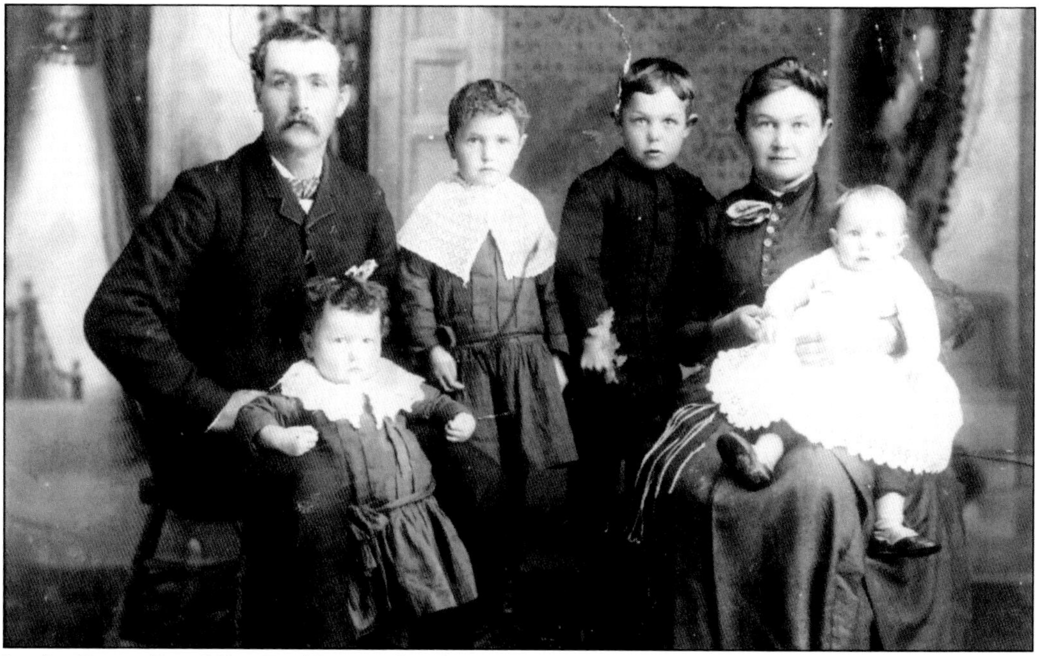

In this Roswell and Eva Bird Darius family picture taken in 1888, pictured from left to right are Roswell, Hazel by Roswell's knee, Mina, Roswell Jr., and Eva holding baby Eva. These are their first four of seven children. Built in 1892 at 65 South Center, the seven-room Roswell Darius Bird Home is now located at 115 South Main Street in Mapleton City Park and is currently the Mapleton Historical Museum. The beautiful large trees by the home were planted in 1892 and are now designated as Mapleton Heritage Trees. The home is constructed of red sand brick with white brick trim around the windows, door, and corners. There are two steel beams that run through it to hold it together. The home is on the Utah Historical Homes Register. (Courtesy of Mary Ann Lush.)

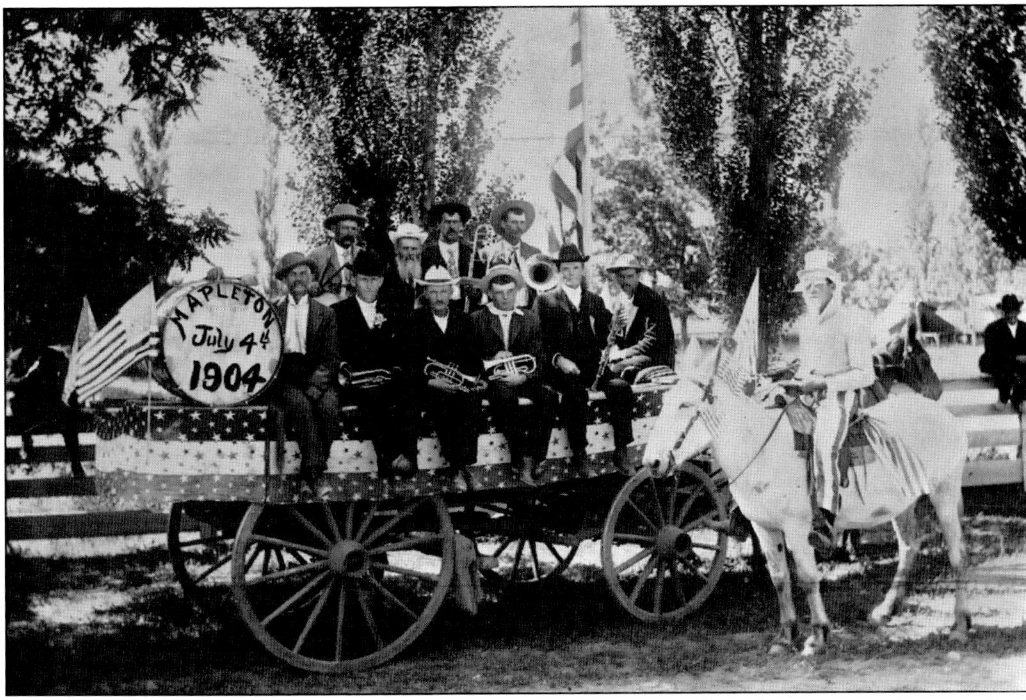

Members of the Mapleton Brass Band, pictured in this George Edward Anderson photograph on July 4, 1904, are, from left to right, (first row) Edward J. Marchbanks, Joseph Malmstrom, Levi Gregory Metcalf, Joseph Allan, Wayne Johnson, and Charles Allan Jr.; (second row) Edwin M. Snow, Charles Allan Sr., Tom Watson, and Will Allan. At left on the fence is Charles Walker, with Parley P. Perry to the right. "Uncle Sam" is on the mule, and Wells Snow is at far right. (Courtesy of the Mapleton Historical Museum.)

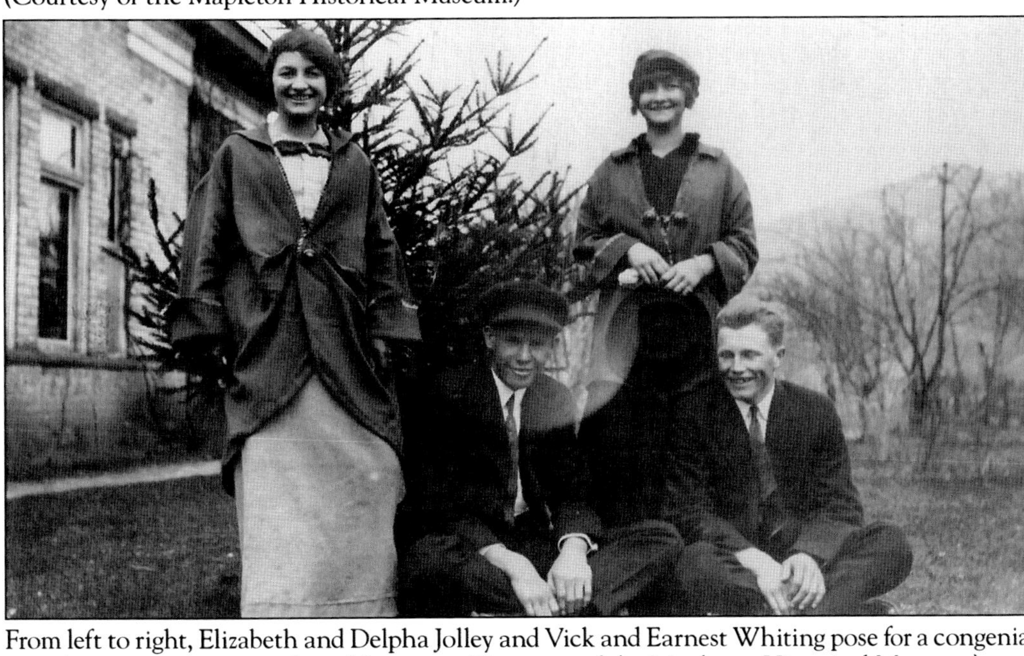

From left to right, Elizabeth and Delpha Jolley and Vick and Earnest Whiting pose for a congenial snapshot sure to be remembered for years. (Courtesy of the Mapleton Historical Museum.)

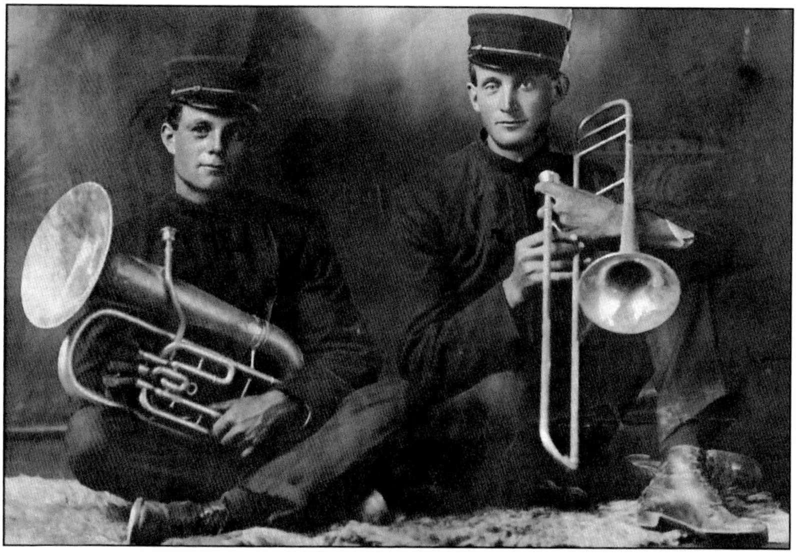

Sporting official band uniforms are Joseph Allan (left) and Leslie Wassom. (Courtesy of the Mapleton Historical Museum.)

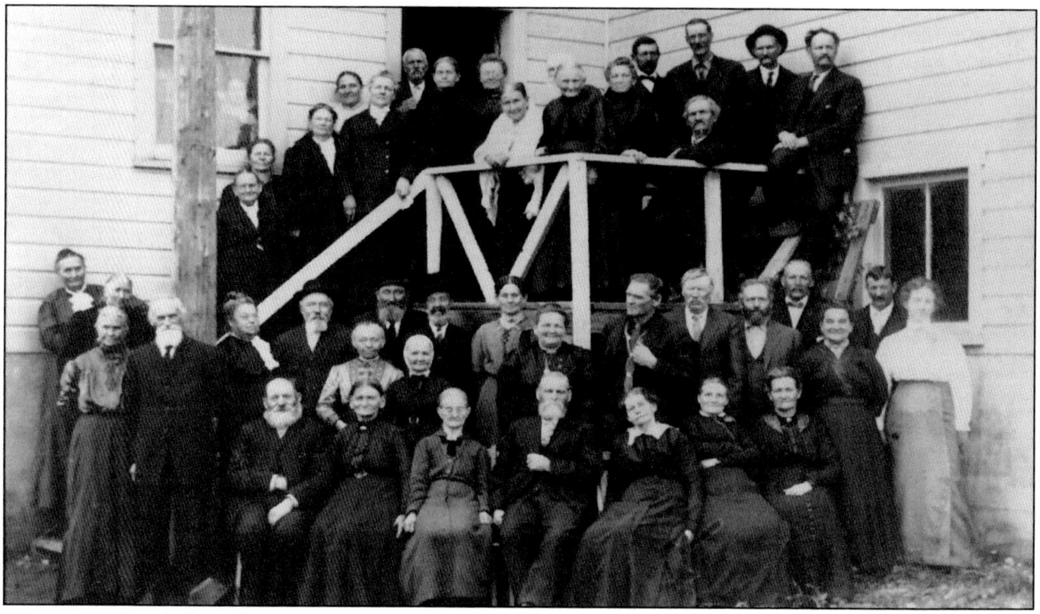

This c. 1910–1915 gathering of Mapleton pioneers is behind the Mapleton Amusement Hall at 106 East Maple. From left to right are (first row, sitting) Mr. and Mrs. Gudmundson, Elizabeth Clements Kendall, Phillip Houtz, Louisa Meletiah Johnson, Mrs. Lars Jensen, and Miriam Norris Mendenhall; (second row, standing) Mrs. Charles Malmstrom, Mrs. Hans Peter Jensen (Karen), Maria Jane Fullmer, William Price Fullmer, Tryphena Whitney, Christian Peter Boels, Anna Johanna Boels, Hans Peter Jensen, Mrs. Christian Boels (Anne Johanna Jensen, second wife), Lewis Nielson, Mrs. Lewis Neilson, Fannie Whiting Houtz, Aaron Johnson Jr., Lars Jensen, John Mendenhall, Hyrum Perry, Annie Whiting, Leonard Diamond, and Mrs. Pearl Lee Diamond; (third row, on porch) Mrs. Spicer Bird (Lavinia Storrs), Susannah Perry Whiting, Mrs. Edwin Johnson, Mrs. Charles Law (Signa), Clara Elizabeth Tew, Charles Law, Rosalia Curtis Bromley, Frances Evaline Perry Snow, Mrs. Hans Peter Jensen, John Tuckett, Sarah Ann Gee Tuckett, Maria Catherine Boyer Mendenhall, E.M. Snow, August Peterson, Richard Mendenhall (seated), Van Fullmer (wearing hat), and William T. Tew. (Courtesy of the Mapleton Historical Museum.)

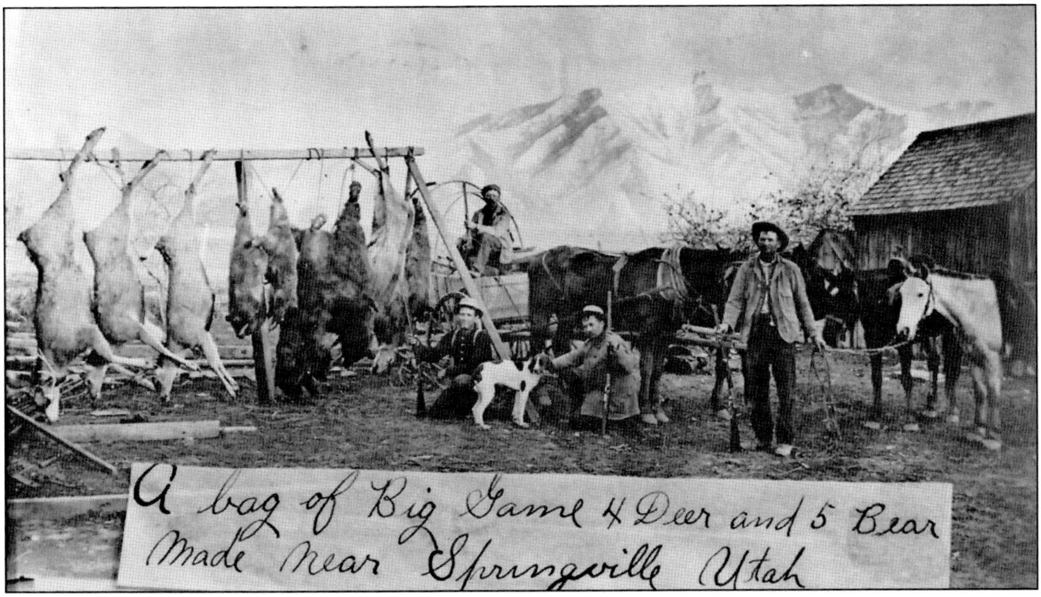

Four deer and five bears are lined up ready to be skinned. Mark Cook is kneeling in front of the wagon, Nephi Packard is in the wagon, George Averett is second from the right, and James Weight is on the far right. (Courtesy of Joe Bagley.)

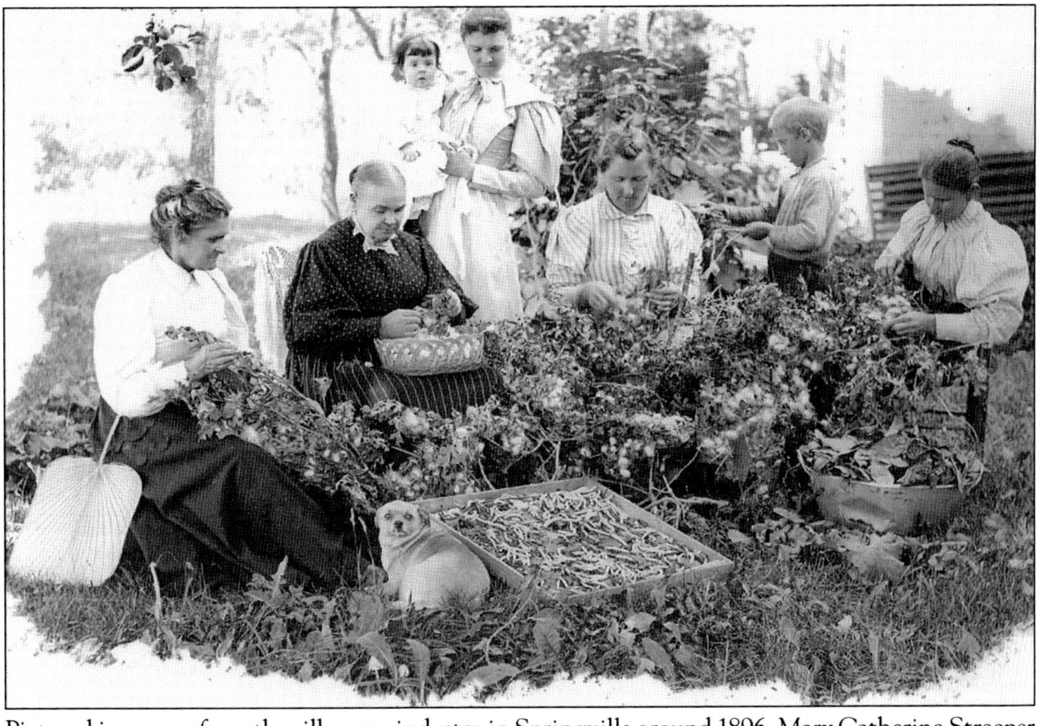
Pictured is a scene from the silkworm industry in Springville around 1896. Mary Catherine Streeper Dougall is at left with the fan. Mary helped to establish the industry, and young people gathered bushels of mulberry leaves for the worms to feast upon. In this picture, they are removing the silk cocoon. The venture failed due to Utah's climate. George Edward Anderson took this photograph, and Rell G. Francis preserved it. (Courtesy of the Mapleton Historical Museum.)

Discover Thousands of Local History Books Featuring Millions of Vintage Images

Arcadia Publishing, the leading local history publisher in the United States, is committed to making history accessible and meaningful through publishing books that celebrate and preserve the heritage of America's people and places.

Find more books like this at
www.arcadiapublishing.com

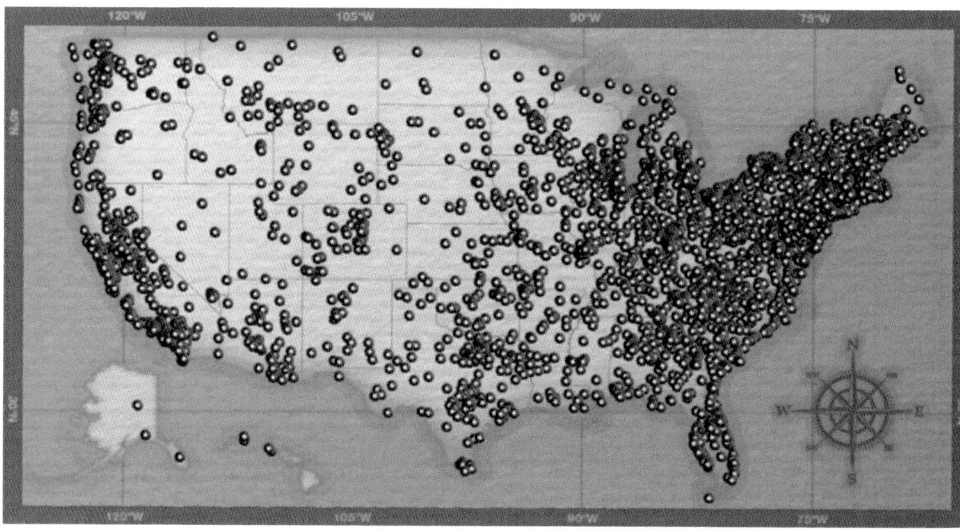

Search for your hometown history, your old stomping grounds, and even your favorite sports team.

Consistent with our mission to preserve history on a local level, this book was printed in South Carolina on American-made paper and manufactured entirely in the United States. Products carrying the accredited Forest Stewardship Council (FSC) label are printed on 100 percent FSC-certified paper.

MADE IN THE USA